Weakness: A Literary and Philosophical History

Dear Sky (Tope),

It was great to stalk you in Hong Kong. Here is a paltry return for your poetry, laughter and calm.

See ya in Rockhampton or Éire,

Mícheál

Bloomsbury Literary Studies Series

Related Titles:

The Imagination of Evil, Mary Evans
Melancholy and the Archive, Jonathan Boulter
Milton, Evil and Literary History, Claire Colebrook
Revisions of the American Adam, Jonathan Mitchell

Weakness: A Literary and Philosophical History

Michael O'Sullivan

Bloomsbury Literary Studies

BLOOMSBURY

LONDON • NEW DELHI • NEW YORK • SYDNEY

Bloomsbury Academic

An imprint of Bloomsbury Publishing Plc

50 Bedford Square
London
WC1B 3DP
UK

1385 Broadway
New York
NY 10018
USA

www.bloomsbury.com

Bloomsbury is a registered trade mark of Bloomsbury Publishing Plc

First published in 2012 by the Continuum International Publishing Group Ltd
Paperback edition first published by Bloomsbury Academic 2014

British Library Cataloguing-in-Publication Data
A catalogue record for this book is available from the British Library.

ISBN: HB: 978-1-4411-2817-1
PB: 978-1-4725-6835-9
ePDF: 978-1-4411-7703-2
ePUB: 978-1-4411-8198-5

Library of Congress Cataloging-in-Publication Data
O'Sullivan, Michael, 1974–
Weakness: a literary and philosophical history/Michael O'Sullivan.
p. cm. – (Continuum literary studies)
Includes bibliographical references and index.
ISBN 978-1-4411-6299-1 (hardcover) -- ISBN 978-1-4411-7879-4
(pdf) – ISBN 978-1-4411-9564-7 (ebook (epub))
1. Power (Philosophy) in literature. 2. Literature and society.
3. Self in literature. I. Title.
PN51.O87 2012
809'.93353–dc23 2011051218

Typeset by Deanta Global Publishing Services, Chennai, India
Printed and bound by CPI Group (UK) Ltd, Croydon, CR0 4YY

To my parents and to Irene

Contents

Acknowledgements

I would like to thank the following friends and colleagues for reading earlier drafts of the chapters: Billy Ramsell, James Carney, Ve-Yin Tee, Eddie Tay, Li Ou, Grant Hamilton and Francis Chan Pak Hang. I would like to thank the following, as well as those above, for their insights in conversation on these ideas: Tomàs Mulcahy, Cian O'Sullivan, Tim Kelleher, Francis O'Sullivan, Majella Henson, Dominic O'Sullivan, Margaret O'Sullivan, Leonard Madden, Jeremiah O'Sullivan, Willard Harris, Graham Allen and Guo Yangsheng. I also thank Colleen Coalter, Laura Murray and Subitha Nair at Continuum for their patience and encouragement.

Introduction

It has long been acknowledged that weakness can be a strength.[1] Depending on the context, the terms of this 'oppositional couple' can possess either a fascinating complicity or a 'worrying familiarity'.[2] Literature has been particularly resourceful in charting their restless confederacy. Helena reminds us in *All's Well That Ends Well* that '[h]e that of greatest works is finisher/Oft does them by the weakest minister' (II: 138–9). However, how are we to understand the complicity between weakness and strength, two terms that have a strong claim as opposites in the popular imagination? Weakness is forever being reinvented even in science, philosophy and psychology. We now have a 'weakening philosophy'[3] that holds all thought together; a renewed interest in the 'weak force'[4] of the Standard Model of particle physics that may hold the secret for how the universe is held together; and the 'weak ties' of the social network that hold us all together. Sometimes, in our rush to explain power and strength, we overlook their connection to weakness. The new Penguin *Great Ideas* book on Shakespeare is entitled *William Shakespeare On Power*, it begins with an extract from Rozencrantz's speech on the life of the King: 'The single and peculiar life is bound/With all the strength and armour of the mind/To keep itself from noyance, but much more/That spirit upon whose weal depends and rests/The lives of many' (3). Shakespeare knew better than most that power means nothing if it is not understood or explained in terms of the weakness of 'the single and peculiar life'.

The exploration of weakness has served as a source of insight for philosophers and artists in their quest to refine theories of the person and to delve further into the depths of personality in narrative. However, while Western philosophy has generally aligned weakness with moral failing and even sin, literature and certain strands of Eastern philosophy have been more forgiving in exploring a weakness that is often descriptive of the noblest human characteristics and expressive of the most enduring of human values. The present book reappraises key accounts of weakness as fallibility (Greek *akrasia*, Christian weakness and weakness in Nietzsche and Kierkegaard) or 'force of weakness' (Derrida) in Western philosophy in light of the more

affirmative readings of weakness as survivability or precariousness in literature and Daoism. These latter accounts present weakness as a state that is
revealing of core elements of a shared humanity. If the engagement with
weakness is time and again revealing of, or creative of, an affirmative potential that comes to be regarded as an unrecognized 'strength', then the dialectical nature of the oppositional couple strength/weakness is made ever
more apparent. However, the presentation of this dialectic has been influenced in recent decades by a negative epistemology that privileges violence.
If the dialectic is engaged with in writing and representation in a system
that is already perceived by influential Western theories of signification as
'violent', then it is too late for the representation of weakness; it has already
been delimited. This book attempts to engage with weakness before this
metaphysical opposition (and the embodied experience of weakness and
potential that goes with it) has been consigned to a violence that affects
inscription, trace, voice and whatever else is aligned with the subject. In
Chapter 5 I examine one influential philosophical account of language –
that of Jacques Derrida – that describes a metaphysics of violence around
signification.

For Beckett, Keats and Joyce, the presentation of weakness is often aligned
with suffering and pain. When Thomas Mann was asked to write an encyclo-
pedia volume on the literature of suffering he replied that he couldn't write
it because every piece of literature in the world is about suffering. However,
Elaine Scarry also reminds us that Virginia Woolf believed that 'we have no
language for physical pain' (Coakley, 64). Weakness is in the same ballpark
as suffering and pain. It is everywhere and nowhere. Show me the writer
who hasn't explored weakness and I'll show you the reader who hasn't
traced its contours on his or her own heart, enlivened by the confessional
exchange that retains its comforting mystery only in secrecy. However, weakness also has the capacity to straddle the divisions between physiological,
psychological and ethical states. Weakness might not accompany pain and
suffering, even though its most profound state acknowledges these experiences. Weakness can appear passive in a way that pain and suffering do not
and this is evident in how it is used to describe a tendency to lapse, err or
stray. The humane weakness that is important for this book emerges from
thinking through two sides of weakness at the same time: first, weakness as
acceptance of bodily need resulting from pain, suffering or general physical
conditions and, second, those acts and states of weakness that have been
regarded as manifestations of a psychological or ethical failing of some
kind. As an articulation of both the personal and the ethical, weakness also
has a political face. In following the recent call of Judith Butler for 'a more

inclusive and egalitarian way of recognizing precariousness' (and weakness in this book is very often read as a kind of 'precariousness') that 'should take form as concrete social policy', (2009, 13) this book regards weakness as a 'shared condition of human life'. It acknowledges, again with Butler, that '[a] certain apprehension of equality follows from this invariably shared condition' (181). The exploration of works of literature and philosophy that foreground ethical awareness in discussions of weakness can go some way towards reaffirming this call for an 'apprehension of equality'.

However, weakness as human vulnerability and fragility that is not bound up with the deliberation on the physiological recognition of need as part of a programme for greater human flourishing can sometimes descend into a celebration of weakness for weakness' sake; it can appear hypochondriacal and self-indulgent. As Martha Nussbaum suggests in *The Fragility of Goodness*, her reading of the political subject of ancient Greece, states such as fragility and vulnerability can form a 'necessary background condition' for 'certain genuine human goods'. However, the Greek accounts of vulnerability and fragility are not 'to be prized in their own right'. She reminds us that much human vulnerability is not the result of accident, ill-fortune, or some 'mysterious necessity of nature', but of 'ignorance, greed, malice' (xxx). The present book explores weakness in a range of different traditions, and the writers I examine keep this tendency to celebrate a disinterested weakness in check by maintaining throughout a close attention to the description of 'survivability', need and 'precariousness' that humane weakness accompanies.

The presentation of weakness in Eastern philosophy is sometimes markedly different from its presentation in Western philosophy; for Daoism and Buddhism it is aligned with survivability and mindfulness. The recent revitalization of the East-West paradigm in comparative studies is a further sign of our shifting, globalized community and it offers great potential for enhancing our understanding of important philosophical notions such as power, strength and weakness. Many of the most influential literary critical and philosophical works of the last fifty years in the 'West' have made sweeping claims about language and metaphysics that neglected the Eastern perspective. This is no longer possible. Longxi Zhang's and Robert T. Ames's pioneering work in East-West studies, to name but two of the most important bodies of work in this field, offer valuable perspectives for comparative research that aims to bring the two traditions closer together while recognizing that cultural differences must still be respected. In Chapters 2, 4 and 5 I use their insights to explore the representation of weakness in the philosophies of Lao Tzu, Friedrich Nietzsche and Jacques Derrida. Zhang's

The Tao and the Logos remains one of the most important works for cross-cultural understanding in East-West studies, a work that is sadly neglected by undergraduate courses in the West. David Faure has recently described the difference between the 'Chinese book' and the 'Western book' in terms of the difference between a 'collection of like-minded documents' and the 'telling of a story', the latter describing the 'Western book'.[5] The examination of weakness and its representation by way of the 'inadequacy of signification' by writers from both traditions offers great potential for re-imagining these differences.

Gender studies also has much to say about weakness. Unfortunately, the advances made by the *écriture féminine* movement and by feminist writers who have explored weakness and the notion of the 'weaker vessel' have not inspired an equally engaging *écriture masculine*. In Chapter 6 I argue that the representation of the masculine in terms of the 'phallic self', 'phallic identity' and a writing that is phallogocentric has much to learn from the 'womb vision' and the engagement with a writing of the body that has given women writers such important notions as the 'Great Vessel' and 'self-touching'. The bloated symbolic currency of phallogocentrism might be regarded, in psychological terms, as inciting the very weakness-as-impotence it fears most by instituting a 'fear of failure' at the heart of male identity. In this regard, Wilhelm Stekel notes the 'unprecedented attention' that psychoanalysis focuses on the 'genitals as the synecdoche of the individual', where the 'penis' becomes an' 'image of the entire man' (in McLaren, 2006, 164). The 'phallic self' and the narratives it supports must be unpacked through a close attention to the physiology of male weakness. The male writer's description of these moments can enhance the general understanding of weakness. For this reason, I focus on male writers in the final sections in the belief that studies in masculinity have much to learn from the advances in feminist writing.

Chapter 3 deals with weakness as mediated by important Christian texts. Jesus's privileging of the meek, Matthew's warning that the 'flesh is weak' and Paul's celebration of weakness launched an influential metaphysics of weakness in literature and culture. The notion that the 'flesh is weak' no longer spoke for the passions of a single body, as it had done in early Greek thought, but for notions of sin and guilt as overarching and transcendental as the God revered. Erich Auerbach argues that the Christian narrative of weakness changes narrative forever and allows for the representation of people of the 'humblest social station'. In Chapter 4 I examine how later philosophers, specifically Nietzsche and Kierkegaard, respond to Christian weakness in very different ways. However, Paul Ricoeur is the only leading twentieth-century Christian philosopher to devote an entire work to weakness as fallibility. His *Fallible Man* discusses the Christian understanding of weakness. He writes that '[w]eakness makes evil possible in several senses' and that man 'is also the weak link of the real' (141). Ricoeur describes fallibility in terms of a primordial sense of disproportion or conflict at the heart of being between βιοσ and λογοσ, or living and thinking (132). However, Ricoeur flies too quickly to the 'possibility of evil' when he describes fallibility: 'What is meant by calling man fallible? Essentially this: that the *possibility* of moral evil is inherent in man's constitution' (133). The affirmative aspects of weakness are overlooked or only hinted at: 'Man is the Joy of Yes in the sadness of the finite' (140). However, he acknowledges a gap 'between the possibility and the reality [of evil]' that is 'reflected in a similar gap between the mere anthropological description of fallibility and an ethic. The first is prior to evil, the second finds the real opposition of good and evil' (142). The 'enigma' or the 'gap' between innocence and fault or between the 'possibility and the reality' of evil is then described in terms of a 'leap' from 'fallibility to the already fallen' (143). Ricoeur does ultimately acknowledge that in order to 'catch sight of that leap we must make a fresh start and enter upon a new type of reflection' (143). The present book takes up this challenge in offering a 'new type of reflection' on weakness that can be regarded as prolonging the contemplation of this first stage, this 'anthropological description of fallibility', before the narrative of 'sin' and salvation is applied. Weakness is not only the 'possibility of evil'; it can be a secular experience that opens the individual up to a confessional and conciliatory attitude that is beneficial when shared and communicated.

I follow philosophers and literary critics such as Alasdair MacIntyre, Martha Nussbaum and Bernard Williams in accepting that literature can describe a concern for ethics (and the present book will explore how weakness can incite a humane regard for shared human endeavour) that philosophy cannot. Keats's deliberation on his 'weak mortality', Wordsworth's desire to speak for the 'frailties of the world' and Dickens's presentation of the 'battle of life' have become important literary archetypes for how later writers present weakness. Joyce perhaps did more than any other modernist writer to explore male weakness; in Chapter 9 I examine his presentation of weakness as a means to greater kindness in *Finnegans Wake*. Samuel Beckett also privileges weakness in terms of bodily privation; he once told Lawrence Harvey that his work was all about describing the 'authentic weakness of being'. Given that his work has also been read as describing a 'syntax of weakness', in Chapter 10, I endeavour to bring these different readings of Beckettian weakness together around an examination of the insights on art evident in his recently published letters.

Animal vulnerability is, for many, at the heart of human vulnerability. Philosophers and thinkers such as Giorgio Agamben, Judith Butler and Jacques Derrida have argued that there is an urgent need to describe the hiatus or 'cleft' between 'the animal' and the human in man. J. M. Coetzee is a writer who explores animal vulnerability most imaginatively. In reference to his earlier work as critic on Franz Kafka and 'the animal', in the final chapter I give a reading of his fiction on animals and I examine how his experimentation with narrative authority is revealing of a broader attempt to 'give up control' in dealing with 'the animal'.

In concluding, it is perhaps Katherine Mansfield who describes most beautifully the necessity of exploring weakness in her story 'The Daughters of the Late Colonel'. Mansfield might be read as bringing together about her character Constantia the shared insights to be gained from the most enduring states of Eastern and Western philosophy. The name Constantia, from the Latin, connotes constancy, perseverance and harmony and in the story Constantia is most at peace when she spends time before her collection of Buddhas, exploring the mindfulness and insight the Buddha's smile puts her in touch with: the smile "gave her such a queer feeling" and "almost a pain and yet a pleasant pain" (116). Such experiences grant her a capacity for understanding the value of weakness. As she struggles with her sister Josephine to go through the belongings of their recently deceased father, she asks: 'Why shouldn't we be weak for once in our lives, Jug? It's quite excusable. Let's be weak – be weak, Jug. It's much nicer to be weak than to be strong'. This is a book that follows Mansfield in exploring how an often neglected engagement with weakness can make manifest overlooked aspects of mindfulness and insight.

Part One

Philosophy

Chapter 1

Fragile Goodness and Weakness of the Will

In the *Gorgias*, when Socrates and Callicles are coming to the end of their long discussion, Callicles, the young politician with 'business in the city' is becoming ever more infuriated by Socrates' style of questioning. Socrates is going out of his way to describe how ineffective the philosopher can appear to a young businessman. When he comes to predicting his own death sentence because he 'won't know what to say in court' (Cooper, 864) to the allegations brought against him about impiety and confusing and corrupting the youth of Athens, and, as we learn in the *Apology*, about 'making the weaker argument the stronger',[1] Callicles asks in almost disbelief: 'Do you think, Socrates, that a man in such a position in his city, a man who's unable to protect himself, is to be admired?' (Cooper, 865). Socrates responds: 'Yes, Callicles, as long as he has protected himself against having spoken or done anything unjust relating to either men or gods' (865). The vulnerable man, the man who cannot protect himself in the city, is also, for the Socrates of the *Apology*, as the oracle suggests, a man who, in being the 'wisest', accepts that his wisdom is 'worthless' (23). Despite the fact that Socrates, as Alcibiades suggests in the *Symposium*, does play games of irony, when we read on in the *Gorgias* we can sense that Socrates is serious about how such a man must be admired. He goes on to describe Callicles' arguments as 'worthless' also (869). Callicles argues that 'the many' 'conceal their own impotence' behind law so that they can 'enslave men who are better by nature' (835). He therefore argues that 'the more powerful among men' (827) must have their 'fair share' (828) because those 'who institute our laws are the weak' (827) in seeking to control nature through law. It may sound a little Nietzschean; however, Socrates is unwilling to accept this regard for 'impotence' and the 'powerful' because 'a person who wants to be happy must evidently pursue and practice self-control' (851), and he says it is philosophy alone that can enable one, as Socrates describes for himself, 'to be and to live as a very good man, and when I die, to die like that' (868). He calls on all other people to do the same in this contest 'that

I hold to be worth all the other contests in this life' (868). It is because he is unwilling to accept the ways of the city, to give in to 'flattery', and to accept Callicles' regard for appetite, which ignores self-control and discipline, that he admits that he will be unable to defend himself to the members of the public, the 'jurymen', who will convict him. He says he 'won't be able to point out any pleasures that I've provided for them, ones they believe to be services and benefits, while I envy neither those who provide them nor the ones for whom they're provided' (865).

Socrates pays with his life for such vulnerability. But he says that he is not afraid to die because he is confident that he has 'protected himself against having spoken or done anything unjust relating to either men or gods'. This is the kind of 'self-protection' he values the most and he says he would only feel shame and be 'upset' in death if someone could refute him and prove that he has been unable to provide such protection for himself or anyone else (865). Bernard Williams believes that shame alters early 'ethical thought' for good; it necessitates the incorporation of vulnerability into a theory of action. However, Socrates' admission that he is vulnerable veils his conviction that he is capable of protecting what is truly valuable – namely, a self that he believes has not been unjust. The paradox, such a life throws up is that the stronger one's convictions are that one is invulnerable to the allure of what is 'unjust', the more vulnerable one is likely to be in 'public affairs'; as Callicles suggests, such men prove to be 'inexperienced in the ways of human beings altogether' (829). Despite this risk, self-protection is essential because 'doing what's unjust is more to be guarded against than suffering it' (829). Socrates ultimately calls on his belief in the afterlife to defend this way of life. He tells Callicles: 'you won't be able to come to protect yourself when you appear at the trial and judgment' that we all must face after death. Socrates is convinced that when Rhadamanthus comes to inspect the souls of the dead he will send Socrates' soul, as 'that of a philosopher who has minded his own affairs and hasn't been meddlesome in the course of his life', to the Isles of the Blessed. Socrates is like the private citizen 'who has lived a pious life, one devoted to truth' (868). Being expert, then, in the 'weaker argument' and vulnerable before the ways of the city and the language and antics of the courts are qualities of the philosopher because what he says and does is worthless in the eyes of the majority. However, it is because it is 'worthless' to such an extent that it endures like the soul that has been devoted to the 'truth'.

Vulnerability and weakness are important for early Greek 'ethical thought' and there are two expressions of weakness that are influential for its theories of action. The first is what Martha Nussbaum describes as 'the fragility of goodness', and the second is the related notion of *akrasia*, which is typically translated as 'weakness of will'. The idea that goodness is fragile – most prominent in Aristotle – means that 'certain central human values are available and valuable only within a context of risk and material limitation' (341). For the good life as a life of happiness to be wholesome and truly human we must accept the 'necessary vulnerability of human *eudaimonia*' (340); we must accept that there are certain human values such as love, or *philia*, that leave us vulnerable to risk and luck. The Greek dramatists had been staging the most extreme forms of this vulnerability for some time – we recall Medea's killing of her children, Alcestis' sacrificing of her life for her husband and Oedipus's blindness – and it was time that such vulnerability was incorporated into a philosophy of life. Nussbaum argues that these risks are bound up with all human flourishing, because, as she suggests for Aristotle's reading of love, all excellence is 'other-related' (351). The result is that 'excellence . . . diminishes self-sufficiency and increases vulnerability' (336). The central question then becomes how much vulnerability or luck should we live with? Nussbaum argues that Plato had no time for such vulnerability and that he describes a kind of 'goodness without fragility' and recommends an 'ascent towards the form' where the individual becomes, like the Socrates of the *Symposium*, 'hard, indivisible, unchanging' (195). She argues that Plato's longing for self-transcendence results in a philosophy where the 'everyday' and all that risks privileging risk must be outlawed; the 'intimate bonds of family love' are discredited, the 'only family' becomes the city and love itself is only a rage or madness that must be expelled by 'right reason'.

The presentation of Socrates' vulnerability as that of a philosopher would seem, on first impressions, to be directly related to this necessary vulnerability of *eudaimonia*. However, Nussbaum's belief that Plato describes 'goodness without fragility' should give us pause for thought. Socrates' life is one that sees him die in 'poverty', surrounded by friends who cannot commute the death penalty. It is a life in which he admits, in the *Apology*, that he has 'neglected all my own affairs . . . for so many years' because he has seen himself as a 'father or an elder brother' to all citizens, believing he can 'persuade you to care for virtue' (29). His life is therefore a reminder of the perils of such vulnerability in the city where an emotional philosophy of friendship can seem sentimental. Plato's 'goodness without fragility' may well be putting such vulnerability on trial in the *Apology*, and Nussbaum recommends that we must not try and 'humanize' Plato. Plato's *Republic* would ensure that Plato himself would always be remembered, like Callicles, as a man with 'business in the city'. As Williams reminds us, 'Plato's anxious question' that the *Republic* keeps asking is 'how moral knowledge could be institutionalized and effective in society'; it was supposed to 'complete the work, and the apology, of Socrates' (2006, 30). Even though it 'fails' to offer the 'theory of effective moral education' that it promises, Plato is clearly aware of the need to make the philosopher's knowledge amenable to 'public affairs'. Such a man could surely not be wholly admiring of a fellow countryman whom he describes as never 'taking part in public affairs' and who has followed since childhood a 'divine or spiritual sign', ridiculed by Menelaus at his trial, and a 'voice' that 'turns me away from something I am about to do, but it never encourages me to do anything' (29). We must, then, be wary of how Socrates presents himself here. Socrates' death can be regarded as the ultimate expression of the kind of fragility and vulnerability that Nussbaum believes Aristotle's good man must leave himself open to in his quest for excellence, but it can also be regarded as the staging of an old-school, sentimental philosophy removed from 'public affairs' that Plato needs to work through as he moves towards his vision of public man. What is clear, no matter how we read the scene, is that these early works fore-ground the deliberation on vulnerability. Whether the 'tragic conflict' is drawn from a life lived in the constant recognition of one's lack of wisdom or in the living out of the relationships of vulnerability that *philia* opens us up to, it is the negotiation of man's weakness in the context of the good life that is being examined.

Bernard Williams, who believes that 'Greek ethical thought' can be of great value to contemporary society's attempts to connect theories of the self, or questions 'of what life it is worth one's leading' with 'questions of how one should relate to others and to society' (2006, 45), describes a similar sense of vulnerability in these works in terms of 'exposure'. Williams believes that a 'deeper sense of exposure to fortune is expressed' in Greek literature and 'above all in tragedy' (45). Exposure is, for Williams, tied to notions of shame and necessity in Greek culture, two emotions that he suggests have lost their motivational sense in modern philosophy. Because, as Williams explains, the Greeks had no need of a God for their notion of the good life, despite the fact that there are numerous references to gods, the person was more at the mercy of such humanly charged factors as fate, chance and necessity. The risk that Aristotle perhaps did most to describe and that, for Williams, was a necessary part of the 'apparatus of social life' (45) could result in one being taken into slavery or in one marrying one's mother. It is this sense of risk in social life that Williams believes has been lost in philosophy. The repeated references to the insecurity of happiness get their force, for Williams, from the 'fact that the characters are displayed as having responsibilities, or pride, or obsessions, or needs, on a scale which lays them open to disaster in corresponding measure' (46); they encounter these disasters in 'full consciousness'. It could be argued that the metaphysical rationalism that dominated twentieth-century Western philosophy and that, for Gianni Vattimo, inaugurated 'the rationalization of existence guided by the mathematical sciences of nature' (Zabala 2007, 406) spawned a literature of modernism that has been able to respond most effectively to this lost sense of risk in the modern age. However, in saying this, it may well be impossible to recapture the sense of experience and vulnerability that Williams finds in ancient Greek literature. Because Homer wrote before Plato, whom Williams credits with having invented the 'subject philosophy', Homer's writing embodies a never to be regained merging of the literary and the 'philosophical'.[2] Socrates will still call on Homer's words on numerous occasions – in the *Gorgias* and the *Republic* – but once Plato invents the 'subject philosophy' he inaugurates a greater separation between literature and philosophy. However, it is this attention to the role fate, chance and necessity play in the structure of happiness that is so enduringly representative of the 'insecurity of happiness' that Greek thought privileges. Even if it is somewhat subdued in Plato, it is revived, as Williams and Nussbaum argue, in the later philosophy of Aristotle. In other words, Greek tragedy and 'ethical thought' was a consistent record of what Dickens would later describe as the 'battle of life' or of the 'struggle of existence'; it is caught up with the uniquely human capacity to achieve less than one's potential, to be susceptible to failings and to human weakness. Williams refers directly to this capacity of Greek literature and 'ethical thought' when he writes that '[a] sense of such significances, that what is great is fragile and that what is necessary may be destructive, which is present in the literature of the fifth century and earlier, has disappeared from the ethics of the philosophers' (2006, 46).

It is this concern for exposure that makes the related notions of shame and necessity so important for early 'ethical thought'. Williams argues that the 'root of shame lies in exposure in a more general sense, in being at a disadvantage: in what I shall call, in a very general phrase, a loss of power. The sense of shame is a reaction of the subject to the consciousness of this loss'. Shame becomes what Gabrielle Taylor calls 'the emotion of self-protection' (in Williams, 2008, 220). The consciousness of this 'loss of power' is a cause of shame because it impedes action. However, since this theory of action, in early Greek thought describes how the 'functions of the mind, above all with regard to action, are defined in terms of categories that get their significance from ethics', (2008, 42) and since the feeling that causes the shame that necessitates this theory is a 'loss of power', it is the experience of vulnerability or weakness that is at the heart of the emergence of this early ethics. We have seen that the Socrates of the *Gorgias* is more afraid of the shame of realizing that he has not provided himself with sufficient 'self-protection' from acting unjustly than he is of death itself. Williams argues that this incorporation of shame in this way into a theory of action is an idea that is not present in 'Homer and the tragedians' (2008, 42). It therefore describes the incorporation of weakness and vulnerability into a philosophy of life.

However, Williams notes that in incorporating the experience of shame based on weakness into philosophy and into this theory of action, not all 'kinds of human experience and human necessity' were being described in this early ethical thought: 'Greek philosophy, in its sustained pursuit of rational self-sufficiency, does turn its back on kinds of human experience and human necessity of which Greek literature itself offers the purest, if not the richest, expression' (2006, 46). In this new philosophy 'reason operates as a distinctive part of the soul only to the extent that it controls, dominates or rises above desires' (2008, 43); it leads, as Nussbaum suggests, to the less than wholesome examination of these 'ethically significant distinctions of character and motive'. Aristotle will be the first to give these their due in a theory of action that speaks for the 'excellences of character' and not only the 'intellectual excellences' (43). However, when Williams describes the work of Aristotle, the philosopher who really describes the 'fragility of goodness', he argues that Aristotle's 'most famous contribution' to the discussions on Plato's new understanding of the soul and the individual comes in the shape of his discussion of *akrasia*, what approximates to 'weakness of the will' or 'incontinence'. Williams tells us that Aristotle's definition of this condition is 'entirely shaped by ethical interests' (2008, 44). Aristotle writes: 'And the incontinent man [the *akrates*], knowing that what he does is bad, does it as a result of passion, while the continent man [the *enkrates*], knowing that his appetites are bad, does not follow them because of his reason' (Barnes, *NE* VII, 1809). It is important, then, that we look more closely at this concept.

When Plato does come to describe his tripartite division of the soul in the *Republic*, it is the third part – the part that is notoriously difficult to define and that mediates between appetite and reason, an area that encompasses spirit, feelings and indignation, and that has been described as self-regard or self-preservation that causes the most difficulty. Socrates admits, in his discussion with Glaucon, that they will have to change their 'methods of . . . argument' in their inquiry into the 'three parts' of the 'soul' or they 'will never get a precise answer using our present methods of argument' (Cooper IV.V 1067). The famous Socratic paradox that 'no one does wrong willingly' is the idea that is turned to most frequently in examinations of how moral weakness or human failing can be incorporated into Plato's tripartite model of the soul by way of this third part. The paradox would appear to rule out *akrasia* or weakness of the will. If Greek tragedy is all about staging the 'tragic conflict' where man's frailties are laid bare, and if Plato's theory of action strives to incorporate this sense of vulnerability into a philosophy of life, then it will indeed, as Williams suggests, have to avoid a great deal of 'human experience and human necessity' if no one is to do wrong willingly. The paradox can still allow for agents, such as a Hamlet or a Raskolnikov, who go through incredible mental torture before they kill, but it would deny the possibility of someone performing a wrong in the full knowledge that it was 'the action judged best on the basis of all available relevant reasons'. This is an ability that the rational man possesses through applying 'practical reasoning', and Donald Davidson argues that it is beyond the incontinent man, who, for him, acts 'irrationally' (Davidson, 2006).

There has been a great deal of commentary on the notion of *akrasia*.[3] *Akrasia* is generally regarded as being rejected by Socrates; however, Roslyn Weiss's recent examination of the Socratic paradox offers a refreshing reading. She argues that the paradox is Socrates' 'weapon of choice for taking on the enemies of justice' (1) and that 'once the paradoxes are viewed as reactions to positions taken by Socrates' opponents, it is possible to show that Socrates endorses neither the implausible doctrine that has come to be known as the denial of *akrasia* nor the host of other odd ideas associated with it' (22). Because the Sophists turn intemperance and overindulgence into virtues, Socrates is pressured into responding with a theory of action that presumes a holistic view of life. It is almost as if he is describing a theory of action from a god's perspective: 'What Socrates means by saying that no one does wrong willingly is that whenever one chooses injustice over justice one fails to fulfill one's arguably most important wish – namely, the wish to live well and do well really' (19). In order to explore how the Socratic theory of action deals with an action that raises important questions for the Socratic paradox, I want to focus on the story about Leontius that Socrates relates in the *Republic*.

Socrates, in this section, reverts to retelling a story. It is notable, despite Plato's admonitions to poets and writers in the previous section of the *Republic*, that dialogue is supplemented with story or narrative when it is proving difficult to define particularly weighty ideas. Nussbaum argues that a contrast between the 'literary and the philosophical' is 'sharply drawn' by Plato but that it is done 'unreflectively', in a manner that 'does not call into question the contrasts themselves' (187). The story Socrates relates is about Leontius, the son of Aglaion, who is on his way up from the Piraeus when he notices some corpses lying under the outer side of the north wall of the city with the executioner standing by. The corpses of the condemned wrong-doers spur Leontius' desire and he struggles to refrain from looking at the spectacle. There is a 'conflict in the mind', as Socrates suggests later (2007, Desmond Lee translation, 149; the G. M. A. Grube translation revised by C. D. C. Reeve reads: 'the civil war in the soul' [in Cooper 1072]); Leontius is filled with desire to have a good look, but at the same time holds 'himself back in disgust' (2007, Lee translation 148). Socrates relates the story to explain to Glaucon that there is another part to the soul besides reason and appetite; he argues that the story shows 'that anger sometimes makes war against the appetites' (Cooper 1070). Socrates will later argue that health, and excellence as a 'kind of mental health', is produced by 'establish[ing] the components of the body in a natural relation of control' (Cooper 1076). Leontius is obviously lacking this 'natural relation of control' since he strides up to the corpses, stares at them and begins scolding himself: 'Look for yourselves, you evil wretches, take your fill of the beautiful sight!' (Cooper, 1071: 440 a).[4] There is clearly a sense that the anger and indignation have a purpose. As Williams argues, shame and indignation that arise from recognition of a 'loss of power' drive the configuration of this tripartite description of the soul. In this story Leontius is not simply disgusted at the fact that there are stinking corpses; he is disgusted at himself for wanting to stare at them. His recognition of a 'loss of power' arises from the fact that he is not in possession of the 'natural relation of control' of the harmonious soul. After acknowledging his own appetite and his own self-disgust in wanting (and then going) to stare at the corpses, it could be argued that – even at this late stage, with his eyes gaping at the corpses – he turns the moment to his advantage. He stares long and hard, hoping to teach himself a lesson. Staring at corpses is no worthy practice, but if one feels impelled to do so, one might as well take in the full horror of the spectacle so that one can feel the harm that such a predilection brings to the soul and to the mind's harmony. However, since we are told by most commentators that Socrates rejects *akrasia* and advises that 'no one does wrong willingly', it is interesting to read the commentary on Leontius' actions. Socrates continues: '[b]esides, don't we often notice in other cases that when appetite forces someone contrary to rational calculation, he reproaches himself and gets angry with that in him that's doing the forcing, so that of the two factions that are fighting a civil war, so to speak, spirit allies itself with reason?' (1071: 440b). Desmond Lee translates this passage as follows: 'And don't we often see other instances of a man whose desires are trying to force him to do something his reason disapproves of, cursing himself and getting indignant at their violence?' (146). Now, if *akrasia*, or incontinence, is not possible in Socrates' world, then one would presume that 'rational calculation' or 'reason', with the aid of spirit or indignation, prevents the wrong from being enacted. However, Leontius has actually done the deed; he upbraids himself while staring at the corpses. We are told that '[f]or a time he struggled with himself' and this suggests that the act was not impulsive and that reason was involved. It is only after this period of 'struggle' that, 'overpowered by the appetite', he pushes his eyes wide open and stares. Whether the final act of staring was done 'willingly' or not is unclear, but his words to himself as he stares reveal that the doing of the 'wrong' act is being employed to heighten the gravity of his self-berating in the expectation that it will teach him not to stray again. Living through the shame of having failed provides a more heartfelt sense of indignation than if one had merely mentally acknowledged that shame will result from doing what is 'unjust'. Since shame and the acknowledgement of a 'loss of power' lies at the heart of early attempts to devise a theory of action around ethics, then it is likely that the conviction not to do what is unjust will be more emphatic if the shame has been lived through. While in hindsight Leontius would probably reason that he should not stare, in the heat of the moment he has acknowledged that he has had to give in to his appetite. The important point is that, in turning the momentary failing to his advantage, he willingly seems to prolong the stare so that he can remind himself firsthand how corrupting such appetites can be. There would seem then to be a degree of give and even forgiveness in Socrates' relating of the story of Leontius.[5] This story and the commentary Socrates gives would suggest, as Weiss argues, that Socrates cannot be seen to uphold the 'implausible doctrine that has come to be known as the denial of *akrasia*' (21). Wrongs can sometimes be done willingly, with the accompaniment of reason, 'rational calculation' and indignation, even if it is in order to force a lesson home. Once again, it is the deliberation on the momentary 'loss of power' that has motivated this particular shaping of the tripartite soul.

In further demonstrating the different nature of this third part of the soul, Socrates refers to the words of Homer once again. He argues that the line 'He struck his chest and calls his heart to order' (Lee, 149: 441b) demonstrates how Homer is here making 'one element rebuke another, distinguishing the power to reflect about good and evil from unreasoning passion' (441b). Socrates explains that in order for there to be this third part of the soul – spirit or indignation – it must be 'different from the rational part' (441a). When Glaucon replies that this 'isn't difficult to show' because even 'in small children, one can see that they are full of spirit right from birth', Socrates replies: '[t]hat's really well put'. However, surely the kind of spirit or indignation that accompanies and supplements the rational calculation of why it is wrong to look at corpses must be different for an adult like Leontius than it would be for a very young child. It cannot only be reason that is bound up with the reflection about 'good and evil'; indignation would have no force if there were no understanding of good and evil, and surely a young child 'right from birth' has a very different understanding of good and evil than an adult like Leontius. In leaving Leontius, we are left with a sense that each individual needs to tackle his or her weaknesses and the desires that lead to disharmony in a profound manner. There is no point wallpapering over the cracks, just as there would have been no point if Leontius sneaked a look at the corpses and then went on his way attempting to persuade himself that he had never in fact *really* looked. There is a sense from this story that, on occasion, Socrates accepts that an act regarded as wrong can be the result of a moment when reason is 'overpowered by the appetite', but that shame can step in and give reason a second wind so that the depravity of the moment can be used to teach a lesson.

In finishing this chapter, I want to now read Aristotle on this Socratic paradox in order to show that the two philosophers who are regularly regarded as being at loggerheads over *akrasia* and moral weakness are, in fact, quite close. The story of Leontius may be as close to the akratic as Plato brings us. Aristotle will discuss Socrates' views on *akrasia* in the seventh book of his *Nicomachean Ethics*. He asks:

> [W]hat kind of right belief is possessed by the man who behaves incontinently. That he should behave so when he has knowledge, some say is impossible; for it would be strange – so Socrates thought – if when knowledge was in a man something else could master it and drag it about like a slave. For *Socrates* was entirely opposed to the view in question, holding that there is no such thing as incontinence; no one, he said, acts against what he believes best – people act so only by reason of ignorance. (Barnes, 1809–10)[6]

Aristotle believes that this 'contradicts the plain phenomena' (1810). He introduces a broader picture of character and of the person. The incontinent man 'knowing what he does is bad, does it as a result of passion'

(1809). There are different kinds of incontinence, for Aristotle says: 'Of incontinence one kind is impetuosity, another weakness' (1818). Therefore, even though *akrasia* (or incontinence) is today translated as 'weakness of will', Aristotle does point to a distinct kind of incontinence, which he calls weakness, and those who are incontinent in this way are those who, because they have not deliberated, 'are led by their passions' (1818). Friedrich Nietzsche, many centuries later, would describe weakness of the will, 'the inability *not* to react to a stimulus', as 'merely another form of degeneration' because it suggested that all impulses need to be extirpated or denounced (*Twilight*, 53). However, since weakness of will is a recognized expression for incontinence in philosophy today, incontinence will be taken to refer here to a kind of weakness. The difference between Aristotle's agent and Plato's Leontius is that Aristotle's agent is invested with a greater sense of character and with a greater array of emotions. Aristotle, therefore, has the vocabulary to unsettle Socrates' privileging of knowledge. Plato's Socrates denies incontinence or *akrasia* because nothing is stronger than knowledge and no one acts contrary to a better course they have knowledge of. Aristotle considers how some people say it might be 'opinion' and not knowledge that the incontinent is invested with when he or she enters the state; it is therefore 'not a strong belief that resists but a weak one, as in men who hesitate' (1810). However, he discards this view because it would lead to the 'absurd' situation where a man can be both practically wise and incontinent at the same time. He therefore makes something of a return to Socrates and recognizes that men frequently use the word 'knowledge' incorrectly: '[t]he fact that men use the language that flows from knowledge proves nothing; for even men under the influence of these passions [including incontinents] utter scientific proofs and verses of Empedocles' (1812).

He then introduces the notions of universal and particular opinion to get to the bottom of the problem concerning in what sense incontinents know. He describes a situation in which an agent is presented with some sweets. The universal opinion will advise him that he should restrain himself when it comes to tasting sweet things. However, he is also in possession of a particular opinion that tells him that 'this is sweet' and this is 'the opinion that is active'. Appetite is also present in the man and this 'leads [him] towards' the sweet so 'that it turns out that a man behaves incontinently under the influence (in a sense) of reason and opinion, and of opinion not contrary in itself, but only incidentally – for the appetite is contrary not the opinion – to right reason' (1812). In other words, by introducing these notions of universal and particular opinion Aristotle can claim that the incontinent is not simply overcome by the passions, but that he or she actually acts in accordance with a degree of reason. As he says at a later stage, the incontinent man is 'better than the self-indulgent man, and not bad without qualification; for the best thing in him, the first principle [what Aristotle appears to hold is right reason], is preserved' (1819). Aristotle then finally offers the notion of 'perceptual knowledge', a kind of knowledge that describes an 'opinion about a perceptible object . . . that determines our actions' (1812), in order to come to some kind of conclusion about the kind of knowledge an incontinent man has. He will state that the kind of opinion or perceptual knowledge that the man who eats the sweets has 'is not universal nor equally an object of knowledge with the universal term' and that 'the position that Socrates sought to establish actually seems to result; for it is not what is thought to be knowledge proper that the passion overcomes (nor is it this that is dragged about as a result of the passion) but perceptual knowledge' and this 'must suffice as our answer to the question of whether men can act incontinently when they know or not, and in what sense they know' (1812–13). In other words, Aristotle has come full circle in a sense. He originally suggests that Socrates might have it all wrong, only to conclude by suggesting that it is critics and 'men' in general who have it all wrong by misunderstanding Socrates' notion of knowledge.

Aristotle ultimately comes to agree that a universal sense of knowledge – a kind of knowledge that, for agents, has 'to become part of themselves, and that takes time' (1812) – is not overcome by the passions or anything else for the incontinent man. It is not 'knowledge proper' that the passion overcomes but this new notion of 'perceptual knowledge' that he has introduced. Roger Crisp refers to this universal knowledge that Socrates and Aristotle both respect as 'knowledge of any ethical universal' (Aristotle, 2000, ix). Aristotle will later compound this shift towards Socrates when he writes that '[n]or can the same man have practical wisdom and be incontinent' (1820). *Phronesis*[7] is an important notion for Aristotle; it describes the kind of knowledge gained, perhaps through years of practising a *technē*, to the extent that the knowledge becomes 'part' of the person, or, to use a word that will have profound meaning for weakness in the Christian context, embodied.[8] Aristotle writes that 'a man has practical wisdom not by knowing only but by acting; but the incontinent man is unable to act' (1820). 'Act' here must therefore describe a particular type of action that expresses ethical awareness. For even though the incontinent is described a few lines later as acting – 'he acts voluntarily (for he acts in a sense with knowledge both of what he does and of that for the sake of which he does it), but is not wicked since his choice is good' – he is only 'half-wicked' and he does not act with 'malice aforethought'. Therefore, we can see that whereas Aristotle introduces the 'incontinent man' as a man who may well suffer from a weakness that we can describe as 'weakness of will', the weakness does not shatter the inviolability of 'right reason' and universal knowledge. If a man has acquired practical wisdom, possibly Aristotle's greatest attribute for man, then he will simply not act incontinently. And since practical wisdom is not something that can be put on and taken off like a cloak but must instead become 'part of [ourselves]', the practically wise man will never succumb to weakness or *akrasia*. This is more than a little similar to Socrates' description of the philosopher or the truly wise man.

However, how can such a state be attained? It is because Aristotle goes to such lengths to describe these states of weakness, which prevent man from attaining such a state of being practically wise, that we can take heart. He writes that 'continence consists in conquering' whereas 'endurance consists' only 'in resisting'. This is why 'continence is also more worthy of choice than endurance' (1817). He also describes an important state of the philosopher, that of 'contemplation', as involving '*no* pain or appetite'; 'the nature in such a case not being defective at all' (1821–2). It is then that he moves to his unique sense of 'impotentiality', a notion and state that Giorgio Agamben has developed in his own work and which I examine in more detail in Chapter 6. Such a state of 'impotentiality', what speaks of 'immobility', impotence and even what philosophers today call 'radical passivity' comes closest to the weakness that this book speaks for, a weakness that allows for potential with full acceptance of the body's condition. Aristotle offers justification for his philosophy with references to mortality and 'God':

There is no one thing that is always pleasant, because our nature is not simple but there is another element in us as well, inasmuch as we are perishable creatures, so that if the one element does something, this is unnatural to the other nature, and when the two elements are evenly balanced, what is done seems neither painful nor pleasant; for if the nature of anything were simple, the same action would always be most pleasant to it. This is why God always enjoys a single and simple pleasure; for there is not only an activity of movement but an activity of *immobility* [my italics], and pleasure is found more in rest that in movement. (Barnes, 1825)

Aristotle is, then, more accepting of man's condition as 'perishing creatures' than as beings whose souls are sent to the Isles of the Blessed. In
accepting 'excellences of character' that draw from a heightened assessment of bodily appetites, he allows room for notions of forgiveness,[9] immobility and impotentiality that all privilege a sense of man's embeddedness in
his physicality, an understanding that takes on ever new dimensions when
placed alongside Daoism's advice to 'abide by the weak' and when contrasted with the Christian descriptions of weak flesh.

Chapter 2

弱者道之用 'Weakness is the Means *dao* Employs': Daoism and Weakness

When we move from ancient Greek and Christian accounts of weakness to weakness as it is used in the *Lao tzu*,[1] we see less of an emphasis on shame and guilt. D. C. Lau argues that the supreme object of the *Lao tzu* is the 'preservation of life, "the way", to use its own words, "of long life and being able to keep one's sight for a long time"' (1958, 357) and this must be achieved by learning to 'abide by the soft' (358) and holding 'one's self humble and weak' as the ancient scholar Ban Gu suggests in his first-century reading of the *Lao tzu* in his history of the Former Han (in Lau, 357). D. C. Lau also reminds us that this approach to living is reputedly described by Lao Tzu in the *T'ien-hsia* chapter of *Chuang Tzŭ* in terms of gender: 'Knowing the male, abide by the female and be the ravine of the world' (349). The *Lao tzu* itself advises, in Chapter 40, that 'weakness is the means the way employs' (Lau, 2001, XL.88, p. 61);[2] in Chapter 76 that '[a] man is supple and weak when living, but hard and stiff when dead' (LXXVI.182, p. 109); and in Chapter 78: 'That the weak overcomes the strong,/And the submissive overcomes the hard,/Everyone in the world knows yet no one can put this knowledge into practice' (LXXVIII.187, p. 113). How are we to understand weakness here? Commentary on the *Lao tzu* has sparked much heated debate in sinology and in comparative studies. I want to examine, first, how weakness is understood in terms of the theory of opposites that D. C. Lau regards as central for understanding the *Lao tzu*; and, second, how the text's foregrounding of, what Longxi Zhang describes as the 'inadequacy of signification', perhaps the point from which all weakness originates, has led to some soul searching in comparative studies in relation to whether the investigation of the inherent weakness of language is revealing of irreconcilable differences between traditions of representation. The 'inadequacy' of language that the text foregrounds has become a point from which to assess how different traditions make meaning.

The other title for the work, *Tao te ching*, is itself revealing; the Chinese character for virtue, *te*, what is used interchangeably with *jen* in Confucius, is described by Xinzhong Yao as 'both the power of humanity and the seed that can grow into full humanity' (Yao, 140). Since it might be argued – if we are trying to distinguish between Daoism and Confucianism – that Daoism is more concerned with the natural than the moral order, then weakness in the *Lao tzu* is a means through which such humanity can be realized.[3] It is quite close to Aristotle's notions of immobility and impotentiality that I examined in the first chapter. It describes the process for realizing virtue, what is also assigned to *te*. The work itself also explains how we move from *Tao* to *te*: 'After *tao* (the Way) was lost, then came *te* (power or virtue)' (Chapter 18) and 'after *te* was lost, then came *jen*' (Chapter 38). *Jen* is translated as benevolence or human kindness. Fung Yu-Lan reminds us that Lao Tzu 'despised' such Confucian virtues as 'human-heartedness' and 'righteousness' because they represented a 'degeneration from *Tao* and *Te*' and that this 'degeneration' begins with 'ceremonials' (101). In being tied to a natural order, weakness in Daoism does not rely on the same system of philosophical Forms that the Platonic system does (Lau reminds us that Plato's argument results in a 'plurality of Forms' but that there is 'only one *tao*' (2001, xviii)) and since transcendence, both in Daoism and Confucianism, is not predetermined by God's grace or by a recognition of mankind's weakness in relation to a benevolent Christ and an omnipotent and sometimes wrathful God, this kind of weakness is also very different from that found in Christian writers. Weakness is also emphasized in Daoism in a way it is not in Confucianism. Confucianism does stress notions of self-control that are reminiscent of the aspect of self-regard found in *akrasia*. Confucius advises that 'to control oneself and return to *li* [propriety or moral codes] is the way to *jen* [benevolence]' (in Yao, 141). However, even though the movement from *li* to *jen* is by way of *ke ji*, what is typically translated as 'to overcome and subdue oneself', Xinzhong Yao argues that this translation does not reflect the 'full meaning of its Chinese counterpart'; '*Ke ji* in a Confucian context is not to suppress all one's desires and interests, but to guard against being overcome by *extreme* motives, emotions or instincts' (141). Confucius advises: 'to subdue one's self and return to propriety is perfect virtue. If a man can for one day subdue himself and return to propriety, all under heaven will ascribe perfect virtue to him' (Lau translation, 1979, 12.1, p. 112).[4] The inclusion of 'one day' here is revealing of a distinct understanding of human weakness and human frailty that one might argue is often lacking in the peripatetic and theological accounts of perfect knowledge, wisdom or divine grace. It might lead one to question whether many Christian writers, in seeking to define humanity in terms of what could be accepting of divinity through Incarnation, set the bar too high for most believers, thereby exacerbating and overplaying human weaknesses. Confucius explains more clearly in an earlier section how 'insufficient strength' is not in itself the reason why people do not choose to be benevolent: 'Is there a man who, for the space of a single day, is able to devote all his strength to benevolence? I have not come across such a man whose strength proves insufficient for the task. There must be such cases of insufficient strength, only I have not come across them' (4.6, p. 73).

The reason why benevolence is so rare is simply because, as he explains at the start of this section: 'I have never met a man who finds benevolence attractive' (4.6, p. 73). For Confucius, then, 'perfect virtue' and 'benevolence' are so difficult to attain not because people lack the strength to attain these states, but simply because they choose not to. This might then appear as a philosophy that is more accepting of the tendency to choose 'unbenevolence'; the failure involved in making this choice has less weight attached than seems to be the case for Christian writers and Greek philosophers. It is clear that Confucius sees that the potential is there for benevolence; however, there is no sense of predestination or even of the individual, like Leontius, being overcome by appetite. Confucius does not set man up as weak and powerless in the face of a divine will or an uncontrollable appetite; he simply states that people do not find such 'benevolence' to be 'attractive' and choose to follow 'unbenevolence'. It might be regarded, then, as a rather life-affirming reading of the human condition, especially if placed beside post-Reformation creeds on man's impotence and humility before God by writers such as Calvin, who speaks of 'how destitute and devoid of all good things man is'.[5] Many scholars translate Confucius's guidance here in terms of asking individuals to follow 'the middle way' (Yao, 142). However, we will also see that Daoism has a less prescriptive approach when describing nature of weakness since it aligns weakness with natural cycles.

Weakness is an important concept for the *Lao tzu*, a work that Ursula K. Le Guin describes, in her 'rendition' of the *Lao tzu*, as 'the most lovable of all the great religious texts, funny, keen, kind, modest, indestructibly outrageous, and inexhaustibly refreshing' (xi). One of the first things we realize when we begin reading the *Lao tzu* is that it immediately alerts us to the weakness of language itself. The name of the text itself is indistinguishable from the name of its author, if indeed, and this is very unlikely, there is a single author. Rather like the original Greek words for the Bible, *ta biblia*, which describes a collection of texts or books, the *Lao tzu* is most likely an anthology written well after Confucius and 'after Hui Shih and Kung-sun

Lung' (Fung Yu-Lan, 94). 弱, *ruo*, the character for weakness, originates as a pictograph of a fragile plant or possibly a variation of a young bird's wings. It is important to note that characters often have multiple meanings in Chinese ancient texts. Xinzhong Yao explains that *Tian* (what Yao regards as the 'Confucian transcendent being' and also 'Heaven' (77)) appears a 'total of eighteen times in the *Analects*'; among these eighteen times 'there are twelve that are uttered by Confucius himself' and '[t]hree kinds of *Tian* can be detected in these twelve uses' (Yao, 58). However, 弱 (*ruo*) is generally translated as weakness in the translations.

The *Tao te ching*, or the *Lao tzu*, has as its 'best authenticated theory', acording to D. C. Lau, the notion of 'valuing the soft' or 'abiding by the soft' (1958, 349) or, as he puts elsewhere in relation to Daoism in general, 'abiding by the limpid and the empty, holding on to the essential and basic' (357). Many commentators on this ancient classic of Chinese literature also note, however, that the work privileges a 'theory of circular change' since there are constant references in the *Lao tzu* to 'return', and to how 'things turn back', and lines that speak of the value of old traditions: 'Let your wheels move only along old ruts' (LVI.129, p. 83). However, D. C. Lau advises that since the precept of 'holding fast to the submissive seems central to the teachings in the *Lao Tzu*, it is the cyclic interpretation that has to be given up' (1963, Introduction, xxiv). He argues: 'Moreover, if change is cyclic and a thing that reaches the limit in one direction will revert to the opposite direction, then the precept [of holding to the weak] is both useless and impracticable. It is useless, if both development and decline are inevitable, since the purpose is in the first instance to avoid decline; and impracticable, if it advocates that we should remain stationary in a world of inexorable and incessant change' (Lau, 1963, xxiv).

What, then, is the nature of this kind of weakness or submissiveness? Even though Lau believes that there is this 'incompatibility between the theory of circular change and the injunction to "abide by the soft"' (1958, 354), he does offer a solution. He argues that the process of change is not necessarily circular because 'decline is inexorable, but development may require effort', therefore it is 'both possible and useful to "abide by the soft"' (355). Lau also explains how this theory, which in some ways seems counterintuitive, emerged in China. As with Plato, where there is a strong analogy between soul and state (Plato has Socrates say in the *Republic*: 'Well, we are bound to admit that the elements and traits that belong to a state must also exist in the individuals that compose it' [Lee translation, 1987, 4.5, p. 142]), morals and politics in ancient China were 'looked upon as two aspects of the same thing' (Lau, 1958, 356). When 'The Way' is applied to an individual's life it is his or her way of life, but when it is applied to government it becomes the way of the state (356). As Chuang Tzu, 'perhaps the greatest of the early Daoists', (Fung Yu-Lan, 104) suggests, 'the way of inwardly being a sage and outwardly being a king' (in Lau, 1958, 356) is most important for public life. The historical context is also central to any understanding of the text. The *Lao tzu* was written in the Warring States Period and therefore the 'common man' was most concerned with self-preservation: 'he has to exercise prodigious care if he were to wish to live out his natural span' (356). Therefore 'survival' or the 'preservation of one's life' is the 'principal lesson' (357) of the *Lao tzu*. Even though Daoism is often criticized by Confucianists as being impractical and by the Mohists as being illogical (Fung Yu-Lan, 126), it is a body of thought that was intended to be lived out practically. As Ban Gu notes in his comments on Daoist works in the 'Bibliographical Chapter' in his history of the Former Han both for rulers of states and for rulers of individual bodies: 'The Daoists and their like . . . record one by one success and failure, preservation and annihilation, disaster and good fortune, the way of antiquity and that of the present, and then come to the realization of the importance of holding on to the essential and basic, abiding by the limpid and the empty, holding one's self humble and weak. This is *the method of the ruler facing south*' (in Lau, 357).

D. C. Lau also argues that *Lao tzu* describes two different kinds of weakness: 'To abide by the weak and yet be content presumably makes it different from simply being weak' (358). The aim, then, is to abide by the weak in a non-contentious and content manner; it is not enough to simply acknowledge one's weakness, one must experience a 'freedom from desire': 'The nameless uncarved block/Is but freedom from desire,/And if I cease to desire and remain still,/The empire will be at peace of its own accord' (XXXVII.81, p. 55). This state also recalls the buddhist state of *nibbāna* which requires 'the relinquishing of all attachments, the destruction of craving' (Lopez, Jr. 111). However, Wing-tsit Chan also reminds us in relation to Daoist weakness that 'one should not be misled by its ideals of weakness and emptiness into thinking that Daoism is a philosophy of negativism' (1963, 137). The above extract also demonstrates that language and writing is bound up with desire and with action; remaining still, ceasing to desire and 'doing that which consists in taking no action' (LXIII.147, p. 93) is the way of the sage who 'desires not to desire' (LXIV.156, p. 95). Writing marks the beginning of the move away from this state. When Lau describes the 'doctrine' of the text in terms of an ability to abide by the soft and the weak 'through knowing where to stop and when to be content' – the *Lao tzu* reads: 'One ought to know that it is time to stop./Knowing when to stop one can be free from danger.' (XXXII.72, p. 49) – it begins to sound a little like the rule of reason in the Platonic tripartite division of the soul. However, even though there are references to 'knowing' and 'enlightenment' in the *Lao tzu* it is difficult to find an equivalent for reason, *ratio* or *logos*.

However, it is worth looking more closely at the use of the notion of weakness in this classic Daoist text. Lao Tzu uses the metaphors of wind and water to describe how such weakness works: 'In the world there is nothing more submissive and weak than water. Yet for attacking that which is hard and strong nothing can surpass it. This is because there is nothing that can take its place' (LXXVIII.186, p. 113). This ancient description of a state of receptivity and passivity is echoed by contemporary descriptions of fragilty and 'radical passivity'. Thomas Carl Wall describes the citizen of Giorgio Agamben's coming community as existing in a state of radical passivity as a being who is 'fragile, unstable' and who is '*the pure possibility of any relation whatever.* It is a being constituted *by* expropriation and also simultaneously, by the impossibility of exclusion because it incessantly borders on all its possibilities' (156). However, it might be more appropriate to read this water metaphor in terms of *qi*, which Roger T. Ames translates as 'vital energy'. The weakness of water is a revealing metaphor; water can erode landscapes over time through a process that appears gradual and gentle, through the lapping of waves against a shore. Water, as we will see in the next section, is also a favoured figure for life for Dickens and Joyce. However, when one is at the mercy of the sea or water one also learns to give up a degree of control since it is most advantageous to work with the water to achieve motion. As with a tree in the wind, people must also learn when to bend but not break or when to give themselves up momentarily to the elements, until the swell or gust has subsided. An acknowledgement of one's weakness in certain respects is essential for self-preservation or for practised self-regard – what might remind us once again of the contemporaneous interest in Greece in the notion of *akrasia* as self-regard. However, Ames reminds us that the Daoist notion of 'Inward Training' (*Neiye*) and its associated notion *qi* (vital energy) are ideas that defy 'the Aristotelian categories' (64). *Qi* is 'at once one and many. When it accumulates and coagulates, it can have a formal coherence by taking on a shape inspired by its context that is persistent and yet changing too'; *qi* 'will not be resolved into categories that would separate forming from functioning' (64). It speaks for a harmonious relationship with nature and for a harmonious relationship with such concepts as *jen* and *Tian*, which also speak for how the individual embodies the transcendental, but a transcendental that is different from the Christian transcendent as God.

It is noteworthy that Daoism and Confucianism differ in relation to where they place the transcendent; Confucianism privileges *jen* (*Jen* is a central concept for Confucianism; Wing-tsit Chan has documented its evolution and how it has variously described such notions as 'kindness from above,' 'benevolence,' 'affection' and even 'one body with the universe' (in Yao, 74)) as a concept represented most effectively by the notion of the 'mind-heart' (Yao, 80) – and we will see in a later chapter how Nietzsche's Zarathustra also emphasizes the heart. Xinzhong Yao writes the following on this mind-heart: 'The unity of all things lies in the mind of *jen* that is our Heaven-endowed nature. The mind-heart in itself has bright and manifest virtues which are present in all men, either great or small, so long as it is not obscured by selfish desires' (80). This use of the heart to speak for a neglected aspect of thought is also reminiscent of the transformation that took place in terms of the covenant between man and God in moving from the Old Testament to the New Testament. The initial covenant was revealed to Moses on tablets of stone while he veiled himself so that the Israelites should not see the 'splendour of the covenant fading'. This 'veil' is also removed in the new covenant where Christ reveals himself in flesh as the embodiment of a new covenant between God and man 'so that anyone who turns to the Lord can immediately behold his glory' (Yao, 120).

The *Lao tzu* is also, as has been suggested, deeply concerned with naming; it speaks, like Beckett, about the 'unnamable'; 'The way that can be spoken of/Is not the constant way;/The name that can be named/Is not the constant name' (I.1. p. 3); and later: 'The nameless uncarved block/Is freedom from desire' (XXXVII.81, p. 55). Longxi Zhang points to another aspect of this 'inadequacy of signification' that the *Lao tzu* makes us confront even before we have seized on its themes and philosophy. The commentary on this aspect of linguistic inadequacy or weakness in the *Lao tzu* has raised a whole host of issues for comparative studies; some comparatists argue that this acknowledgement in the *Lao tzu* demonstrates how both Western and Chinese language systems foreground, in a similar manner, the 'slippery' nature of signification. In other words, it is only when language self-reflectively calls attention to its own weakness that we can truly understand how different writing systems are connected. While this once again points to the value of acknowledging structural weakness, this tendency to align Chinese and Western systems of signification has been challenged by sinologists such as Robert T. Ames and James J. Y. Liu, and I return to this in greater detail in Chapter 5 in discussing the work of Derrida.[6]

Longxi Zhang uses the *Lao tzu*'s foregrounding of the 'inadequacy of signification' to compare Chinese and Western systems of signification.

Zhang refers to Qian Zhongshu's celebrated commentaries on the *Lao tzu*. Qian, in turn, is commenting on the Wang Bi text of the *Lao tzu*. Zhang informs us that the Wang Bi provides us with a brief note to the opening lines of the *Lao tzu* – 'The *Dao* that can be spoken of is not the constant *Dao*./The name that can be named is not the constant name' – that reads as follows: 'The sayable *Dao* and the nameable name point to things and define their shapes, but they do not capture their constant nature; therefore [the constant *Dao*] cannot be spoken and cannot be named' (in Csikszentmihalyi, 100). Qian gives the following commentary to this extract from the Wang Bi text:

> In explicating these first two verses, the 'Explaining the *Laozi*' (*JeLao*) chapter of the *Han Feizi* already says in effect that all that is present or absent, lives or dies, flourishes or persishes, 'cannot be said to be constant', and whatever is constant 'has no duration or change, follows no fixed rules, and therefore cannot be spoken'. Wang's note means to say the same, but it does not give a word-by-word exegesis. (100)

Zhang argues, in relation to this piece of commentary, that the 'question of speaking and naming, or the relationship between thinking and language, is thus the first question presented at the beginning of the *Laozi*' (100); he argues that the text raises philosophical and not solely philological questions and that the philological has often been overplayed in commentaries.

With the use of such words as 'present' and 'absent' and the reference to Lao Tzu's 'distrust of words' and his 'radical linguistic skepticism', Zhang sets out to make the *Lao tzu* amenable to post-structuralist and even deconstructive reasoning and analysis, thereby adding a new dimension to the linguistic weakness the *Lao tzu* raises so early in the text. He argues that what the *Lao tzu* reveals in its 'opening verses' is the 'essential problem of language: the inadequacy of all verbal expressions, either spoken or written' (102) and that 'it is especially appropriate to emphasize the philosophical aspect of the *Laozi* beyond the mere explication of single words' (101). He has already written at length, in *The Tao and the Logos*, on related issues such as the 'primal discourse' and how writing and commentary destroy this and 'records but the loss of what was originally contained in thought as internal speech . . . the internal speech which alone holds the ideal harmony of the sign and the thing' (16). Of course, this kind of argument recalls Derrida's work on logocentrism that notes the privileging of speech over writing in Western metaphysics. However, if Derrida's thesis is extracted from its European context, as it is here for Zhang, and from the debate over the respective merits of Christian and Judaic exegetical and hermeneutic styles, then the aspects of embodiment, presence and 'linguistic incarnation' that haunt Western metaphysics like spectres and that grant Derrida's 'deconstructive' arguments such influence, take on a very different meaning. We would then, most likely, have a very different version of the logocentric argument.

Zhang suggests that Qian's efforts to 'understand Laozi in the context of Eastern and Western philosophy and mysticism' is important because it enables us 'to read the *Laozi* as we have never read it before, and understand its many ideas as meaningful and significant to us in our own time' and thus make it 'capable of enriching our own experience, far beyond the confines of a mysterious and arcane Daoism' (1999, 123). Zhang explains that Qian's reading of the first verse of the *Lao tzu* is particularly revealing of how different philosophical traditions can be brought together. Qian's commentary reads:

'The *Dao* that can be spoken of (*dao*) is not the constant *Dao*'; here the first and the third character *dao* 道 is the *dao* as in *dao li* 道 理 [reason], and the second *dao* is the *dao* as in *dao bai* 道白 [speech] .... We may compare this with the ancient Greek word *logos*, which means both 'reason' (*ratio*) and 'speech' (*oratio*); in more recent times, some have argued that the proverbial statement that 'man is the animal reason' originally meant that 'man is the animal that speaks. (in Zhang, 1999, 104)

Zhang takes this commentary to imply that the 'problem – or the dialectics – of thinking and speaking is common to the East and the West, even though its manifestations necessarily takes different forms' (104). Zhang argues that Lao Tzu's demonstration of the 'inadequacy of language and speaking', perhaps the point from which all inadequacy and weakness begins, leads to the language of the *Lao tzu* being 'highly literary' since it calls 'attention to itself by foregrounding the problem of all language and expression' (106). One of the only solutions then is to remain silent or to speak in 'non-words' (107). Qian compares this to the mystical 'method of dealing with the problem of language' by getting rid of words in a 'constant process of constructing and deconstructing' (107).

In his reading of Qian's commentaries on the *Lao tzu* Zhang explores how this ancient text's privileging of the 'inadequacy of signification' results in what might be described as a deconstruction of opposites, the very opposites that D. C. Lau regards as fundamental for understanding the text and as 'basic' (2001, xxxiv). Zhang argues that such a style leads to the

elimination of all difference between opposites: 'to eliminate the difference between speaking and silence, Laozi goes further to erase differences
between any two opposite categories' (108) so that there is a 'radical erasure of the difference between things and human beings in Laozi's philosophy' (109). As we have seen, D. C. Lau's argument in relation to weakness
and the system of opposites does not go this far; it argues for the preservation of these opposites in favour of the desire to 'abide by the weak' for
human survival. Lau argues that if you '[t]ake away this basis . . . you render
superfluous almost everything that is said in the book' (2001, xxxiv).
However, Zhang argues that 'a fundamental idea in Laozi's philosophy is
thus the levelling of all things under heaven, a concept of universal nondif-
ferentiation' (109). Zhang then moves to the political sphere with his use of
Qian's commentary. He argues that this 'total erasure of the difference
between human beings and inanimate things is hard to practice in reality'
(109) (on the way suggesting that Confucianism is a more practically
minded philosophy) so that when Daoism enters the 'realms of action and
politics' (111) a degree of force must be used. Qian argues that 'words'
become 'empty' when 'they are attached to events by force' because words
then become 'sophistical and evasive'. Language is then to be imagined
prior to force; this is an argument I return to in Chapter 5 in examining the
'violence' Derrida aligns with the sign. Perhaps the recourse to force only
becomes necessary because of this elimination of opposites that stymies the
engagement with each element taken separately. Qian writes:

> As words are empty in themselves, when they are attached to events by
> force, they become sophistical and evasive. . . . 'No words' thus leads to
> quoted authoritative words, words with hidden meanings, words respond-
> ing to occasions, and words that are fanciful and absurd; 'no body' thus
> turns to justify oily manners and slick acquiescence in order to save one's
> skin and to obtain longevity. (in Zhang, 111)

However, one must wonder whether Qian's and Zhang's emphasis on the
radical erasure of the difference aligned to opposites that are so prevalent
in the *Lao tzu* risks privileging the inadequacy of signification at the expense
of engaging with the thematics of weakness that Lau regards as the chief
principle of the *Lao tzu* in terms of its advice to readers to 'abide by the soft'.
In saying this, Zhang does point to a moralistic theme in the *Lao tzu* that is
echoed by many later Western writers; he suggests that Qian's commentary
is justified in noting that Lao Tzu is chiefly 'concerned with the way in
which the search for *Dao* is expressed as a dialectic reversal, the idea that

what one looks for outside turns out to be present inside, but only to be discovered after a long detour of seeking externally, in all the wrong places' (1999, 120). In other words, we must discover that we have been wrong all along before we can gain enlightenment.

However, it must be noted that this Chinese-Western comparison of an external/internal dialectic through writing that leads to self-discovery is only made possible because of the shared dialectic between speech and reason that Zhang has noted in Greek and ancient Chinese thought. The Christian tradition, as I will explore in more detail in the next chapter, may not fit the model so easily. Christian writers introduce a distinct sense of embodiment into the *logos* with the notion of the hypostatic union; speech and mind would now always connote the unity in difference emblematized in the Word. As the Christian phenomenologist Michel Henry explains, Greek thought describes an 'ontological monism' that Christian thought would challenge through Word and Incarnation, thereby inaugurating an enormous struggle to assimilate 'the notion of Incarnation into a system of thinking' where early Christians 'tried hard to understand what they did not yet even have the means to understand' (2000, 11). Ancient Greek and Chinese thought did not have to contend with the notion of 'hypostatic union'. As I will examine in more detail in the next chapter, Richard Cross explains how the early Church Fathers, theologians and believers struggled to fit words to this mystery's meaning for centuries because, as one medieval scholar, Giles of Rome, noted, in tackling the mystery: 'The poverty of words has many bad results for us, so that, on account of the defect of words, it is necessary to use one word to signify one thing, even though [the word] in itself properly signifies something else' (Cross, 38). This account of language by Giles of Rome may bring a surface-level correspondence with Zhang's and Qian's analysis of the *Lao tzu* in terms of the 'inadequacy' of signification. However, any more profound comparison is surely problematized by the fact that, as Richard Cross explains, 'Chalcedonianism is . . . consistent with extreme anti-realism' (3).

Zhang has responded to these claims that strive to retain important differences between different traditions in his later book *Allegoresis*. He argues for the 'validity of cross-cultural understanding' and the 'viability of intersubjective transference of consciousness and sensibility' in East-West studies (2005, 1). However, when he argues for the 'fundamental equality of things' across these traditions that is 'not tied to colonialism or ethnocentrism', (11) writers from different traditions will be eager to retain what they feel are unique aspects of these traditions that are sometimes tied to different religious beliefs. He notes the Orientalist stance of writers, sinologists and translators such as the Jesuit Fathers in China, Jacques Gernet and Stephen Owen, who can even be read as suggesting, that there is a 'lack of transcendence' in Chinese writing and literature (*wen*). For Zhang, these writers imply that Chinese literature cannot share the mimetic qualities of Western literature since they see it as 'the result of a primordial continuum of all the phenomena in the natural cosmos, of which Chinese writing or literature is conceived as an integral part' (2001, 21). He cites Stephen Owen, who argues, for Zhang, in his book *Traditional Chinese Poetry and Poetics* that '[w]hile the Western poet creates, in imitation of God the first Maker, a fictional world *ex nihilo*, the Chinese poet only "participates in the nature that is"' (22). In response to such claims Zhang is even drawn to ask rhetorically: 'On what basis can you claim to have knowledge about me, but at the same time deny me the possibility of knowing?' (19). Of course, Zhang is speaking for Chinese scholars here and he is right to reappraise these one-sided accounts of Chinese writing. As Roger T. Ames suggests, the debate should never be cast in terms that deny any group of individuals any kind of 'possibility of knowing'. After all, Zhang is arguing for a recognition of what is '*equivalent*' in the two traditions, and not for the 'identical' (19); he does also admit that there is no '"theology of revelation"' in China 'if by that is meant a specifically Christian theology' and that 'a Chinese sign is, of course, different from a Christian sign' (38). All these aspects of different traditions are therefore what need to be assessed for their equivalence since, if we brush over too many of the distinctions, comparative studies no longer serves a purpose. In the background here is also the logocentric debate spearheaded by Derrida, who, for Zhang, argues that 'the nonphonetic Chinese and Japanese scripts offer [Derrida, as will see later, actually writes 'largely nonphonetic'] '"the testimony of a powerful movement of civilization developing outside of all logocentrism"' (29). However, as suggested above, the debate on logocentrism becomes something very different when extracted from the Judeo-Christian context of Europe and transferred to the 'East-West' comparison Zhang is concerned with.

Ames has suggested, in referring to Zhang's general argument on comparative studies, that any broad comparison of meaning-making in writing in Western and Chinese language systems must retain a 'healthy pluralism' (35) in mapping the interpretive tools of 'a theo-ontological tradition' onto those of a tradition that 'pursues practical wisdom and the alternative spiritual and religiousness sensibilities produced therefrom' (34). He argues that 'we pluralists['] need' to believe in a distinction in language between *langue* (language) and *parole* (speech) where *langue* is an 'evolved, theoretical, and conceptual structure of a language system that is shaped by an aggregating intelligence over millenia and that makes speech possible' and where *parole* refers to 'any natural language in the individual utterances we make' (34); it is this distinction which then galvanizes Ames's claim 'that the Chinese language has not developed and does not have available to it either an indigenous concept or a term that can be used to capture the Abrahamic notion of "God", while at the same time allowing us to insist that the same Chinese language has all of the semantic and syntactic resources necessary to give a fair account of such an idea' (34). However, the devil is in the detail once again; Ames does not make clear here what the difference is between being able 'to capture' and being able 'to give a fair account of' God. It would seem then that sinologists and comparatists have recognized that different religious beliefs lead to different ways of understanding language and, therefore, to different hermeneutic practices. This makes any easy application of a shared interpretive dynamic that works across 'Western' and Chinese thought in relation to 'the dialectics – of thinking and speaking' (Zhang, 1999, 104) notoriously problematic. Ultimately, it must be noted that this debate becomes most enlightening when the 'inadequacy' of language is being explored and the weakness privileged by the *Lao tzu* is a fertile ground from which to begin this exploration.

Xinzhong Yao describes the differences between Confucianism and Christianity in terms of the differences between *jen* and *agape*: 'the fundamental differences between *jen* and *agape* lie in the aspect of transcendence, the one rooting in humanity and the other in God's grace' (137). However, there is an important difference in interpretative styles for Scriptures of the Word and Scriptures of the Way when weakness and humanity must be understood in terms of language as revealing the Word as God. Language becomes tied to notions of embodiment that presume a human/divine sharing that influences interpretative and hermeneutic practices. Zhang argues, in his ground-breaking work *The Tao and the Logos* that many East-West comparative studies 'juxtapose texts from different cultural traditions without justifying the choice of those texts for comparison' and that such works 'mechanically apply terms, concepts, and approaches of Western criticism to non-Western works' (1992, xi). However, even though he rightly points out that Foucault 'does not disengage from the tradition of creating cultural myths of the Other' in relation to the 'representation of the Chinese mind' (1992, xvi), there is also a danger of cultural shoehorning when we use the umbrella term Western to refer to hermeneutic traditions as divergent as the Christian and the ancient Greek in making broader East-West comparisons. This may become evident when Zhang parallels

Western and Chinese traditions in relation to the idea that 'writing signifies not only what it records but the loss of what was originally contained in thought as internal speech – the loss or absence of that primal discourse which the written text fails to preserve and commentary fails to retrieve' (1992, 16). Two strands of this 'Western' tradition – namely, the Judaic tradition and the Christian – have decidedly different interpretations of such notions as 'internal speech' and 'the loss or absence of that primal discourse'. However, the 'emphasis on the accumulated wisdom' that Zhang traces in the Chinese tradition to Confucius' words: 'I transmit but do not innovate . . . I trust and devote myself to the study of the ancients' (1992, 13) can be related to the Judaic notion of commentary. Gershom Scholem describes in *On the Possibility of Jewish Mysticism in Our Time* how 'commentary' became:

> [O]ver the course of generations . . . the first ranking form of Jewish cre-
> ation. In a society based on the acceptance of a truth which had been
> revealed in a written document originality could not be a central value.
> The truth is already known. We have naught to do but to understand
> it, and what is perhaps more difficult, to pass it down. In other words:
> originality and the creative impulse which acted here did not declare
> themselves as such, but preferred to manifest themselves in a form which
> was less pretentious but in fact was no less creative – namely, that of com-
> mentary. (Scholem, 17)

Therefore, while both the Chinese tradition and strands of the Western tradition might share a belief in interpretation as commentary and in writing as a displacement of 'thought as internal speech', it is important to note that such important figures as Hegel in the Western tradition had quite radical ideas regarding what constituted external and internal for the Chinese tradition. In describing the traditional Chinese conception of self, Hegel writes: 'Morality is in the East likewise a subject of positive legislation, and although moral prescriptions (the *substance* of their Ethics) may be perfect, what should be internal subjective sentiment is made a matter of external arrangement' (in Ames, 2011, 13). Despite Hegel's obvious over-sights and misconceptions, his notion of the dialectic was important for what came later in the West.

While East-West Studies is eager to foreground, albeit in a very different paradigm, the same kind of 'interconfessional' attitude that Paul Ricoeur called for between the different religions, it is apparent that there is also an urgency to preserve a sense of difference. I have argued that the weakness described thematically in the *Lao tzu*, working also through its staging of signification, is an important entry-point for understanding these most urgent of differences. It is when we apply the notion of weakness to notions of identity and the 'person' that the true nature of the difference becomes most apparent. Weakness in the *Lao tzu*, when understood in terms of personal endeavour and fulfilment, has less of the shame of the Greek system and less of the guilt and humility of the Christian system. It might suggest that the subject of the Greek dramas and the Christian narratives all too quickly discovers him- or herself confronting a Fate or a 'grand design' that asks him or her to prematurely don the attributes of identity. In tackling Fate in a tragic manner, one must have some understanding of the life that is being foiled. Ames points to two characteristics of Chinese philosophy that might prevent the Chinese notion of 'person' from straying so quickly into a similar kind of quest narrative that foregrounds weakness in terms of personal identity. He argues that Tang Junyi describes a conception of 'ecological relationality' as '*the* distinguishing feature and most vital contribution of Chinese culture' (Ames 78). Tang describes this in terms of 'an unwillingness to isolate the particular from the totality (this is most evident in the cosmology of the Chinese people), and from the perspective of ties of feeling and affection, it means the commitment of the particular to do its utmost to realize the totality' (in Ames 78–9). Ames also points to the New Confucians' 'naturalistic view of the vital life forces that animate the cosmos wherein the goal of the consummate human being is to participate fully in optimizing the harmony of the totality' (78). Ames argues that we are guilty all too often of 'inadvertently shoehorning the Confucian foot into a Greek sandal' (88). This is problematic because 'the Confucian notion of relationally constituted "human becomings"' for understanding 'the notion of the "person"' must be distinguished from an 'essentialist understanding of discrete human beings' and that the 'philosophical implications of this distinction between Confucian *ren* [this is Ames's translation of what Yao, as we have seen, translates as *jen*] and a foundational individualism that had its beginnings in classical Greece are pervasive and enduring, and unless and until we are clear on this difference, we will continue to theorize Confucian philosophy according to assumptions that are not its own' (88).

One of the key differences that Ames focuses on to make this clearer is the lack of a Creator or 'grand design' in the Confucian system and in Daoism. He returns to the importance of 'opposites' for understanding this difference: 'The mutual entailment of opposites – day becoming night, young becoming old, full becoming empty, contracted becoming outstretched, and so on – *sui generis* always comes back upon itself. As it says in the *Lao Tzu*, "Returning is how way-making (*dao*) moves," or giving it a more explicit interpretation, "Returning is how experience unfolds"' (in Ames, 82). In returning one last time to the *Lau tzu*, there is one final concept that might help us understand its advice to 'abide by the weak'. The notion of *tiyong*, which Ames tells us appears first in the 'third-century commentary on the *Daodejing* by Wang Bi,' describes, for him, 'vital and persistent transformation' or the 'inseparability of forming and functioning [it can also be translated as 'to take up and use']' (65). It is an idea that requires that all 'experience must begin from locating it within the totality of relations' and it describes the 'rhythm of the dramatic and ceaseless unfolding of our experience in both its formal and its animated aspects' (65). However, the focus on the forming and the functioning of life in all its 'dramatic' detail begs the question of why it should be dramatic. One might suggest that it is dramatic precisely because it survives at all, as D. C. Lau also reminds us in his reading of the *Lao tzu*. The *Lao tzu* is a work about survivability and its attention to survivable weakness and need that can continue to form and function will always be dramatic.

Chapter 3

The Flesh is Weak: Incarnating the Word

Weakness appears in many forms in the work of Christian writers. Whether it be Matthew's warning that the 'flesh *is* weak', Paul's agonizing over the weakness he must boast of, Kierkegaard's 'despair in weakness' or even Christ's own words reminding us of how the 'meek' are 'blessed', weakness typically describes a fundamental attribute of the Christian believer. As Catholic seminarians are reminded, man as believer and as priest must recognize his nature as *Alter Christus* or 'substitute of Christ' on earth. In other words, this rhetoric of weakness has its genesis in Christianity's most influential mystery for writing, the mystery of the Incarnation. In recent years, following the emergence of radical orthodoxy and in the aftermath of the 'theological turn' in continental philosophy, the 'weakness of God', to use a phrase from John D. Caputo, has emerged as a new idea for consideration. Caputo describes God in terms of 'weak grace' or the 'weak force of a call' (13) so as to unthink the 'being' of God: 'by untying the name of God from the order of being, it releases the event' (9). Caputo is responding here to the recent language of the 'event' foregrounded by the work of Alain Badiou[1] and to the language of the 'theological turn' that, as Derrida suggests, speaks for the '*possibility* of religion without religion' (*Gift*, 50). Caputo is right to suggest that "the truth of religion is the genuine power of powerlessness, of the bottomless and infinite depth of the unconditional affirmation of the world" (91), however, Derrida's writing on religion, in privileging such notions as 'call', 'gift', and *l'avenir*, is often described in terms of a messianic eschatology that is heavily influenced by Jewish interpretive practices. If Christian philosophers such as Caputo are simply being mindful here of, what Paul Ricoeur calls, 'an interconfessional, interreligious hospitality' (Janicaud, *Turn*, 132) and are speaking more for a universal God who transcends religious boundaries, then all is well and good. However, if this God as 'event' is still firmly in place as a Christian God, a God that traditionally has such appeal because the New Testament makes so much of a weakness of the flesh and of a divine weakening that privileges materiality and a Word made flesh through Incarnation, then this new weakness is surely of a very different nature. The question then is how does this recent de-ontologizing and de-materializing of God as 'event' work against an older current that Christian writers have drawn from in writing of the weak and the 'lowly'?

In *Mimesis: The Representation of Reality in Western Literature*, one of the great works of literary criticism of the twentieth century, Erich Auerbach explains how this older Christian attention to weakness has been revolutionary for literature and narrative. He describes how the most important shift to occur in literature, the shift from the Homeric or classical style to the 'Christian mixture of styles', (73) is a direct result of the narrative of the life of Jesus. The narrative of Jesus's life is revolutionary because he is a divine figure who is made to embody the human characterization that he shares with people like his first apostle Peter, a man who 'derives the highest force from his very weakness' (42). Hans-Georg Gadamer argues that the mystery described by this narrative also revolutionizes our understanding of language precisely because the idea that 'does more justice to the being of language' is the 'Christian idea of *incarnation*' (Gadamer, 418). For Gadamer, incarnation goes further than any notion of embodiment we have seen in Greek writers because the soul and body are no longer 'completely different' (418). Bodily actions now stain the soul and original sin has marked the body for good. Auerbach extends this reading into narrative and characterization. Jesus was a new kind of hero and king; he was a human being of the 'lowest social station' (Auerbach, 72) but all that 'he did and said was of the highest and deepest dignity, more significant than anything else in the world' (72). The Christian narrative of weakness necessitated a style of 'figural interpretation' that works in a 'vertical' rather than a 'horizontal' manner and according to 'Divine Providence, which alone is able to devise such a plan of history and supply the key to its understanding' (74). It is very different to the classical system's adherence to the 'earthly relations of place, time and cause' (74). This material and worldly sense of classical culture was mapped directly onto its writing 'with all its ingenious and nicely shaded conjunctions, its wealth of devices for syntactic arrangement, its carefully elaborated system of tenses' (74). However, the advent of the Christian vertical system ushered in a disregard for such linguistic finery and, for Auerbach, 'literary language declined' (75). It was to be the model for all subsequent Everyman narratives. Gradually such narratives would supersede the classical rhetorical culture with its 'separation of styles' by engendering a 'new elevated style' which did not scorn 'everyday life and which is ready to absorb the sensory realistic, even the ugly, the undignified, the physically base' (72). Auerbach argues that this narrative of weakness changes narrative forever and allows for the representation of people of the 'humblest social station'. Ludwig Feuerbach had already noted such a capacity in his *The Essence of Christianity* where he writes that the Christian religion is so 'little superhuman that it even sanctions human weakness'; he also reminds us that '[w]hile Socrates empties the cup of poison with unshaken soul, Christ exclaims, "If it be possible, let this cup pass from me". Christ is then the "self-confession of human sensibility"' (52).

The Christian mystery of Incarnation in particular allowed a new understanding of weakness into the world. Debate has surrounded the Chalcedonian description of Incarnation in regard to whether the assumed nature of Christ is or is not a 'human substance' with a degree of 'human autonomy' (Cross, 316–17). Richard Cross argues, in his dense examination of the medieval account of the second person of the Trinity, that opinion is still split on the subject. He argues that Duns Scotus is the 'most powerful exponent' of the tradition that regards the human nature of Christ as a 'substance in its own right'. Aquinas, on the other hand, denies Christ's human nature any 'proper personhood' (in Cross, 8) since he wants to maintain that the Word is the only 'substance' (311). This 'non-existence of Christ's human nature' in Aquinas might seem to compromise the reality of the Word's being human, but Cross does not think so, because, as he puts it, the 'non-existence' of any person's human nature does not mean that person is not human (313). While it is notoriously difficult to find definitions of person and nature that all scholars agree on, what is important to note in the medieval descriptions of the human nature of Christ is the role the 'assumed human nature' is granted. Scotus holds that Christ's nature is a 'subject of accidents' and that the Word's 'human nature is a non-essential property of the Word' (in Cross, 18); Augustine argues that the human nature is related to the Word in the same way as 'clothing is related to a person' (30); and Karl Rahner, writing much later, describes the relation between the human nature and the divinity of Christ as follows: 'The human nature of Christ possesses a genuine, spontaneous, free, spiritual, active center, a human self-consciousness, which as creaturely faces the eternal Word in a genuinely human attitude of adoration, obedience, a most radical sense of creaturehood' (in Cross, 316). It is clear, then, that the debate on, and the descriptions of, the different natures of Christ as Word have influenced and indeed become analogues for descriptions of the relationship between Christians and their God. With the mystery of Incarnation God became bound up with human weakness in an inextricable way. The popular idea that the flesh is weak now had to contend with the notion that the flesh could also be divine. The resulting narrative of Jesus's life changed narrative forever, as Auerbach suggests. The mystery of the Incarnation is an important notion for understanding weakness in Christianity since it refers to possibly the greatest weakening or humbling imaginable – that of God. The mystery has also undergone something of a philosophical rejuvenation in recent years with philosophers such as Michel Henry,[2] Jacques Rancière and Jean-Luc Nancy[3] incorporating new definitions of its influence on the body into their philosophies.

However, it is important to acknowledge, again as Feuerbach reminds us, that the Incarnation itself arose out of a profound human weakness or sense of need: 'The Incarnation is nothing else than the practical, material manifestation of the human nature of God. God did not become man for his own sake; the need, the want of man – a want which still exists in the religious sentiment – was the cause of the Incarnation' (Feuerbach, 43). We can see, however, even as early as Athanasius' *On the Incarnation*, that this originary sense of need or weakness associated with the mystery is already being transformed into something for which mankind must feel a sense of shame: 'the Word, the Power of God, the Master condescended on account of the weakness of mankind and appeared on earth' (Athanasius, 83). Feuerbach is therefore right to note that by the nineteenth century, because of 'theological dogmas and contradictions', (51) the mystery had become 'incomprehensible' for believers because of the 'mingling or confusion of the idea or definitions of the universal, unlimited, metaphysical being with the idea of the religious God, that is the conditions of the understanding with the conditions of the heart' (44). Feuerbach's words also speak for the dilemma that Caputo's new description of weakness raises today: how is the weakness of the 'unlimited, metaphysical' first person to be equated with the weakness of the 'religious' second person, Jesus? Feuerbach reminds believers that the mystery arose out of nothing other than a feeling of urgent necessity: 'Man was already in God, was already God himself, before God became man' (43). Feuerbach also reminds us of Martin Luther's description of the nature of Incarnation which also stresses the 'gentle manhood' of Christ as a spur against violence and anger:

> He who can truly conceive such a thing (namely, the incarnation of God) in his heart, should for the sake of the flesh and blood which sits at the right hand of God, bear love to all flesh and blood here upon the earth, and never more be able to be angry with any man. The gentle manhood

of Christ our God should at a glance fill all hearts with joy, so that never could an angry, unfriendly thought come therein. (in Feuerbach, 50)

Weakness is also treated as a theme in its own right by many Christian writers. The most evocative early description of weakness in the Christian canon is surely that of Paul. Paul extends Jesus's description of himself as 'meek and gentle' to the weakness that is essential to his own ministry. He reminds us of Jesus's weakness and he uses this to explain to sinners how they will be treated. The believer now has to somehow hold together in his or her faith this new description of the second person of the Trinity as weak while also being mindful of earlier biblical descriptions that describe the first person of the Trinity as 'O my strength, I will watch for you; for you, O God, are my fortress' (Ps. 59.9). In the *Second Letter to the Corinthians* Paul writes:

> This is the third time I am coming to you. 'Any charge must be sustained by the evidence of two or three witnesses.' I warned those who sinned previously and all the others, and I warn them now while absent, as I did when present on my second visit, that if I come again, I will not be lenient – since you desire proof that Christ is speaking in me. He is not weak in dealing with you, but is powerful in you. For he was crucified in weakness, but lives by the power of God. For we are weak in him, but in dealing with you we will live with him by the power of God. (2 Cor. 13.1-4)

We are reminded here of the weakening that God suffered in order to win salvation for mankind; Jesus was crucified in 'weakness'. He assumed mankind's fallen state in order to redeem. However, whenever Paul speaks of God there is an intimation of power. Sinners will be dealt with powerfully and the threat given here is reminiscent of the wrathful God of the Old Testament. Paul does admit, however, that 'we are weak in him'; mankind is weak by nature, human nature is weak, but if this can be seen in terms of a weakness bestowed on believers by Jesus, and if believers can live according to the dictates of this weakness Jesus has outlined, then they too can gain salvation.

There are two aspects of weakness at issue here and both are intimately connected. Mankind is already fallen and weak and, starting on the back foot, must seek redemption and, in turn, God is made to suffer the defining moment of weakening when He assumes flesh to atone for the sins of mankind. Jesus is God weakened as only God can be. His suffering and death as flesh do not relieve mankind of its weakness, but redeem its fallen state. C. S. Lewis was also deeply conscious of this weakening and he explains it in a perhaps more accessible way than Paul:

But supposing God became a man – suppose our human nature which can suffer and die was amalgamated with God's nature in one person – then that person could help us. He could surrender His will, and suffer and die, because He was man; and He could do it perfectly because He was God. You and I can go through this process only if God does it in us; but God can do it only if we men share in God's dying, just as our thinking can succeed only because it is a drop out of the ocean of His intelligence: but we cannot share God's dying unless God dies; and He cannot die except by being a man. (*Mere Christianity*, 60)

Paul, like Socrates and Confucius before him, will end up proclaiming his own weakness: 'Who is weak, and I am not weak? . . . If I must boast, I will boast of the things that show my weakness' (2 Cor. 11.29-30). He is prepared to be punished and whipped with those fellow believers who are being prosecuted. He recognizes his own authority as the voice of God with the communities he visits and despite being 'beaten with rods' three times and having 'received a stoning' (2 Cor. 11.25) he continues with his mission and comes to realize that he must appeal to these communities 'by the meekness and gentleness of Christ' (2 Cor. 10.10). This is a more world-weary Paul than the Paul of *Romans* who begins confidently describing himself as a 'servant of Jesus Christ, called to be an apostle, set apart for the gospel of God' (Rom. 1.1) and who reminds all that 'we . . . boast in our hope of sharing the glory of God' (Rom. 1.2) through the peace 'we' have gained 'with God through our Lord Jesus Christ' (Rom. 5.1). In *Romans* he also gives an intimation of the sufferings that will be experienced because of this faith and of the logic of redemption that follows from this and of why it is still necessary to boast even of this suffering because it is a mark of the covenant: 'we also boast in our sufferings, knowing that suffering produces endurance, and endurance produces character, and character produces hope, and hope does not disappoint us, because God's love has been poured into our hearts' (Rom. 5.3-5). The Paul of the *Second Letter to the Corinthians* also speaks of a need to boast, but his missionary life, living as he did according to the truth of his moral universe in God, has made him even question the worth of boasting of weakness. It is similar to Socrates' recognition that his philosophy is 'worthless' because he admits that before the jurymen he will be unable to put forward any evidence of his good work that does not appear as another case of him merely making the 'weaker argument the stronger'. Paul writes that '[i]t is necessary to boast [of weakness], nothing is to be gained by it, but I will go on to visions and revelations of the Lord' (2 Cor. 12.1). So nothing is to be gained from boasting of weakness and yet it is essential because it brings on the visions which are then the spur for his writing and ministry. Boasting of weakness makes him privy to the words of souls that have died and been to Paradise and heard things 'that no mortal is permitted to repeat' (2 Cor. 12.4). He then feels sufficiently confident once again in boasting of his weakness: 'but on my own behalf I will not boast, except of my weaknesses' (2 Cor 12.5). He then writes that he has, however, decided to 'refrain from it, so that no one may think better of me than what is seen in me or heard from me, even considering the exceptional character of the revelations' (2 Cor 12.6-7). The form of the writing here might itself be described as 'weak'; it hesitates, runs over the same ground and even seems to contradict itself. However, the temptations Paul suffers finally allow him to receive another vision and he hears the Lord appealing to him, saying: 'My grace is sufficient for you, for power is made perfect in weakness' (2 Cor. 12.9). Paul now has fresh conviction and he decides once again to 'boast all the more gladly of my weaknesses' because he has realized that 'whenever I am weak, then I am strong' (2 Cor. 12.10). His entire message might then be regarded as a contemplation on how best to share weakness. Alain Badiou reads Paul's deliberations on weakness as being removed from older notions of sin and flesh (sarx) and their 'automatism of repetition' (79); Pauline universalism is one grounded in activism that works on the 'idea that every existence can one day be seized by what happens to it and subsequently devote itself to that which is valid for all' (2003, 66). When weakness becomes the only strength, how is one to persuade others of its worth? When the visions of believers at their lowest ebb are visions that advise that 'power is made perfect in weakness', how is this to be communicated? When the greatest philosophers, prophets and missionaries have their words reduced to a play on what is worthless and weak then it also pushes readers to examine all that is most hidden and all that we had assumed was unique and worthless. Socrates and Paul do this on a grand scale. The good life itself is acknowledged as weak and worthless and yet because it is so it will forever be shared with the thrill that accompanies all disclosures that one had presumed inconsolably would remain forever hidden as a mark of one's unique and unparalleled failing.

It is important to look at the development of the description of Christ's weakness and the weakness believers possess since this runs parallel to the development of the Christian narrative that Auerbach examines. Jesus's contemporary Philo advises against this new narrative that was coming to Christianity. He writes that even though 'man was created after the image of God and after His likeness (Gen I.26) . . . [l]et no one represent the likeness as one to a bodily form; for neither is God in human form, nor is the human body God-like' (55). Athanasius, writing before the Council of Chalcedon in *The Incarnation*, describes how Jesus, 'by what seems His utter poverty and weakness on the cross', 'overturns the pomp and parade of idols' (25). He also describes the 'frailty' of man as the tendency of man to neglect the 'grace' that 'knowledge of the Word' grants (39). However, his use of the phrase 'what *seems* his poverty and weakness' is important, for he will later explain, in describing how Jesus defeats death for mankind, that 'He is not weak' and that 'in pursuance of His nature neither laid aside His body of His own accord nor escaped the plotting Jews' but this 'showed no limitation in weakness' (52). Athanasius transforms the cross into a symbol of power and strength; it is a cross that 'has vanquished all magic entirely and has conquered the very name of it' (86); the older 'so-called gods are routed by the sign of the cross' (92). However, as he reminds us earlier, it was Jesus's 'utter poverty and weakness on the cross' that has enabled the cross after the event to wield such power that it 'overturns the pomp and parade of idols' (25). This account of Jesus's life from about 250 years after Paul's Letters offers one possible reading of the message Paul receives from God in the *Second Letter to the Corinthians*: 'My grace is sufficient for you, for power is made perfect in weakness' (2 Cor.12.9).

However, we might still be unsure about how Jesus's weakness is expected to appear in the character of his believers. How are believers to embody this weakness? The nature of the weakness that believers share with Jesus changes over time in the early Christian period. Weakness for mankind, if it is to appeal to some uniquely human failing, cannot be regarded as simply recalling the human 'nature' of Jesus; it must point to some distinct aspect of humanity and it is the body or the flesh that in various forms becomes the weakening substance that surrounds the soul, heart or spirit. Matthew's Gospel advises: 'Stay awake and pray that you may not come into the time of trial: the spirit indeed is willing, but the flesh *is* weak' (Mt. 26.41).[4] This kind of weakness sounds remarkably similar to the desire of Leontius before the corpses; it refers to something like the appetite that overcomes the regulating force of 'right reason'. Paul gives the earliest and starkest commentary on this notion of flesh as being prone to temptation in *Romans*: 'For I know that nothing good dwells within me, that is, in my flesh . . . but I see in my members another law at war with the law of my mind . . . Wretched man that I am! Who will rescue me from this body of death?' (Rom.7.18–24). This again recalls the Psalms where the writers remind us of God's capability to forgive 'iniquity' that is rooted in the flesh: 'He remembered that they were but flesh, a wind that passes and does not come again' (Ps. 78.39). Paul's brilliance, however, lies in his ability to use his rhetorical talents to transform weakness and hence the flesh into something that is larger than the body. The flesh becomes not only representative of such physically grounded appetites that lead to sins such as lust and drunkenness, it also comes to stand in for what Peter Brown describes as a turning away from or a 'rebellion against God':

> 'The flesh' was not simply the body, an inferior other to the self, whose undisciplined stirrings might even at times receive a certain tolerance, as representing the natural claims of a physical being. In all later Christian writing, the notion of 'the flesh' suffused the body with disturbing associations: somehow as 'flesh', the body's weaknesses and temptations echoed a state of helplessness, even of rebellion against God, that was larger than the body itself. (Brown, 48)

It might be argued that Paul describes a new Christian law through the flesh to replace the old Judaic law of circumcision that he challenges in his letters. Paul scorns the Jewish adherence to the law, both in regard to circumcision and in regard to Judaism's reluctance to renounce any single aspect of life, including sex, because of its belief that all aspects of life 'must be given form according to the declared will of God' (Brown, 62). Through Paul, Christians and Gentiles had a new law to assign to the flesh; the flesh removed in circumcision was no longer the only mark of adherence to a creed. Now the entire flesh was a reminder of the inherent tendency in mankind for rebellion against God's will.

Early Christian writers moved beyond this strictly dualist description of the flesh as eager temptress of the soul and the spirit. Tertullian was a monist and a Stoic. 'Look to the body' was his direction to believers and, as Brown writes, 'it was directly through the body and its sensations that the soul was tuned to the high pitch required for it to vibrate to the Spirit of God' (77). However, Tertullian uses the metaphor of obtruncation of flesh to describe how the movement away from the rite of circumcision and the 'amputating' of the 'extremest superficies' may only have ushered in a period rife with parallel 'defilements of the flesh' in early Christendom that sought to destroy the 'inmost image of modesty' by 'obtruncat[ing] the pure and true integrity of the flesh' (Tertullian, 75). His engaging descriptions of modesty and the flesh prior to Chalcedon in relation to marriage also help institute the Christian notion of marriage for life: 'it is not permitted, after believing, to know even a second marriage, differentiated though it be, to be sure, from the work of adultery and fornication by the nuptial and dotal tablets' (75). Tertullian was possibly the first to usher in a controlled attitude to the body that led to a devotion to continence and virginity (for men and women) because 'no Christian could claim to be free from the social conventions that human frailty demanded' (Brown, 81); he therefore 'sunk sexuality deep into the human body', thereby exacerbating the already tortured life of the body as 'frail clay' (68).

Clement of Alexandria extended Tertullian's concern for continence and correct conduct to the minutiae of the household. The individual believer was expected to achieve a state of 'high-hearted readiness' (Brown, 129). However, getting in the way of this were the 'passions', those 'tendencies built up within the *ego*, which could force even a 'sage' to 'overreact to any situation, to cathect it with a charge of personal, egoistic significance that distorted its true meaning' (129), However, Clement seems to suggest that it was only when a 'weak mind' resulted that the body and its passions were truly blameworthy: 'The passions might have their distant origin in the body; but it was only when they had brought about a change in the inner climate of the mind that they were to be eradicated' (129). The 'biological self' could never be abandoned; only a 'meticulous rhythm of life' could ultimately train the mind to perform properly according to Clement. Clement can be regarded as mixing Christian religious faith with the 'sharp aesthetic sensibility' (Brown, 133) of the Greeks.

Origen added a further twist to the nature of the body's frailty and how it should be handled. He could not accept Clement's close attention to the household and to the divine nature of such practices as married sex. Origen contrasted the coupling of the marriage bed with the '"true" spiritual joining' between believer and God (Brown, 174). The only kind of body that would have access to this kind of joining would be the 'isolated virgin body' (174). This theme is taken up years later by Shakespeare; the fear of infidelity in marriage is often described in Shakespeare in terms of the flesh – Adriana advises in *The Comedy of Errors* that 'if we two be one, and thou play false,/I do digest the poison of thy flesh' (2.2.143–4) – and Shakespeare also describes a cult of virginity in terms of the flesh: we are told that Bertram 'fleshes his will in the spoil of her [Diana's] honour' (4.3.17) in *All's Well That Ends Well.* Emmanuel Levinas, a later Jewish writer, also returns to the notion of 'virginity' in describing a notion of radical alterity that speaks for both the political 'Other' and what often sounds like a description of God: 'The Beloved, at once graspable but intact in her nudity, beyond object and face, and thus beyond the existent, abides in virginity' (Levinas, 1961, 289).

In Origen the body was made for a much nobler purpose than merely to eat and procreate; 'it was made that it should be a *temple to the Lord*' (qtd in Brown, 175). Perpetual continence now became a regular practice among believers and Origen himself was 'widely believed' (168) to have been castrated for his faith, another common practice at the time. The human body could therefore be 'offered up' and 'made holy' for God. As Brown writes, the 'humble "ass" of the body could become the "resplendent" vehicle of the soul' (177). The nature of the body was being transformed once again to contend with the true nature of human frailty and weakness. The weakness was no longer a larger than life notion of 'flesh' that was evidence for man's rebellion against God, or a 'passion' that could be dealt with by 'meticulous' living. It was an almost supernatural quantity that inhabited both mind and body and that could be eviscerated from the body through continence. Once again, we can see that the philosophy that provides the background to all this redrafting of the body in order to accommodate weakness was one that was uncomfortable with exploring the practices and habits that were generally described as weak. As we have seen with Tertullian and Clement, weakness was not simply a 'passion' that the body was responsible for, but a larger quantity that necessitated a range of influential metaphors throughout the literary and philosophical writing of the time.

The early Church Fathers would only finally decide on the true nature of the Incarnation at Chalcedon in 451, and it would take an equally long time, if not longer, for the Church to find the vocabulary necessary through this understanding of Incarnation to formulate guidance for sins or failings that dealt with similar acts to those covered by incontinence and weakness of the will. Right reason was now found in God and weakness was subject to temptation and a lack of grace. Augustine is possibly the most important writer and thinker for understanding how weakness is transformed in moving from the classical era to the Christian era. The form of Augustine's confessional writing enables greater shows of weakness. His style, concerned with 'growth and development', is radically new. For Auerbach, Augustine's discussion of the 'transition from childhood to adolescence' (*Confessions*, 1.8) 'would be unthinkable before Augustine' (71). In Augustine such practical dilemmas are paralleled with hugely important 'purely theoretical problems' about salvation and 'under his hands [all] become drama' (Auerbach, 71). We will see in a later chapter how Wordsworth's similarly confessional style also challenges the writerly expectations of his day. Augustine would seem to describe the state of being 'weak-willed' as a permanent state of man. Ann A. Pang White argues that since being 'weak-willed' for Augustine is a concept which 'refers to both a universal condition of fallen human nature and one's actual behavior, being weak-willed in the Augustinian sense does not necessarily entail moral blameworthiness'.[5] In his preface to *City of God*, Augustine privileges humility above all human characteristics and man's weakness in relation to God was the belief and figure that would allow such humility never to be forgotten. In setting out to write the work, he acknowledges how difficult it is to keep his own pride in check; he recognizes 'what efforts are needed to persuade the proud how great is that virtue of humility which, not by dint of any human loftiness, but by divine grace bestowed from on high, raises us above all the earthly pinnacles which sway in this inconstant age' (1998, 3).

Augustine develops the Christian narrative of weakness of the Old Testament and he responds directly to the weakness Paul praises. In the fourth book of *On the Trinity*, in a section entitled 'We Are Made Perfect By Acknowledgment Of Our Own Weakness. The Incarnate Word Dispels Our Darkness', he responds to Paul on weakness:

> And hence He so dealt with us, that we might the rather profit by His strength, and that so in the weakness of humility the virtue of charity might be perfected. And this is intimated in the Psalm, where it is said, 'Thou, O God, didst send a spontaneous rain, whereby Thou didst make Thine inheritance perfect, when it was weary' (Ps. lxviii. 9). . . . But He Himself makes us perfect, who says also to the Apostle Paul, 'My grace is sufficient for thee, for my strength is made perfect in weakness (2 Cor. xii. 9).' (1948, 729–30)

Once again, it is humility that is held up here as the most fundamental expression of this weakness through which we can be made 'perfect'. He returns time and again to passages from scripture that describe humility and being humble: 'God resisteth the proud, but giveth grace unto the humble', (Jas. 4.6); 'Learn of me, because I am meek, and humble of heart' (Mt. 11.29). Weakness and being humble of heart are connected and these are the divine attributes believers must embody.

It is Aquinas, however, who returns Christian narratives of weakness to something approaching the Greek privileging of 'right reason'. He argues that '[m]an's weak point ought to be associated with that part of his nature which is most easily broken' and that this is 'the flesh'. However, he argues that 'sins of weakness' are caused more by 'bodily defects' than 'emotion' because 'a man is not thought to be weak with regard to those things which he can control volitionally'. Since 'yielding to emotion is something that is within man's power to will . . . sins which arise from emotion are not from weakness'. He sums up his argument on weakness as follows:

> Man's body is said to suffer infirmity when it is weakened or hindered in its proper functions by some organic disturbance . . . . Hence, an organ is described as sick when it does not function as well as a healthy organ . . . . Likewise, the soul is subject to infirmity when its functions are hampered by some inherent disorder. . . . functions of the soul are said to be abnormal when they are not controlled by reason, for reason is the regulative force behind the activities of the soul. Thus when the concupiscible or irascible appetites of man are aroused by uncontrolled emotion so that they hinder a man from behaving properly in the manner just described, the man is said to sin from weakness. (*Summa Theologica*, Vol. 25, 1969, p. 169, Question 77, Article 3)

Reason is the guiding force, once again, for 'behaving properly'. However, the 'infirmity' that inflicts the soul, in privileging reason, is different here precisely because there is now the narrative of Jesus's life and all its mysteries reveal to remind the believer of how to behave properly. The narrative itself is therefore the key to redemption and it was precisely this kind of narrative that the Greek philosophers could not turn to, or refer to, in making somewhat similar claims for 'right reason'. Auerbach details this difference between the classical style and the Christian style by arguing that whereas Tacitus and Petronius give us the 'sensory impression' of a 'specific stratum of society' (48), the new narrative 'becomes visually concrete' and 'speaks to everybody; everybody is urged and indeed required to take sides for or against it' (Auerbach, 48).

Before we move to a reading of an episode from Augustine, I want to explore in more detail Auerbach's description of the important 'change' in narrative that occurs as we move from the 'domain of classical antiquity' into the emergence of Christian narrative. He is writing of Peter's tragic denial of Christ: 'A tragic figure from such a background, a hero of such weakness, who yet derives the highest force from his very weakness, such a to and fro of the pendulum, is incompatible with the sublime style of the classical antique literature' (42). Peter is a lowly figure and yet his psychological crisis and his deep, personal wrangling become representative of a universal struggle, which all must one day experience. Gone are the heroes, the oracles and the kings. The lowly particulars of a fisherman from the humblest stratum of society are made to mediate our understanding of profound spiritual and philosophical issues: 'it was rooted from the beginning in the character of Jewish-Christian literature; it was graphically and harshly dramatized through God's incarnation in a human being of the humblest social station, through his existence on earth amid humble everyday people and conditions, and through his Passion' (41). Auerbach believes that this new kind of narrative of weakness, which would find its ideal trope in the mystery of the Incarnation, had a 'wide diffusion and strong effect' for literature 'in later ages' to the extent that it had 'a most decisive bearing upon man's conception of the tragic and the sublime' (41). He suggests that this movement was representative of 'the unfolding of historical forces' (44). Auerbach asks why such narratives 'arouse in us the most serious and most significant sympathy' (42); it is because they portray 'something which neither the poets nor the historians of antiquity ever set out to portray: the birth of a spiritual movement in the depths of the common people, from within the everyday occurrences of contemporary life, which thus assumes an importance it could never have assumed in antique literature' (42–3). Charles Dickens, who I examine in Chapter 8, strives to keep some of this 'spark of life' alive in his narratives which can also be regarded as describing this 'spiritual movement in the depths of the common people'. Other writers who have sought to base their philosophy on such a movement of the 'common people' might also be regarded as tapping into this new style of narrative. Even Marx, in his *Critique of Hegel's Doctrine of the State*, might be regarded as critiquing Hegel precisely because he neglects such a dynamic in narrative. For Marx, Hegel creates the impression 'that there is an idea over and above the organism' (Marx, 66); the real subjects 'are reduced to mere *names* of the Idea' (67). Fate becomes predestined by the 'nature of the concept' (70). However, Auerbach is right to remind us that in the early Christian narratives 'any raising of historical forces to the level of consciousness is totally "unscientific": it clings to the concrete and fails to progress to a systematization of experience in new concepts' (44).

Auerbach explains that the 'new spirit' of this narrative applies to 'every other occurrence which is related in the New Testament. Every one of them is concerned with the same question, the same conflict with which every human being is basically confronted and which therefore remains infinite and eternally pending' (43). This drawing up of all narrative moments into a singular narrative trajectory that is forever 'pending' and always pointing forwards to a salvation and redemption that arrives with the completion of the story of the Passion has, of course, been seen as limiting of narrative's potential by many Jewish philosophers and critics. Emmanuel Levinas puts the point most eloquently in relation to the notion of 'prefiguration'. How might the implications of such a narrative of weakness affect the 'very essence of the spirit which Judaism installed' through the Old Testament? He continues:

> If every pure character in the Old Testament announces the Messiah, if every unworthy person is his torturer and every woman his Mother, does not the Book of Books lose all life with this obsessive theme and endless repetition of the same stereotyped gestures? Does the spiritual dignity of these men and women come to them through reference to a drama operating on a miraculous level, in some mythological and sacred realm, rather than from the meaning that this life, which is conscience, gives itself? Does the monotheist God haunt the roads of the unconscious? (Levinas, 1990, 121)

However, the change from the narrative of classical antiquity and the new detailing of weakness is unmistakable. The fact that a 'random fisherman' or 'adulteress' can 'come from their random everyday circumstances to be immediately confronted with the personality of Jesus' in a narrative where 'the reaction of an individual in such a moment is necessarily a matter of profound seriousness, and very often tragic' (Auerbach, 44) is profoundly different to Oedipus's battles with a fate that is invisible, unexplained and unattached to any logic of personal salvation. One might suggest that God's weakening is mirrored in the characterization where 'lowly' figures are made to shoulder burdens that will lead to the redemption of mankind. However, this also raises a further question for such narratives that Auerbach does not examine in great detail. If the narratives are so radical precisely because 'lowly' characters like fishermen and prostitutes are made to carry the story, then what does this say about Jesus's weakness? Is he weak with conditions? How do generations of believers respond to and embody a weakness classified as Incarnate by Chalcedon and held up as a model by the early Church Fathers when Jesus's weakness may well have to accompany His awareness or consciousness of Himself as the Second Person of the 'Trinity'? The heroes and gods of the Classical age may be gone but are they replaced by a hierarchy that is all the more inviolable precisely because divinity has now simply 'assumed' human nature and taken on human form as weakness Incarnate to act as saviour for 'lowly' mankind in the shape of prostitutes and fishermen? The Passion brings home to believers the terrible suffering that human bodies must endure but recent studies, such as Richard Swinburne's *Was Jesus God?* also explore the 'human consciousness' the mystery of the Incarnation assigns to Jesus. Swinburne suggests that 'when he [Jesus] acts in a human way, he need not always be fully aware of having more power than that' (46). These explorations into Jesus's 'mind' raise the question of whether Jesus is capable of suffering or doubting as Kierkegaard's Abraham doubts when a wholly human life goes to sacrifice another human life for ends that are always possessive of the uncertainty and doubt that makes life human. Of course, these are questions that are impossible to answer conclusively. However, what is important to acknowledge in accepting the nature of the change in narrative that arrives with Christianity for Auerbach is that weakness, if it is entirely human and if it is to be connected with the 'unfolding of historical forces', is described anew for each age. While the Christian era undoubtedly ushered in a remarkable shift in narrative through this confrontation with weakness, it was effective precisely because it attached a spiritual need to the unique historical forces of its day and each age does likewise. This new style involves 'entering into the random everyday depths of popular life, as well as readiness to take seriously whatever is encountered there' (44). Auerbach argues that because this new narrative of weakness 'cannot be fitted into a system of judgments which operates with static categories' that the 'ethicism of the ancient had lost its supreme rank' (45). It would seem, then, that the new Christian narrative of weakness followed none of the recognized systems of ethics. In other words, it fastened the debate between Plato and Aristotle over the 'incontinent' and what kind of knowledge the man guilty of weakness of will or moral weakness has to the Christian narrative of salvation. However, it is clear that the Christian believer's greater certainty about ends, despite his or her lower status, transforms the sense of 'exposure' that Socrates' Leontius or Homer's Ulysses experience.

In acknowledging the importance of Auerbach's description of the move from the classical 'separation of styles' to the era of Christian 'figural interpretation' by way of this incorporation of weakness, it is also important to consider the new kind of psychological grappling with weakness that these new Christian characters must endure. We have seen in the story of Leontius in Chapter 1 how Leontius upbraids himself for having lapsed in regard to the self-discipline deemed so important in the classical era. For Socrates, Leontius may not be guilty on this occasion of *akrasia* or weakness of the will, but his appetite has triumphed, he feels shame, and he chides himself. In finishing this chapter, I want to turn to an early Christian narrative that might be regarded as describing a similar moment for early Christians. Augustine recounts the details of an episode in the life of his friend and disciple Alypius that reveals how Christian writers understand human weakness and human moral failing in light of the paradigmatic shift that was occurring in narrative styles. Alypius is dragged along to a gladiatorial fight against his wishes by his friends and while there he tries to close his eyes to the slaughter before him. However, after hearing one of the deathly shrieks of the contestants he 'opened his eyes' and 'was struck with a deeper wound in his soul than the other, whom he desired to see, was in his body' and 'fell more miserably than he on whose fall that mighty clamor was raised, which entered through his ears, and unlocked his eyes, to make way for the striking and beating down of his soul, which was bold rather than valiant hitherto; and so much the weaker in that it presumed on itself, which ought to have depended on Thee' (Auerbach, 68). Alypius is smitten by the gladiatorial contest: '[h]e looked, shouted, was excited, carried away with him the madness which would stimulate him to return'. But despite all this he is saved by God: 'And from all this didst Thou, with a most powerful and most merciful hand, pluck him, and 'taughtest him not to repose confidence in himself, but in Thee' (in Auerbach, 68). Weakness is no longer treated in terms of a failure of 'right reason' where the individual self-reprimands him or herself for a lack of self-sufficiency; from now on the believer must learn to rely not on him or herself but on God. The texts that give the narrative of Jesus's life now act as a textual and spiritual bulwark enabling the believer to relinquish control to God. Auerbach writes in his commentary on this piece: 'For his defeat is not final. When God has taught him to rely on Him instead of on himself – and his very defeat is the first step toward that knowledge – he will triumph' (69). However, what is important for both Leontius and Alypius in these similar personal struggles, separated by some 800 years, is that 'the very defeat is the first step toward that knowledge' both for the individual concerned and for the philosopher or theologian employing such instances for ethical or moral guidance. Leontius has himself to blame for not listening closely enough to his own 'right reason', whereas Alypius is now regarded as failing because his soul was 'weaker' because it 'presumed on itself' and not God. The moment of weakness is employed time and again to support theses on ethics and the good life in Christ. The 'defeat is the first step toward that knowledge' because the defeat must be explained.

Chapter 4

Nietzsche's Revaluation of Power and Kierkegaard's 'Despair of Weakness'

If there is any philosopher who prioritizes the challenge to the Christian worldview, it is Friedrich Nietzsche. Nietzsche might appear, on first impressions, as a philosopher who regards weakness as a wholly 'negative' concept. His 'will to power', 'the most profound fact to which we penetrate' (Kaufmann, 229), which Walter Kaufmann describes as 'essentially a striving to transcend and perfect oneself', (248) is starkly opposed to weakness as it appears in Christian writers and in much of Greek philosophy. Nietzsche consistently attacks Paul's notion of weakness and its 'glorification of the "foolish"' and the 'weak' from 1 Corinthians 1.27 (Kaufmann, 231) and weakness in the form of weakness of will or in light of the 'morality-and-ideal swindle' of Plato and the Socratic schools is also scorned (Neitzsche, 1990, 118); he calls Plato an 'antecedent Christian' (117). It is interesting, then, to discover that his reading of strength and weakness by way of 'dialectical monism' is often closer to the reading of these 'opposites' that we have found in the *Lau tzu*. Walter Kaufmann finds this parallel with Lao Tzu at work in Nietzsche in relation to the sense of 'self-overcoming' and 'self-mastery' that is central to the 'will to power': 'there can be no question but that Nietzsche agreed with that ancient tradition, which we can trace through continents and centuries to Laotze: that the man who conquers himself shows greater power than he who conquers' (252). Kaufmann directs us to Nietzsche's description of strength from his third *Meditation*:

> I have found strength where one does not look for it: in simple, mild, and pleasant people, without the least desire to rule – and conversely, the desire to rule has often appeared to me a sign of inward weakness: they fear their own slave soul and shroud it in a royal cloak (in the end, they still become the slaves of their followers, their fame etc.). The powerful natures *dominate*, it is necessity, they need not lift one finger. Even if,

during their life time, they bury themselves in a garden house. (x, 412; Kaufmann, 252)

There is, then, in Nietzsche, especially in *The Will To Power* with its privileging of the notions of stillness and moderation, a parallel of sorts with the Daoist sense of self-preservation through 'abiding by the soft'.

However, one cannot dismiss, despite Nietzsche's claim that his 'nature' is '*affirmative*' (1990, 76), the frequently acerbic 'grand style' that colours his descriptions of power and by consequence weakness in his rhetorical play with 'the negative' (Kaufmann, 243). Nietzsche's complex dialectical style also offers only glimpses of what the will to power can achieve through sublimation since it spends the majority of its time demonstrating how previous philosophies and belief systems have corrupted this self-overcoming and striving for a higher state. However, the emphasis on the 'negative' does not mean, for Kaufmann, that Nietzsche 'would have preferred things to be different from the way they were' (243). As Kaufmann reminds us, Nietzsche emphasizes 'the negative' precisely because he recognizes that the process of self-overcoming is so difficult. Despite all our weaknesses and our impulses we must refrain from resorting to a belief in a parallel universe, ideal or transcendent realm symbolized by either a heaven or Platonic Forms. Nietzsche was at heart pragmatic and we cannot ignore his regard for his *amor fati*. As he writes in his final work *Ecco Homo*: 'My formula for the greatness of a human being is *amor fati*: that one wants nothing to be different, not forward, not backward, not in all eternity' (*EH* II 10; Kaufmann, 243).

Besides this emphasis on 'the negative' there is another aspect of Nietzsche's reading of power and weakness that departs from the Daoist reading of strength and weakness. Right from the beginning, in *The Birth of Tragedy*, Nietzsche looks to the symbolic power of the ancient Greek gods, gods closely associated with creativity and the arts, in drawing up the dimensions of his 'dialectical monism' and the 'ordering of the chaos' that the 'will to power' as manifestation of this dialectic would have to eternally elaborate. As he writes in *The Birth of Tragedy*, '[o]nly as an aesthetic phenomenon is existence and the world justified'; the categories that loom large, then, over all the later rephrasings of the elements of this dialectic are the Apollonian and the Dionysian and these are notions arrived at through art and from which 'art derives its continuous development' (xxvii). Heidegger has warned, however, that the opposition between the Apollonian and the Dionysian 'all too often becomes a vacuous catchword' (1991, 102–3) if we do not recognize the dramatic transformation that takes place in Nietzsche's thought between *The Birth of Tragedy* and *The Will To Power* regarding this opposition. Heidegger reads the later sense of the opposition in terms of the unique sense of willing that Nietzsche promotes in the later work: 'willing is to-want-oneself' (Heidegger, 136) and it works through the 'indissoluble unity of the corporeal-psychical, the living' (96); it brings this initially aesthetic opposition into the realm of the personal. The Daoist does not call on any such categorical artistic notions in the estimation of strength and weakness.

As I have suggested in the introduction, Gianni Vattimo also regards Nietzsche as the chief influence for his 'weak thought' and his 'weak philosophy'. Before I examine how weakness appears in Nietzsche's descriptions of the 'will to power', I want to examine why Vattimo believes Nietzsche is so important for contemporary philosophy's 'weak thought'. Vattimo believes hermeneutics has reached the 'standpoint of weak thought' because of 'a question of method, namely, the criticism of metaphysical violence' (in Zabala, 2007, 400) and he argues that 'Nietzsche is the master of this radical critique of metaphysics' (402). Vattimo acknowledges that Nietzsche's unmasking of the violence that always haunts metaphysics has an 'apocalyptic' tone (405) to it, but he argues that Nietzsche's 'conception of the end of metaphysics through the unmasking of its violence . . . anticipates the complex meaning of many, if not all, the discourses that have been at the centre of philosophical attention from the end of the nineteenth century to today' (405). Nietzsche is therefore central to any understanding of how weakness in the form of 'weak thought' has emerged as fundamental for contemporary philosophy. The early, more 'scientific' Nietzsche tackled what Vattimo describes as the first aspect of this 'crisis of metaphysics' – one where the understanding of philosophy as a search for a 'true world', or foundation, in the face of the 'uncertain mutability of the visible world' (402) was seen as a fiction – by revealing how this 'crisis' or 'unmasking' of metaphysics is itself part of nihilism. For Vattimo, Nietzsche questions, once philosophy's unmasking is itself regarded as contrived and 'functional', whether 'we really have to think that the destiny of thought and of the very belief in the value of truth or foundation is to install itself without illusions as an "esprit fort" in the world of the war of all against all, where the "weak perish" and only power is affirmed' (402). In other words, Nietzsche, for Vattimo, points to an alternative where in a philosophical climate where unmasking is accepted for what it is those who are destined to triumph are, as he writes at the end of his 1887 essay 'European Nihilism', 'the most moderate, those who have no *need* of extreme articles of faith, who not only concede but even love a good deal of contingency and nonsense, who can think of man with a considerable moderation of his value and not therefore become small and weak' (in Vattimo, 402). Nietzsche refers to this sense of contingency and moderation again in his late work *Zarathustra* when he writes that '[i]t is the stillest words which bring the storm. Thoughts that come on doves' feet guide the world' (2003, 'The Stillest Hour', 168). This might remind us, once again, of the weakness described in the *Lao tzu*, and when Nietzsche writes 'Humility has the toughest hide' we might even recall Christian humility. However, we should not get carried away; Nietzsche's thought works against any naturalistic philosophy grounded on the Enlightenment's 'original spontaneity of thought' that is seen to shape 'life itself' (Cassirer, 1979, xiv) and where a rational and 'fully enlightened earth radiates disaser triumphant' (in Safranski, 344).

This emergence in Nietzsche of a regard for moderation and stillness, coupled with his importance for 'weak thought', is perhaps most evident in works such as *Zarathustra* and *The Will To Power*. Rüdiger Safranski suggests that it may also be the result of a change which occurred in the later works in regard to the notion of the will to power: 'The will to power, which had started out as a principle of free self-configuration and self-enhancement, a magical transformational power of art, and an inner dynamics of social life, was now becoming a biologistic and naturalistic principle as well' (290); it was even becoming, for Safranski, a '*causa prima*' (290). It may even have led Nietzsche to find something of worth in Christianity: 'Nietzsche greatly admired the power of Christianity to set values, but he was not grateful to it, because its consideration for the weak and the morality of evening things out impeded the progress and development of a higher state of mankind' (296). Nietzsche recognized the contradictory forces at work within this revised 'will to power', with power now acting as the 'power of life' (205) in the drive towards a 'higher stage of mankind' where the will to power, in unleashing the 'dynamics of culmination' in its 'peaks of rapture', (296) must yet form a 'moral alliance on the side of the weak' (296).

However, in recognizing this aspect of the 'will to power', Safranski argues that this 'alliance' ultimately leads, for Nietzsche, to 'widespread equalization and degeneration' in social movements such as democracy. One must wonder, then, whether this 'aspect' of the will to power is less 'degenerative' for the individual than it would be for social movements. Does it only become degenerative when it is unthinkingly transplanted from the genius and the sage to mass movements? After all, as Vattimo reminds us, for Nietzsche, the 'most moderate man is the artist' (403) or the sage. What Nietzsche assigns to the individual may often become sullied only through its contact with a wider community that he never really explored or embraced. His letters reveal how his sensitivity to others and his ultimate reclusive behaviour was the result of his ideals and vice versa. In a letter to Gast from August 1880 he explains how '[e]ven now my entire philosophy wavers after just an hour of friendly conversation with complete strangers' (Safranski, 204) and later, after finishing the first part of *Zarathustra*, he writes to Overbeck in 1883: 'Because of my exclusive contact with idealist images and processes, I have become so sensitive that I suffer incredibly from contact with actual people and forgo it' (258).

However, in returning to 'weak thought', Vattimo argues that the second 'inseparable' aspect of the 'crisis of metaphysics' that Nietzsche reveals and that is, for Vattimo, related to this ultimate movement towards 'weak thought', is one that acknowledges that 'once metaphysical beliefs are weakened, there is no longer anything that limits the conflictual nature of existence'; the 'supremacy' that results from this 'struggle between the weak and strong' is now only 'legitimated' by the 'mere fact of imposing itself' or, in a manner that Vattimo sees as 'decisive for Nietzsche', where 'the weakening of metaphysical beliefs not only uncovers the violence of existence for what it is and makes it no longer possible but is born as the result of an outburst of violence' (404). Nietzsche thus runs these two aspects of the crisis together; he asks whether the unmasking of violence integral to metaphysics has any meaning if it only leads to further violence. Vattimo's 'weak thought' aims to go further down this track first uncovered by Nietzsche. He argues that we are still chiefly concerned with this 'radical critique of metaphysics' (405) and that we must continue to make the connection between these two aspects of the crisis – 'the theoretical unmasking of the school of suspicion and the practical-political coming to light of a violence without limits' – 'thinkable' (405). The 'thinking' of this necessity to unmask a play of violence that yet results in the re-affirmation of violence, what might appear now as an eerie replaying of another Nietzschean motif, namely, the doctrine of eternal recurrence, is what must remain as the 'undeniable beginning of twentieth century philosophy and the "question of method" from which one must begin' (405). However, Vattimo's 'weak thought' may stray into a kind of language that Nietzsche would have scorned. He argues that '[i]f Being speaks, its discourse takes the form of a general buzzing, a polyphony of sounds, a murmuring, and perhaps even the form of the "neuter" whose announcement Maurice Blanchot says we ought to expect' (420). Vattimo echoes Richard Rorty's suggestion that a 'certain degree of frivolity when dealing with traditional philosophical questions' is needed; however, frivolity would seem to be something that Nietzsche could not entertain (qtd. in Vattimo 420). Vattimo's final words on this movement between 'weak thought' and violence via Nietzsche is a little more illuminating; he proposes a 'path of "moderation" and of listening, one that does not present the schema of foundation again and again but resigns itself to it, accepts it as destiny, distorts it, and secularizes it' (421). In order to discover how Nietzsche sits with such a process of resignation and distortion, I want to look more closely at his descriptions of power and weakness.

Some of Nietzsche's most influential readers and commentators (Walter Kaufmann, Gilles Deleuze and Martin Heidegger) privilege his interest in power and force. Therefore, if we are to come to any understanding of weakness in Nietzsche it is essential that we examine the dialectical relationship between force/power/strength and weakness. It is important to note also that, for Nietzsche, power does not refer to 'power over others' or to any Darwinian notion of power as what gives advantage in a 'struggle for existence' (Kaufmann, 329). Nietzschean power is also unrelated to notions of progress. As Kaufmann again suggests, Nietzsche's 'dual vision of overman and recurrence' means the 'moment' and not progress is glorified; it is about 'all simultaneously'. Nietzsche is forever returning to historical figures, such as Caesar and Leonardo, who come closest to his notion of the overman. Nietzsche also privileges the 'continuity of nature and culture' instead of any sense of progress in society (Kaufmann, 193).

However, it must be acknowledged that Nietzsche's 'weak man' is typically a figure of scorn and rebuke who lacks the necessary strength to gain any kind of self-overcoming. In understanding weakness in Nietzsche, we cannot neglect his sharp disdain for the 'weak man' and for 'weakness' in general. Weakness can be the pity that Christianity promotes (*Anti-Christ*, 1990, 130) or it can be the root of all that is bad – 'What is bad? – All that proceeds from weakness' (127); because we are also in a 'weak age' even our virtues are '*demanded* by our weakness' (*Twilight*, 1990, 102); our weakness is also the cause of a general 'decay of *vitality*' that deadens our spirit and even our language for describing virtue; to explain his point Nietzsche must describe what we lack as 'our hostile and mistrust-arousing instincts' (101). In other words, Nietzsche's 'grand style' employs a 'revaluation of all values'; he explains how we have fallen prey to a '*psychology of error*' where 'cause is mistaken for effect' (*Twilight*, 64). He therefore has an incredibly difficult task; in recognizing that our very language is corrupted and that effect has become cause, he must nevertheless negotiate the revaluation of all values while using existing concepts and language. So whereas Christian discourse and Platonic philosophy might suggest the individual is weak for acting according to impulses, Nietzsche would regard this as a strength in being a sign of vitality.

Weakness is perhaps the notion that alerts the reader most to this play of doubleness in Nietzschean language, and Nietzsche is quite explicit at times about this duplicitous sense of language. In speaking of the 'strong' man in *Twilight*, he describes him as a 'man to whom nothing is forbidden, except it be *weakness*, whether that weakness be called vice or virtue' (114). In other words, he recognizes how political spin and propaganda affect the description of this dialectical movement between what is strong and what is weak. However, in the end, despite Nietzsche's sophisticated 'grand style', there are certain 'truths' that he retains and one of the most basic is that the 'will to power' is undermined by weakness if weakness is conceived in a Christian manner – 'They do *not* call themselves the weak, they call themselves "the good"' (*Anti-Christ*, 139) – or according to a philosophy that advocates the extirpation of the impulses. Because Nietzsche is engaged in a 'revaluation of all values' which does not simply wash over the language that describes it, his philosophy leaves us with new descriptions of strength and weakness.

Nietzsche echoes Socrates, whom he considered among all philosophers to be the 'perfect master of his passions' (Kaufmann, 281), when he argues that the 'weak man' is typically the man who appears most powerful. As Kaufmann argues, 'worldly power may thus cloak the most abysmal weakness'; "the weak man either settles, *faute de mieux*, for some more or less petty form of power, such as that power over others which is found in positions of command . . . or he resigns himself to failure and dreams of greater power in another world" (281). So what is the Nietzschean ideal for the 'powerful man'? In the earlier books Nietzsche suggests that the ascetic may be such a man; however, as we learn later, more powerful still is the man who need not resort to such a radical process as the extirpation of the passions. In the *Dawn*, Nietzsche writes that one should 'measure the health of a society and of individuals according to how many parasites they can stand' (Kaufmann, 280). One must be able to 'master the passions', 'organize the chaos' and give 'style' to the character; the Good Life is found by the powerful man who does not need to 'weaken the impulses' but can master them and incorporate them into a life lived by 'being natural' (281).

In the final work Nietzsche himself published, *The Twilight of the Idols*, he describes Goethe as the prime example of such a 'powerful man':

[H]e disciplined himself into wholeness, he *created* himself . . . Goethe conceived a human being who would be strong, highly educated, skillful in all bodily matters, self-controlled, reverent toward himself, and who might dare to afford the whole range and wealth of being natural, being strong enough for such freedom; the man of tolerance, not from weakness but from strength because he knows how to use to his advantage even that from which the average nature would perish; the man for whom there is no longer anything that is forbidden, unless it be *weakness*, whether called vice or virtue. . . . only the particular is loathsome, and that all is redeemed and affirmed in the whole – *he does not negate any more*. Such a faith, however, is the highest of all possible faiths: I have baptized it with the name of *Dionysius*. (in Kaufmann, 281)

Since we have already seen that, for Nietzsche, the most 'powerful man' is the man who can incorporate into a Good Life the greatest assault by the impulses – what Goethe describes as representative of 'human weakness' – there are thus clearly two meanings of weakness at work in Nietzsche. Impulses are clearly representative of a weakness in that they have the potential to lead man astray and make him fail to realize fully what the 'will to power' can grant, but 'weakness' as used in the above quotation on Goethe is also the attribute of the 'weak man' who lacks the necessary 'power' to face up to the struggle to incorporate the most extreme impulses into the Good Life. Weakness as impulse is what necessitates the eternal struggle between the 'will to power' and the impulses, and weakness is also the inability to follow this struggle through. In other words, weakness is what gives the struggle meaning and, since the 'will to power' would be nothing without this struggle, weakness is also what gives the 'will to power' meaning. However, since the theory of eternal recurrence describes a dialectical process at work across time, it is evident that 'power' and weakness are even more closely linked; since there are no stable co-ordinates in Nietzsche's Heraclitean 'cosmos', these qualities are forever being transformed into each other as new forms of weakness and power emerge. As soon as the subject has incorporated one weakness into the 'will to power', the rationalization of this incorporation will reveal further weaknesses since the 'will to power' thrives on struggle and incorporation. It is only the most powerful man, the overman, who '*does not negate any more*'. The 'powerful man' is the man who can incorporate or integrate the strongest of impulses and passions into the 'style' of life, into life lived as *amor fati*, because 'nothing is dispensable' (*Ecco Homo*, 2004, 2). Because 'Nothing that is may be subtracted', (2004, 2) that which draws man away from the Good Life, the chaos caused by the 'impulses', which are representative of 'human weakness', must be 'read' and plumbed to the depths so that 'self-overcoming' can be authentically lived. The concentration, through the notion of recurrence, on finding permanence in the transitory by privileging the moment – 'all simultaneously' – and not progress as 'the development in time of the one God's will' (Kaufmann, 332) also anticipates postmodern and deconstructive theories that seek to undermine the 'mastery' and theoretical dominance of the master narratives.

Nietzsche's later descriptions of power and force are very often in terms of stillness, moderation and non-contention – characteristics that again remind us of the weakness we read in the *Lao tzu*. The 'will to power', however, does realize itself through reason and sublimation. Reason is then opposed to impulses in a somewhat similar manner to the opposition between 'right reason' and appetite in Plato; however, the difference is that the virtues or values arrived at through the examination of the good life are fluid concepts that are engaged in an eternal war with the impulses. Unlike · Christian philosophy, these impulses or appetites must not all be renounced or extirpated since knowledge without sensuality – as Kaufmann suggests, 'the man who can develop his faculty of reason only by extirpating his sensuality has a weak spirit' (233) – is evidence of weakness. Kaufmann's reading of the 'will to power' alerts us to how central the acknowledgement of weakness is to this never-ending process of self-overcoming. Kaufmann argues that Nietzsche 'proposed to measure power and weakness in terms of man's willingness to subject even his most cherished beliefs to the rigors of rationality' (232). Each journey of self-overcoming is uniquely painful and profoundly spiritual; Nietzsche emphasizes the 'cruelty and suffering' that go along with the process of self-overcoming. The 'most cherished beliefs' must be subjected to the rigours of the 'will to power' through reason and sublimation. Ultimately one's final and 'most cherished belief' will be the weak faith in the 'will to power' itself, since it is this belief that is the drive for the process of adaptation and subjection to the rigours of the 'will to power'. In other words, as the process continues, the boundary between the goals and the individual impulses or weaknesses that must be controlled will become ever more permeable. The goals and the means, since they belong to a 'dialectical monism' and since, as Heidegger suggests, the 'will to power' is the doctrine of eternal recurrence, will always be inextricably intertwined.

Kaufmann suggests that Nietzsche's only solution for this is to claim that the nature of the individual's struggle is simply a 'universal feature of the human constitution' and that these 'fictions must be considered necessary (for man) because they are not subjective'; the dilemma, then, 'however ridiculous it might seem to the angel Gabriel – would be inescapable for us' (206). Kaufmann argues that this dilemma means that the subject's 'own conception of the will to power must be admitted by him to be a creation of his own will to power' (204). It is then no longer regarded as a gift or as something granted *ab extra* but simply as another one of the subject's 'most cherished beliefs' and it must therefore be subjected to the 'rigors of ratio-nality'. Kaufmann admits that Nietzsche was 'not at his best with problems of this kind' (204); the attempt to fix the dilemma by describing it as repre-sentative of a universal condition simply begs the question in relation to whether it is a process that, in being 'inescapable', must be accepted on blind faith, which would go against the basic premise of the 'will to power'.

There is another aspect of the process of the 'will to power' that also alerts us to the importance of understanding and acknowledging weakness. Sublimation is key for the 'will to power', but what does it entail? Kaufmann gives a persuasive reading once again of this aspect of Nietzsche's 'will to power' (220–1). In the *Dawn* Nietzsche has a long aphorism on the 'will to power' and how it has 'self-mastery and moderation as its ultimate motive' (220). Nietzsche outlines 'six essentially different methods to fight the violence of a drive' so that the 'will to power' can suppress all but the most noble impulses. The last of these six methods for fighting the violence of a drive is '[self] weakening and exhaustion', whereby 'whoever can stand it, and finds it reasonable, to weaken and depress his *entire* physical and psychi-cal organization, will of course attain thereby also the goal of weakening a single violent drive' (in Kaufmann, 221). However, even though weakening and an appreciation of weakness are important for this aspect of the 'will to power', sublimation is a very different and more important aspect of the 'will to power' and its striving for self-overcoming. Nietzsche does not describe the precise workings of sublimation, but he makes clear, as Kaufmann demonstrates, that the sublimation and the control of impulses is very different from the 'abnegation, repudiation and extirpation of the passions' (223). However, there is also a difference between abandonment to the impulses and sublimation; sublimation refers to a process where there is an 'ordering of the chaos' brought about by the impulses; 'what remains is the essence and what is changed is accidental' (221).

However, the emasculation and abnegation of desire and passion raises another point in relation to the place of weakness in Nietzsche. Nietzsche asks in *The Twilight of the Idols* '*whether we have really grown more moral*' (37, 101). We have simply become too weak to be immoral: 'our virtues are conditioned, are *demanded* by our weakness' (102). As Kaufmann suggests: 'to be moral is to overcome one's impulses'; 'we are no heroes if our impulses are merely too weak' (224). Impulses, then, which approximate to the appetites that lead to weakness of the will in Aristotle, are in Nietzsche what imply strength. If one is weak then one either has no impulses or one is unable to rise above them. Nietzsche acknowledges that the greater the effort to overcome the impulses, the greater the potential for successfully acquiring a supreme 'will to power'. Nietzsche, as Kaufmann points out, 'insists throughout that we must "employ" our impulses and not weaken or destroy them' (225). As Nietzsche writes in *The Will to Power*: 'Moral intolerance is an expression of weakness in a man: he is afraid of his own "immortality", he must deny his strongest drives because he does not yet know how to employ them' (1968, II.385, p. 207). The sense here is that the strongest drives bring out the greatest displays of power and strength. Since these drives are embodied impulses and appetites, they draw the subject away from the 'will to power' and towards the 'weak spirit'. Nietzsche reminds us that weakness must be respected and that any movement towards self-overcoming necessitates a profound examination of weakness.

Because the meaning of the will to power changes throughout Nietzsche's work, weakness, its corollary, also has many faces. Heidegger's Nietzsche is, to an extent, a phenomenological Nietzsche with a nationalist flavour.[1] However, Heidegger does explore Nietzsche's understanding of will to a greater degree than other commentators. He describes Nietzsche's aesthetic understanding of will in terms of a 'physiology of art' where there is an 'unbroken and indissoluble unity of the corporal-psychical, the living, that is posited as the realm of the aesthetic state: the living "nature" of man' (96). Despite the neutralizing phenomenological language, Heidegger does connect Nietzsche's metaphysical thought and his rational argument with a deep awareness of the body. The body as 'living' is, for Heidegger, central to Nietzsche's philosophy as 'will to power'. He argues that to 'will is to want to become stronger'; it is bound up with an '*increase of power*' (60). Later he describes willing as 'to-want-oneself' where 'oneself is never meant as what is at hand' (136). He then gives a typically complex reading of the nature of the power that is integral to the 'will to power':

> Wanting-to-be-away-from-oneself is therefore basically a not-willing. In contrast, wherever superabundance and plenitude, that is, the revelation of essence which unfolds of itself, bring themselves under the law of the simple, willing wills itself in its essence, and *is* will. Such will is will to power. For power is not compulsion or violence. Genuine power does not yet prevail where it must simply hold its position in response to the threat of something that has not yet been neutralized. Power prevails only where the simplicity of calm dominates, by which the antithetical is preserved, i.e., transfigured, in the unity of a yoke that sustains the tension of a bow. (1991, 136–7)

Power must obey the 'law of the simple' and only prevails where the 'simplicity of calm dominates'. The metaphor of the tensile bow again recalls

Lao Tzu's use of the same metaphor to describe his philosophy of abiding by the soft: 'Is not the way of heaven like the stretching of a bow?/The high it pressed down,/The low it lifts up;/The excessive it takes from,/The deficient it gives to' (Lau, 2001, 111).

In *The Will To Power* Nietzsche gives the most detailed description of his power/weakness dialectic. He writes that 'prolonged reflection on the physiology of exhaustion', which he relates to weakness, has taught him that 'all of the supreme value judgments . . . can be derived from the judgments of the exhausted'. He describes the 'will to power' as a '*pathos*', what Gilles Deleuze describes as 'the sensibility of force' (2006, 63). The 'will to power' expresses itself in interpretation and evaluation that acknowledges how 'that which constitutes growth in life is an ever more thrifty and more far-seeing economy, which achieves more and more with less and less force' (*Will*, 1968, III.639, p. 341). The attention to 'less and less force' suggests that Nietzsche's 'will to power' can be regarded again here as approximating to Lao Tzu's notion of *wu wei* or non-doing, which is perhaps the second most important concept after *dao* for Daoism. Nietzsche's description of weakness does at times even seem to offer a non-contentious calm that eludes power: 'The greater the impulse toward unity, the more firmly may one conclude that weakness is present; the greater the impulse towards variety, differentiation, inner decay, the more force is present' (III.655, p. 346).

Gilles Deleuze's reading of Nietzsche gives the most detailed reading of force. He concentrates on Nietzsche's discussion of force as force without agent or subject. Nietzsche writes in *The Will To Power* that 'one must understand that an action is never caused by a purpose; that purpose and means are interpretations whereby certain points in an event are emphasized and selected at the expense of other points, which indeed, form the majority' (III.666, p. 351). Deleuze explains how the negative figures of reactive forces – namely ressentiment and nihilism – become transformed by the will to power as eternal recurrence: 'in the eternal return nihilism no longer expresses itself as the conservation and victory of the weak but as their self-destruction' (2006, 70). Self-destruction is thus revalued and appears as '*active destruction*' (*Ecco Homo*, III 1); 'it alone expresses the becoming-active of forces: forces become active insofar as reactive forces deny and suppress themselves in the name of a principle which, a short time ago, was still assuring their conservation and triumph' (Deleuze, 2006, 70). A certain degree of weak activity is therefore necessary for the realization of active force within the eternal recurrence. However, Deleuze also explains, in a very different manner to Heidegger, how willing and will have been misunderstood and misrepresented. Will has for too long been described in terms of 'struggle' and 'contest'; these bring Nietzsche too close to Darwin. Deleuze explains that '*struggle, war, rivalry or even comparison are foreign to Nietzsche and to his conception of the will to power* [Deleuze's italics]' (82). Deleuze goes further and explains how this oversight relates to signification and representation:

> [M]aking the will a will to power in the sense of a 'desire to dominate', philosophers see this desire as infinite; making power an object of rep-resentation they see the unreal character of a thing represented in this way . . . Everyone puts contradiction into the will and also the will into contradiction. Represented power is only appearance; the essence of the will does not establish itself in what is willed without losing itself in appearance. (2006, 83)

Deleuze stresses the creative and 'becoming' aspects of the will to power to such an extent that signification itself cannot contain or even momentarily capture the essential nature of its force. Deleuze can therefore put Nietzschean force in conversation with both Freudian psychology[2] and con-temporary theories of signification, even if these comparisons do seem to neglect what R. J. Hollingdale describes as 'the human, phenomenal, and even the animal' in Nietzsche's revaluation of values (*Zarathustra*, 2003, 13). Deleuze also describes power in Nietzsche as 'inexpressible' and giving; it is 'the bestowing virtue'. Power, in this light, appears almost compassionate, altruistic and nurturing, and since these qualities beg the question in rela-tion to who is the object of such compassion, it is a power that appears beneficial to what is less powerful or even weak. Deleuze describes the nature of such power:

> Will to power does not mean that the will wants power. Will to power does not imply any anthropomorphism in its origin, signification or essence. Will to power must be interpreted in a completely different way: power is *the one that* wills in the will. Power is the genetic and differential element in the will. This is why the will is essentially creative. This is also why power is never measured against representation; it is never represented, it is not even interpreted or evaluated, it is "the one that" interprets, "the one that" evaluates, "the one that" wills. But what does it will? . . . What the will to power wills is a particular relation of forces, a particular quality of forces. And also a particular quality of power: affirming or denying. . . . In Nietzsche's terms, we must say that every phenomenon not only reflects a type which constitutes its sense and value, but also the will to power as the

element from which the signification of its sense and the value of its value derive. *In this way the will to power is essentially creative and giving:* it does not aspire, it does not seek, it does not desire, above all it does not desire power. It *gives:* . . . power is in the will as "the bestowing virtue", through power the will itself bestows sense and value. (Deleuze, 2006, 85)

Deleuze will go on to argue that the 'the will to power is unitary, but unity which is affirmed of multiplicity' (85–6), and we have already seen Nietzsche describe weakness as that which accords with unity. In not desiring, in giving and in evoking the unitary, this power may seem impossibly human and all too Judeo-Christian. In giving us a rarefied, stripped-down logic of force in Nietzsche, Deleuze may also depersonalize force to the extent that it no longer appears incorporated or embodied. However, despite the resemblance here between such power and Christian weakness or Daoist weakness, Deleuze emphasizes once again the play of opposites at work in Nietzsche in regard to power and weakness. Nietzsche also explicitly returns to this point in *The Will To Power* in reference to the bow metaphor that we have seen Lao Tzu privilege: 'I believe that it is precisely through the presence of opposites and the feelings they occasion that the great man, *the bow with the great tension,* develops' (IV.967, p. 507). Nietzsche reminds us in this work that '[w]eakness can be an inaugural phenomenon: "as yet little"; or a terminal phenomenon "no more"' (IV.863, p. 459).

Ressentiment is also central to Nietzsche's revaluation of power. In describing the 'paralogism of *ressentiment*', (123) Deleuze explains how this most recalcitrant of negative tropes corrupts force and therefore power. Nietzsche wants to free force from an erroneous logic of force that is promoted by all existing moralities and the opposites strong and weak are favourite types in such moral systems. He wants to revive the 'original difference between qualified forces' that has been substituted by the 'moral opposition between substantialised forces' (124). For Deleuze, *ressentiment* has misrepresented force so that we are given '*the fiction of a force separated from what it can do*'. Because of this, 'reactive forces "project" an abstract and neutralized image of force; such a force separated from its effects will be *blameworthy* if it acts, *deserving,* on the contrary, if it does not' (123). In other words, the sense is that a moralizing narrative is attached to force before its dimensions are properly understood, or as Deleuze argues, '[a]n imaginary relation of causality is substituted for a real relation of significance' (123); '[f]orce is repressed into itself, then its manifestation is made into a different thing which finds its distinct, efficient cause in the force' (123). Nietzsche's philosophy is, then, all about the revaluation of values as outlined in such a system. Force, and hence power, must be freed up. Deleuze argues that Nietzsche takes the revaluation so far that it is not only the causality or the neutralization that is challenged, but also any notion of the 'subject' that is attached to this understanding of force: force is made 'the act of a subject which could just as easily not act. Nietzsche constantly exposes "the subject" as a fiction or a grammatical function' (123). The problem is that forces are 'projected into a fictitious subject' and the actions of this subject are moralized. The end result is that any attributes assigned to the subject on the basis of this erroneous causality of force are also deemed to be voluntarily adopted attributes and this applies to power and weakness. As Nietzsche argues in *On the Genealogy of Morals*: 'Just as if the weakness of the weak – that is to say their *essence*, their effects, their sole ineluctable, irremovable reality – were a voluntary achievement, willed, chosen, a *deed*, a *meritorious act*' (2007, I 13, p. 46). Deleuze explains how weakness, as typically assigned to the 'herd', is then misconstrued as a 'voluntary achievement' when in truth it is simply a result of a pre-subjective play of forces and an acquired habit gleamed from the 'original difference between qualified forces' (124). However, we may well question whether the 'human' has any agency for Deleuze's Nietzsche.

The eternally recurrent force of the will to power means that these states of weakness and strength are forever 'becoming' and are forever in a state of flux that even language itself cannot ensnare. Force, as will to power, is, as Nietzsche reminds us, 'the most elemental fact from which a becoming and effecting first emerge' (*Will To Power*, 1968, III.635, p. 339). The final section of Nietzsche's *Zarathustra* will ultimately present us with an old man with white hair talking to his animals, lamenting how his 'happiness is heavy and not like a fluid wave of water' (2003, 251). The affirmative aspects of the elusive 'will to power' that are sustained throughout Nietzsche's work are here described in terms of water, a metaphor the *Lao tzu's* 'old man' also employs, as we have seen, in describing his privileged state of weakness.

Søren Kierkegaard's understanding of weakness is, on the surface, far removed from Nietzsche's. Even though Nietzsche would presumably support Kierkegaard's belief that 'to conquer one's spirit is greater than to take a city' (*Discourses*, 1961, 74), they have very different aims in mind for such self-overcoming. Nietzsche had not read Kierkegaard since his attention was only drawn to the Dane in 1888 and this was too late for him to acquire his works. For Kaufmann, Nietzsche would presumably have felt that Kierkegaard 'had abandoned philosophy altogether to "leap" . . . into religion' (125). Kierkegaard suggests, in a very different context to that of Nietzsche, that when the subject strives for self-overcoming he must navigate the 'despair in weakness' and, in so doing, he must also confront the 'despair over one's weakness'. Faith is the solution to such weakness but the paradox is, as he writes in the essay 'Keep thy foot when thou goest to the house of the Lord', that a 'man seldom succeeds, and always only in weakness', (*Discourses*, 1961, 183) a solution Nietzsche scorns. Kierkegaard also describes a state of 'despair of weakness' that is a state of being 'in Despair Not to Will to Be Oneself' (*Sickness*, 1980, 49). He describes it as a 'feminine despair' (49) in being different to the 'despair to will to be oneself' that is aligned more with a 'masculine despair'. However, Kierkegaard reminds us that the 'opposites are only relative' (49). It is a 'despair in weakness', which is also translated as a 'passive suffering of the self', (2008, 46) and not a 'despair in defiance' (1980, 61). The possessor of such despair is in a double bind; he wants to free himself of 'immediacy' (55) and in doing so he regards even the loss of self as a 'conversion of property'. But in not wanting to be himself and in not grappling with the self he is lacking the 'self-reflection or the ethical reflection' that would allow him to break with this 'immediacy'. The result is that the whole question of the self becomes for him a 'kind of false door with nothing behind it in the background of the soul' (56). It is a despair one must go through to find the 'self' and it is, for Kierkegaard, the 'most common form of despair' (57).

The *Christian Discourses* give great detail on the nature of Christian weakness (which we have examined in Chapter 2) and what provides an important backdrop for the phenomenology of religion of the twentieth century. In a section from part II of the *Discourses*, which were written before the metamorphosis of 1848, the last and strongest of his three spiritual awakenings, a section entitled 'The Joy of it – That the Weaker Thou Dost Become, The Stronger Does God Become', Kierkegaard argues '*that the fact of a man's being weak signifies* inwardly *that God becomes strong in him*' (1961, 131). Ironically, both Nietzsche and Kierkegaard are applying weakness here to a similar state – namely, that state of being in thrall to the Christian God. However, whereas it is weakness for Nietzsche because of the various ways in which such Christian belief abnegates responsibility for self-overcoming and extirpates the senses and thus the 'will to power', for Kierkegaard, even though he is also, as his translator Walter Lowrie explains, engaged throughout the later works (*Training in Christianity, For Self-Examination* and *Judge for Yourselves*) in sometimes veiled yet 'trenchant attacks upon the corruptions of Christianity', (*Discourses*, 1961, xvii) *weakness* is a positive attribute in that it means that '*God becomes strong in him* [the believer]' (131). Very much like Socrates then, and perhaps less like

Nietzsche, what the world sets up as power and strength is, in truth, a kind of weakness. However, as might be expected, Kierkegaard takes the examination of Christian weakness to new depths. Christian belief inaugurates a 'reciprocal relationship' between man and God that is exacting and even a little demanding. We read that 'love' which 'made a man to be something' also 'requires something of him'. What Christian love requires is that the 'love' which allowed man to 'come into existence *for* God' is reciprocated and that man cannot 'selfishly keep for himself this something which love made him to be' (133). The worldly man hangs onto this form of existence 'as if it is his own'.

Kierkegaard explains for the believer how Christian weakness is earned and why it is to be cherished: 'On the other hand, if man himself relinquishes this something, the independence, the freedom to act for himself, which love bestowed upon him [for Deleuze's Nietzsche's 'force' or 'power', as the pre-subjective energy in his system is also that which gives and bestows]; . . . if God perhaps helps him in this respect by bitter sufferings, by taking from him his dearest one, by wounding him in the tenderest spot, by denying him his only wish, by depriving him of his last hope – then he is weak' (134). The believer has 'whole-heartedly consented to it that God took from him everything there was to be taken'. God only waits for him 'to give lovingly and humbly his glad consent' (134). So man becomes weak voluntarily in this 'reciprocal relationship', and God can 'help' by taking all that is most dear so that any unforeseen suffering is simply what is pre-ordained by God. Weakness is a giving up of everything to God so that lowliness, poverty and even irresolution are vanquished because in the 'leap of faith' the believer discovers that we 'suffer but once', as emblematized by what Kierkegaard refers to as the 'Pattern', or Jesus's Incarnation and Passion.

However, Kierkegaard, like Nietzsche, recognizes that this relation can be 'inverted' and that there is a '*true sense*' to language and meaning that the masses employ (at other times he refers to this way of speaking as 'humanly speaking'). In this sense, he '*who is strong without God*' is precisely he '*who is weak*' (134); however, Kierkegaard emphasizes his own spiritual understanding of weakness where the believer is 'entirely weak [only] in perfect obedience' to God. With such weakness the believer is 'reviled' but 'lovingly understand[s]' that such revulsion does no harm to his 'true welfare'; thus, such weakness is, for Kierkegaard, once again in the 'true sense', also a 'prodigious strength' (135). Kierkegaard stresses that the believer must will such weakness for himself. It must be a kind of 'will to weakness'; if the believer does not will such weakness then he is guilty of 'defiance': 'weakness and impotence which makes itself unhappy by not willing to be weakness and impotence, it is the unhappy relationship of weakness and impotence to superiority' (136). Kierkegaard borrows from the Lutheran dogma of human impotence in declaring that in such a state, man 'is able to do nothing at all'; he must add 'If God will' to every resolution. However, such weakness is 'blissful' because it is a 'love-secret' with God (137). Once again, it is interesting to note how this state, despite the very different set of values attached, recalls Aristotle's notion of immobility.

Kierkegaard employs various other terms to describe man's weakness; he speaks of man's superfluity and lowliness. The 'unusually talented person is more or less superfluous because he is not apt to fit into any of all the situations to which the bustle of business would assign him' and this 'superfluousness' magnifies the 'Creator's honour' more than all the 'self-importance of bustle' (83). Kierkegaard argues, by seizing on the uniquely 'weak' narrative of Christ's life, as Auerbach has suggested, that the Christian must also be 'lowly' in a manner that departs from general lowliness. The lowly Christian once again possesses this weakness as 'love-secret with God' because he has recognized that 'His life in lowliness [Jesus's life], has showed how much a lowly man matters, and, alas, humanly speaking, what it means to be a superior man, how infinitely much it may mean to be a lowly man, and how infinitely little to be a superior man' (1961, 45). The lowly Christian also recognizes that 'the only way one who is on high can truly be without anxiety is not to be higher than any one else' (53). Such states of weakness also extend to material wealth. Poverty is not to be scorned because the poor Christian is 'without the anxiety of poverty' (21); he is, in fact, rich and 'thou shalt recognize him by the fact that he does not wish to talk about his earthly poverty, but rather of his heavenly riches' (20). In the *Discourses* Kierkegaard also explains how one of his most famous descriptions of faith – namely, faith as 'fear and trembling', a phrase used for the title of the earlier work from 1843 – can only be fully realized in 'weakness' where one must 'transform the leap into a gait in life'. Faith is the 'blissful assurance' that is 'found in fear and trembling' and there are two sides from which to view faith: 'When faith is seen from the one side, the heavenly side, one sees in it only the bright reflection of blessedness; but seen from the other side, the merely human side, one sees sheer fear and trembling' (182). It is for this reason that 'it is a difficult thing to steer [faith] aright'; a 'man seldom succeeds, and always only in weakness' (183). Weakness, then, is essential for faith; it is the only route to faith.

If we try and extend Kierkegaard's philosophy beyond the Christian predicament and look for the universal, existential conditions that all peoples must engage with, then we also discover a description of the power/weakness opposition that might be regarded as responding to Nietzsche's notion of 'self-overcoming'. Kierkegaard's edifying and upbuilding discourses may give us what George Pattison describes as Kierkegaard's 'true point of view' (*Spiritual*, 2010, xii) since Kierkegaard 'consistently claimed' that it was not to be found in his pseudonymous works. These works are written under his own name and, regardless of whether we believe they possess the 'hermeneutical generosity' that has been assigned to them that allows us to see them as 'not in fact Christian in an emphatic sense', (xv) as his pseudonymous author Johannes Climacus claims for them, they re-imagine human weakness through a discussion of the notion of 'gift'. Kierkegaard's description of 'the gift', which is only truly experienced by making oneself more lowly than the gift, is a philosophical notion that responds well to notions of giving and the 'gift' in recent philosophy. Lewis Hyde's reading of the gift also returns to this sense of weakening that the gift symbolizes. He describes how the notion of 'gift' can be traced back to the self-giving of gods where the gods 'become incarnate and then offer their own bodies as the gift that establishes the bond between man and the spiritual state to which the god pretends' (Hyde, 74–5).

When Kierkegaard is cast as an existential philosopher he is all too often saddled with the weight of twentieth-century anomie and alienation. A close reading of the edifying discourses, however, reveals how he challenges popular notions of doubt and despair in order to speak for a 'reintegration of the self' through an 'all-embracing self acceptance' that must acknowledge the weakness described above (2010, xxii). In George Pattinson's new translations of Discourses from *Eighteen Upbuilding Discourses*, Kierkegaard explains that presumptuous suffering that wants 'God's ideas about what was good for you to be the same as yours', (2010, 8) what thereby 'weaken[s] God's eternal Being', (9) is a form of despair that understands life as a 'dark saying'. It celebrates despair and suffering according to an unexamined adherence to knowledge that has not 'voluntarily' accepted the true nature of 'God's gift'; in other words, one has not become sufficiently weak and lowly. It is only when you are finally 'crushed in spirit' and you have 'humbled yourself under God's powerful hand' that you no longer see life as a 'dark saying' (10). Of course Nietzsche sees this as evidence of what is most despicable about Christianity; for Nietzsche, Christianity 'crushed and shattered man completely, and submerged him as if in deep mire' (*Human*, 1984, 85). Kierkegaard then gives a reading of the tree of knowledge episode from Genesis that links this reading of despair to doubt. Knowledge became desirable for humanity and was sparked by the doubt that the temptation of Eden prefigured. Mankind was led into an intoxicating hermeneutic circle: 'how could they know about goodness and perfection if they didn't know where they came from, but how could they know the eternal source without knowing what goodness and perfection were?' (25). Doubt became a weapon that mankind wielded to fend off the despair brought about by giving in to the desire for knowledge: '[d]oubt became internalized, and the knowledge that ought to have guided humanity tied it up in neediness and contradiction. Now knowledge appeared as something unattainable, something one could only sigh for. . . . now it overpowered them with its riches, now it starved them out with its emptiness' (25–6). Such knowledge leads man to revere doubt and to assign a notion of strength to the battle for self-overcoming that must now wrestle with such doubt.

Kierkegaard responds to such arguments for self-overcoming that privilege power and strength, which recalls Nietzsche's understanding of 'self-overcoming', with the following description of this 'subterfuge of doubt': 'Is doubt, then, the stronger? . . . And isn't it precisely the subterfuge of doubt that it makes people imagine that they themselves can overcome themselves, as if they are capable of performing a miracle unheard of in heaven and on earth and under the earth – namely, the miracle that someone who is fighting against himself can be stronger in this fight than he himself is?' (26). Kierkegaard will always advise against 'your false friend Mr. Doubtful' (35) in championing 'meekness' (39) and the believer who 'prefers to have little but with a blessing', who 'prefers to have a truth that one might care about, to suffer instead of celebrating imaginary victories' (27). He will also employ the metaphor of the 'gift' to explain how weakness and lowliness is essential for attaining the higher state of 'equality in love'; it is meekness [that] discovers things that are hidden [George Pattinson traces this quotation in Kierkegaard to Ecclesiasticus 3:19 from the King James Bible, where the passage reads: 'many are in high place, and of renown: but mysteries are revealed unto the meek'] (2010, 39). Giving and sympathy are what enable the believer to attain a kind of supreme lowliness or weakness that give to the 'equality in love'; you must '*be lowlier than your sympathy*' and 'put yourself out of the picture' when you give (52); you cannot 'bestow on those who need it conditional on their being weaker' (52) since the one who gives must even acknowledge that 'he is *lowlier than the gift*' (59). There is no longer any market value in giving, no longer any need to 'fumble in a greasy till'; 'the more perfect a gift is, the clearer and more indisputably equality, too, reveals itself, and does so straightaway' (60). This is the 'good and perfect gift' and the 'only good and perfect gift a human being can give is love' where 'giver and receiver are indistinguishable in the gift'. We must 'wean ourselves from understanding the imperfect as a means of grasping the perfect' (61); we must give up our commitment to 'differences' and accept that 'there is one thought that cares to know nothing of the differences that bring only trouble but thinks solely of the equality that is from above: equality in love, which alone abides' (61). The acknowledgement and practice of one's weakness in the interpersonal encounter of giving is therefore fundamental for understanding equality.

Chapter 5

Why is Derrida's Sign Violent? Grammatology and a 'Force of Weakness'

Weakness is principally a structural weakness for Jacques Derrida. However, the Western metaphysics Derrida deconstructs promulgates a 'vulgar concept of writing', (1998, 140) a 'Western ethnocentrism', that therefore has 'deception' at the heart of its representations of power, violence and force. When Derrida comes to assess the range of this great 'deception' in metaphysics, he finds it useful to depart from pure structuralism (if such a thing exists) and to speak of 'experience', behaviour and 'society'. Because of the 'deception' implicit in Western metaphysics, 'violence is writing'. It can never be otherwise because of the initial 'deception'. Vulgar writing is 'repression' and 'arche-writing', the alternative Derrida proposes through the 'trace', is a 'violent opening' because it must 'think the unique within the system' (112). This recalls the 'outburst of violence' that the 'weakening of metaphysical beliefs' triggers for Vattimo's Nietzsche. Derrida's arche-violence is 'confirmed' by a reactionary violence that strives to keep the delusion of presence intact. Out of this arche-violence can emerge a third form of violence 'within what is commonly called evil, war, indiscretion, rape' which consists of 'revealing' the 'originary violence which has severed the proper from its property'. It is at this level that Derrida suggests the 'common concept of violence' should be thought (112). It is clear then that if we want to understand weakness in Derrida that we must explore the roots of this multi-layered violence that is so pervasive in culture.

What is the nature of this 'deception' that Derrida observes? For Derrida, Western culture has been living a lie. A system has taken root in Western ethnocentrism where the 'literal' meaning of writing has been set up as 'metaphoricity itself' and the precise nature of this metaphor has been left unexplored. For this reason writing always incurs violence in 'Western metaphysics' (23) because whenever there is writing, the 'truth' of writing threatens the foundations of this fraudulent manoeuvre within culture; writing is always trying to step out from behind its shadow. Because 'originary' states of being and necessity, such as self-awareness in ancient Greece and living according to God's laws in the Judeo-Christian context, have been described in terms of writing, or *as* writing – we have 'the writing of truth in the soul' and 'God's writing' (15) – writing has been over-whelmed by what it is not. These experiences of self-awareness or commu-nion with God, foundational moments for Western culture and for the Judeo-Christian context, have swelled beyond the proportions of the meta-phor constructed to contain them. Once they had been described figura-tively as experiences where an inner agency of self-awareness 'writes' on the soul, or where God 'writes' on our hearts or on tablets of stone, then the nature of writing was also changed forever. These experiences became emblematic of writing itself because they were foundational for the people of these cultures. In being described in terms of writing, these myths of originary cultural self-determination became emblematic of all future writ-ing; they became 'literal' writing. Any future writing, in order to be regarded as 'real' writing, had to possess the same sense of foundational communion integral to these moments. Anything else was simply 'metaphor'. One result of this was that the original need or necessity that was at the root of the 'turn' to writing as the figure for these moments of cultural revelation was forgotten, as was the original 'unmotivated' understanding of writing as practice, system or activity prior to Greek *aletheia*, Christian revelation or the 'book' of Nature. Any writing that did not correspond to this new 'lit-eral' writing, a writing which, for Derrida, must be 'phonetic', must evoke presence and must privilege the voice over inscription, or expression over indication (to use Husserl's terms) is a 'fallen writing'. In other words, 'lit-eral' writing was, in truth, not a writing at all but an inner communication or 'auto-affection' that bypassed the inscription and yet regarded itself as 'originary' writing. Writing was therefore doubly wounded. It was set up as metaphor for something unrelated and, on top of this, anything that resem-bled its 'proper' dimensions was also regarded as defective or 'fallen'. Derrida therefore, as 'grammatologist', asks 'What is writing?' and 'where and when does writing begin?' (28).

In this chapter I want to examine how the trace and the 'de-constructive' system it brings with it is still a violent system and how the concentration on the violence of this system risks misrepresenting the 'weakness' or 'impo-tence' that alerts Derrida to where such violence must be employed. If there has been a deceptive 'reversal of power', then there has also been a reversal of weakness and with reference to Derrida's own notes on weakness and in light of the version of natural writing put forward by Zhang and Ames earlier in Chapter 3, I want to examine how Derrida's reading of the original deception that produced this system of violence might simply be one way of reading the history. In beginning his exploration in *Of Grammatology* Derrida emphasizes that the resulting 'vulgar form of writing' is inherently violent. The self-communion and auto-affection integral to the moments that ground 'literal' writing have meant that phonetic language, language directly linked with what produces the inner communication or 'inner voice' – also described as the phōnē – has been privileged. There is therefore an inviolable connection between speech and phonetic writing *as* writing. This has necessitated a struggle between what is internal to the system of writing and what is external. Language has therefore set itself up as 'self-proclaimed language' or 'speech' (39), but it is a privileged position that necessitates a continual struggle to defend itself against other kinds of writing that do not comply with this 'phonetic' model: '[s]elf-proclaimed language but actually speech, deluded into believing itself completely alive, and violent, for it is not "capable of protect[ing] or defend[ing] [itself]"' . . . except through expelling the other, and especially *its own* other' (39). Writing in 'Western metaphysics' is thus haunted by the violence and sense of 'usurpation' inaugurated by this original deception where 'literal' writing is itself, unquestioningly, 'metaphoricity'. There is a 'reversal of power' integral to this metaphysics that 'cannot' be 'accidental' (40); a 'usurpation' haunts such writing through the 'violence by which writing would substitute itself for its own origin, for that which ought not only to have engendered it but to have been engendered from it' (40). Derrida asks how this 'trap and the usurpation is possible?' and he offers his own system based on the 'trace' as an alternative.

This is a compelling and at times confounding history of writing. How can it be that all writing in the West is living the lie and perpetuating deception? However, if we have learnt anything from Derrida, it is that arguments always have weak points; it is at the fringes of any argument that the 'boundary event' occurs so that one can begin to ask more probing questions. In laying out his stall at the very beginning of *Of Grammatology*, Derrida describes the different components of his conception of the emergence of Western ethnocentric writing or 'vulgar' writing. He tells us, for a reason he does not make clear, that 'reading and writing' in early times become 'preceded by a truth' (14). This is the truth of the logos, whereby 'the signified' of the thing or the referent has 'an immediate relationship with the logos' and a 'mediated one with the signifier' (15). If it goes 'otherwise' then there is a tendency to simulate 'immediacy'; in other words, if the signifier is primary then because the immediate relationship with the logos is privileged an effort is made to make the subject's relation to this signifier seem 'immediate'.

Derrida speaks of three different origins of writing in developing the argument: Greek origins, the origins of Natural writing and the Judaeo-Christian origin. We have the corresponding metaphors of 'the writing of truth in the soul', the 'book of Nature and God's writing'. Derrida argues that 'all that functions as *metaphor* in these discourses confirms the privilege of the logos and founds the "literal" meaning then given to writing' (15).

What is it, then, that 'functions as *metaphor* in these discourses'? In the case of the Platonic example – 'the writing of truth in the soul' – what matters is that basic truths are regarded as being self-evident and so well known as to actually appear to be 'written' on the soul. Of course, in truth, no writing takes place (unless a PET scan suggests otherwise) and what is more likely to have happened is that the truth was so enlightening that it revealed a great deal about being in general; it was returned to 'inwardly' and reflected on at length so that its meaning became a basis for living. Writing here, if we follow Derrida's argument, is transformed. The 'literal' meaning of writing is 'found[ed]' by these metaphors; we lose sight of writing as the engraving or the inscription and we now conceive of it in terms of this reflection and this sense of self-communion. 'Literal' writing must in future possess this same kind of self-communion. However, in making these metaphors, Derrida suggests that what was presumed was that 'writing', 'in the literal sense', was a sensible and finite practice that therefore falls on the side of 'culture, technique and artifice'. The other idea key to the making of these metaphors was that 'natural and universal writing, intelligible and nontemporal writing' is 'named by metaphor'. In other words, the 'writing of truth in the soul', the 'book of Nature' and 'God's writing' are not described literally but only 'by metaphor'. These are mysterious and somewhat elusive experiences and processes and they have therefore been consigned to metaphor. There is no sense of us ever being able to tell it like it is. This is the reason for the mystery – and not only mystery but 'deception also' – at the origin of writing; from this point on, writing would never be able to possess the same kind of mystery that the communion with God, or the self-communion with the soul or the process of Nature leaving 'signs' possessed. In other words, these earliest of metaphors have implicitly set up writing as something secondary to, and as something that can only stand in as metaphor for, this ill-defined sense of self-communication or 'inner' learning.

However, in accepting the breathtaking nature of this account of the origins of language, we must ask whether the three cases given are so similar. In other words, do the three cases allow for the same kind of phonetic writing which Derrida challenges? Are God's 'writing', Plato's 'writing' on the soul and the 'book of Nature' equally responsible for this privileging of the voice and self-presence? Recent comparative studies of Chinese and

Western writing systems might suggest that 'the book of Nature' in the Chinese context presumes a very different system to that found, say, in the Christian texts that privilege a unique kind of phoneticism or self-communion through incarnation. Derrida acknowledges that Chinese writing 'incorporated' the voice into a 'system' that is 'largely nonphonetic' (90). Longxi Zhang, as we have seen in Chapter 2, sees a 'similar hierarchy' (between speech and writing) at work in both Western and Chinese writing. He explores the meaning of 'word' in Chinese to support his argument that the hierarchy 'seems to apply . . . not only to phonetic writing but to nonphonetic writing as well' (*Tao*, 29). Later, he again describes the 'Chinese script as a form of nonphonetic writing' (32). Is the Chinese writing system, then, 'largely nonphonetic' or 'nonphonetic'? This is an aspect of the system that must be clarified before we can decide if Derrida's reading of language and phonocentrism applies to both 'natural' languages and non-natural languages.

In his argument, Zhang also makes reference to a second-century Chinese dictionary in arguing that the 'debasement of writing' in Chinese texts is 'based on the same consideration as in the West'. The dictionary gives the following definition for 'word': 'meaning inside and speech outside' (29). However, while this early definition may have echoes of Aristotle's poetics, it is perhaps going too far to see in the definition elements of a deconstructive hierarchy which would, at any rate, be more likely to locate speech with what is inside. However, it is when Zhang moves to his description of the legendary account of the origin of Chinese script that we notice an important difference between the two writing systems. He argues that Chinese script might even 'overturn the metaphysical hierarchy' that Derrida has highlighted for him 'more easily and efficiently than Western phonetic writing does' (the hierarchy Zhang has in mind here is that between 'inner reality and outer expression' (32); the hierarchy Derrida privileges between speech and writing may not be entirely equivalent and its expression in Western 'phonetic writing' would appear, in Derrida, to perpetuate rather than 'overturn' any existing hierarchy) (32). It can do this precisely because it is 'nonphonetic' and was 'never conceived as a mere recording of oral speech but as originating independently of speech'; it originated instead as an imitation of the 'pattern of traces left by birds and animals on the ground or by natural phenomena in general' (32). In other words, we now see that the two systems privilege different accounts of origin. It raises the question whether the deconstructive hierarchy between speech and writing, derived as it is from the close examination of a Western system – that is, for Derrida, rooted in phonocentrism – can be transplanted onto the Chinese writing system. Might it not be the case, if the two systems are found to exhibit similar aspects of this 'metaphysical hierarchy' between speech and writing, that they do so for entirely different reasons?

Differences can also be observed between the origins of language from a Natural language perspective and a Christian perspective. What these comparisons of the different explanations for the origin of language make clear is that the three different contexts for the origin of writing that Derrida points to may on occasion use writing as a metaphor for describing an inscription, communion or revelation, but it is not always so clearly motivated by a privileging of a similar 'inner voice'. In the spirit of his own style of commentary, it is important, then, while acknowledging that Derrida does reveal a great 'deception' at the heart of language and metaphoricity, to examine his description of writing as violent in light of the different accounts of weakness examined thus far. Each account of weakness, be it the Greek, the Christian or the Daoist, has related weakness to an original state of need or necessity. We recall the Greek notion of necessity that Williams privileges, D. C. Lau's notion of 'self-preservation' in the *Lao tzu* and Paul's description of weakness as an expression of basic human need before God. Derrida does not take us back to the possibility of need before the arrival of this originary metaphoricity. Where is the inspection of need in Derrida's history of writing and how does its absence affect his description of weakness?

Metaphoricity is an important notion for Derrida's argument and it is worthwhile recalling a different Western description of language and metaphor. Derrida conducted a series of debates on language with Hans-Georg Gadamer. Gadamer writes the following about the origins of language:

> Language and thinking about things are so bound together that it is an abstraction to conceive of the system of truths as a pregiven system of possibilities of being for which the signifying subject selects corresponding signs. . . . Rather, the ideality of the meaning lies in the word itself. But this does not imply, on the other hand, that the word precedes all experience and simply advenes to an experience in an external way, by subjecting itself to it. Experience is not wordless to begin with. . . . Rather, experience of itself seeks and finds words that express it. We seek the right word – i.e. the word that really belongs to the thing – so that in it the thing comes into language. (1995, 416–17)

To 'conceive of the system of truths [and metaphoricity may be one such truth in Derrida's argument] as a pregiven system' may be something of an 'abstraction'. The important point to take from Gadamer is perhaps that experience 'seeks and finds words' that 'express it'. In Derrida's system, how is the 'originary deception' or the 'metaphoricity' that institutes phonocentrism bound up with this seeking and needing and how might such necessity confound any assertion of original structural metaphoricity?

Derrida returns to metaphor in his essay 'White Mythology'. In the essay he acknowledges the 'bottomless overdeterminability' (1974, *New Literary History*, 44) of metaphor. The understanding of the 'metaphor of metaphor' will always be found wanting: '[a]ny "metaphorology" would therefore be derivative with regard to the discourse over which it would claim ascendancy' (28) because the 'concept of metaphor' is itself 'an element of philosophy' (28). Even Derrida's attempted reduction of what is variously referred to as phonetic or natural language is troubled by this dilemma: the position 'becomes worse when we turn to "archaic" tropes which have given to "founding" concepts (*theoria, eidos, logos,* etc.) the character of a "natural" language' since '[e]ven the signs (words or concepts) which make up this proposition, starting with *trope* and *arché*, have their metaphorical charge' (23). The origin of metaphor is therefore a difficult point from which to infer error or injustice. In *Of Grammatology*, Derrida introduces what one might call his own system of tropes – trace, supplement and hinge – that also presuppose their own logic of metaphoricity. Derrida then suggests that the type of metaphor that can rescue us from the history of metaphysics as phonocentrism is the heliocentric metaphor, the metaphor that revolves around the sun. However, in metaphysics and philosophy in general the treatment of this metaphor displays the same kind of self-returning and self-present dynamic that he has been at pains to discredit: 'the turning of the sun is then seen as a reflecting circle, returning to itself with no loss of sense, no irreversible expenditure. This *returning to itself* – this interiorization – of the sun, has not only left its mark on Platonic, Aristotelian, Cartesian discourse, and so on, not only on the science of logic as a circle of circles, but also and in the same stroke on the man of metaphysics' (71). This is, it might be argued, a very metaphorical, if not poetic, reading of the life of such a sun. George Lakoff and Mark Johnson do not privilege such a heliocentric metaphor when they come to explore how 'metaphors are pervasive in everyday life' (1980, 3); for them, NO METAPHOR CAN EVER BE COMPREHENDED OR EVEN ADEQUATELY REPRESENTED INDEPENDENTLY OF ITS EXPERIENTIAL BASIS [emphasis in original] (19) as metaphors are grounded in the body and in actions. Derrida cannot, of course, regard metaphors of the body as primary, since it would allow too much room for an assumed connection between language and one of the first markers of the body, namely, the voice. However, this might then introduce a degree of hermetism into his discussion of the origin of metaphor, which for all its struggles to get free of the body is forever ensnared by the body as *revenant* or as return of the repressed, since, it might be argued, we must have some understanding of self-presence and self-communion before we can conceive of them as the basis for a 'metaphoricity' of 'deception'.

Derrida's reading of Rousseau also stresses how, for Rousseau, metaphor is 'the characteristic that relates language to its origin' (1997, 271). However, he also notes that this description of metaphor is very different from, and may even pre-date, metaphor as signifier related to an 'invisible' signified. This is another reason for the sign's violence. To prevent any 'sublation of metaphor into being' (1974, 71) in his own work, Derrida frequently describes the entry of language in terms of an 'irruption' or 'force'. Derrida references the French rhetorician Fontanier, whose notion of the '*Supplément*' – and we recall that in *Of Grammataology* the supplement becomes a favoured trope for Derrida's arche-writing – is 'first of all concerned with the use of a sign by violence, force, or abuse, with the imposition of a sign on a sense not yet having a proper sign in the language' (57). So whereas Gadamer appeals to how the 'experience of itself seeks and finds words', Derrida seems concerned with the 'imposition [with violence or force] of a sign on a sense not yet having a proper sign'. These references to a violent sign continue in *Of Grammatology*. Rousseau's conception of writing is, for Derrida, a weak conception because only speech has 'vitality': '[i]n writing, one is forced to use all the words according to their conventional meaning' because 'it is not possible for a language that is written to retain its vitality as long as one that is only spoken' (315). Rousseau describes this 'impossible' origin of language as metaphor by way of an '"impossible natural voice"' that is '[n]o longer that animal cry before the birth of language; but not yet the articulated language, already shaped and undermined by absence and death' (247). Because this is an 'impossible' 'voice' and a voice that moves towards 'super-humanity', it is also a metaphor that cannot be repeated; it is an impossible metaphor. When Derrida reads Rousseau according to a style of commentary that has always already set up such impossible metaphoricity as origin, does metaphor become a trace of an original calling that haunts our words? In other words, does such metaphoricity perform best according to a messianic eschatology that looks to the future event as a validation of the responsibility that language harbours? The three instances of 'writing' that come to describe the genesis of such metaphoricity – Nature's book, God's writing and Plato's truth written in the soul – are then originary metaphors that are impossible to repeat. They possess a transcendence that metaphors may never be allowed in the everyday communicative act and in the economy of culture that institutions such as the University embody. Because Derrida's initial reading of metaphoricity has led him to view Rousseau's regard for language as one that, in a more complex way than other philosophers, denigrating written language in favour of a spoken language that comes closer to the voice and thus 'pure nature', writing is always divorced from the bodily connection implicit in speech.

Derrida does, however, explain how 'alphabetic writing' is more culpable in this regard for Rousseau and hence for Western metaphysics. Alphabetic writing 'transcribes heterogenous signifieds within a system of arbitrary and common signifiers: the living languages. It thus opens an aggression against the life that it makes circulate' (1997, 300). Alphabetic writing works aggressively against the *telos* of pure presence that it always embodies. This would, of course, once again recall the distinction between Chinese writing and Western writing. What Derrida refers to as 'the most archaic degree of writing' (Derrida includes Egyptian hieroglyphs here and possibly early Chinese characters), what is similar to painting, is '[c]apable of reproducing all sensible being' as it is 'a sort of universal writing' (301). Natural and universal writing is then capable of this seeming reproduction of 'sensible being'. But can it then be presumed that languages with such origins, as opposed to 'alphabetic' or onto-theological languages, invoke presence and *phonē* to the same extent? Derrida will return on numerous occasions to this violence that is integral to the emergence of writing and to the emergence of his notion of *différance*; he writes that *différance* brings with it the 'necessarily violent transformation of this language' (1973, 159) and necessitates a 'passage through the truth of Being' that is 'so violent' (154). He argues that for Rousseau the 'moment of languages' or the emergence of language 'corresponds to that state suspended between the state of nature and the state of society'. Sometimes this is described beautifully in terms of the moment between the cry and speech. This moment is the 'epoch of natural languages': 'between prelanguage and the linguistic catastrophe instituting the division of discourse, Rousseau attempts to capture a sort of happy pause, the instantaneity of a full language . . . beyond the cry but short of the hinge [another one of Derrida's tropes] that articulates and at the same time disarticulates the immediate unity of meaning' (279). Derrida then tells us in his commentary on Rousseau that 'language cannot be truly born except by the disruption and fracture of that happy plenitude, in the very instant that this instantaneity is wrested from its fictive immediacy and put back into movement' (280). The emergence of language here is therefore violent and harrowing. The deconstructive reading either aligns writing with the trace or the *phōnē*: Rousseau is then regarded as denigrating writing and suggesting that sovereign or structured language is always violent and invasive because his conception of writing is, for Derrida, described in terms of a break with voice and all that is connected to 'pure nature'.

Derrida does accept that 'need' is essential for language, however, his reading of need is once again made against the background of the originary split within language between trace and *phōnē*. In 'Différance', the essay that introduces us to *différance*, his reluctance to explore need is already evident. In giving a long quotation from Heidegger's *Holzwege* (which translates as 'wood paths') that nicely brings together the notions of trace (*Spur*) and difference, Derrida, in his commentary, focuses on Heidegger's phrase describing how the 'matinal trace of difference effaces itself from the moment that presence appears' (156). He uses Heidegger here to support his argument that 'effacement belongs to the very structure of the trace' (156). However, the previous sentence in the quotation from Heidegger begins: 'Difference is wanting'. Derrida says nothing about this phrase. Heidegger is still, of course, bound to 'worldhood' and 'Being', whereas Derrida gives these up for the 'trace' and difference. However, if there is nothing outside the text, then what has happened to this 'wanting' and why does Derrida overlook the 'wanting' that *is* difference for Heidegger?

In returning to Rousseau, Derrida argues that his notion of 'pure nature', a privileged conception of an original state that is threatened by the social contract and culture, is what is responsible for the distinction between need and passion in regard to language. Passion here is different from the passion of Leontius or Alypius in that it has been assigned to an aspect of the structure of language. In not being structuralists, and in not privileging human attributes in terms of how they straddle language as structure, Plato and Augustine do not describe human self-overcoming or human flourishing in terms of a rhetoric that is derived from a grammatology. Derrida would possibly argue that the trace is always already inscribed in the duplicitous self-presence that grounds passion and need for the *akratic*. However, Rousseau's somewhat reluctant questioning of all that has corrupted Western metaphysics – he is 'the only one to indicate an absolute break between the language of action or the language of need, and speech or the language of passion' (273) – leads him to want to control or disqualify what are also attributes of Derrida's *différance* – namely, dispersion, deferral and difference.[1] However, need is what 'maintains, prolongs, or repeats' the 'original dispersion'; it is supportive of difference. Once again, because need as dispersion is constructed above this split in language that aligns culture with self-presence, need can only appear as a disruptive force; it is the 'pure force of dispersion' (274).

There is a tendency then for Derrida's Rousseau to describe writing and the voice in terms of violence, force and aggression; Derrida reads Rousseau as suggesting that '[v]oice penetrates into me violently, it is the privileged route for forced entry and interiorization' (240). Derrida argues that Rousseau 'believed it possible to dissociate structure from origin' and in order to demonstrate this he had described the 'origin' as the 'energy of passion' (251). However, later we are told that for Rousseau 'need' is 'structurally anterior to passion': '[w]ithout need, the force of presence and attraction would play freely' (274). However, does Derrida take the time to explore this need that is so important for Rousseau and that is not only bound up with 'the nostalgia for a society of need' (240)? His readings of Heidegger, Rousseau and others do make their works amenable to the play of supplementarity and difference, but the exploration of the origins of the 'wanting' and the 'need' that these writers also align with the emergence of language is often absent and hence weakness is neglected in Derrida. The suffering of a child may very well be equivalent to 'the summon of the supplement' (247) but if we do not explore the 'need' evident in the 'call,' how are we understanding the emergence into speech? Derrida's style of commentary works to reveal oversights in philosophy, thereby allowing the dimensions of the trace to reveal itself. However, such deconstruction, as will be examined in the next section, can also be a violent process. Because the attributes of vitality, strength, force and aggression are, in this process of commentary, derived chiefly from a grammatology or a structuralist mechanics of language and not from narratives or parables of human agency as in Socrates, Lao Tzu or Augustine, or even in relation to human attributes and 'types' as with Nietzsche and Kierkegaard, there is a possibility that these structural attributes will be unquestioningly mapped onto ethical and political discourses that seek to describe an essence of encounter or a basis for negotiation. If there is an originary violence of the sign, must there be a necessary mirroring of this dynamic in any revisionist account of community and commonwealth?

Derrida introduces the notion of articulation in Rousseau as '*the becoming-writing of language*' and even as the 'becoming-language of language' (229). For Derrida, Rousseau's language is also governed by the situation of 'pure dispersion' which characterizes the 'state of nature' or the 'natural condition' and is marked by an 'original dispersion out of which language began' (232). Derrida then reads Rousseau against the grain, in terms of this notion of 'articulation', a force that 'seemingly introduc[es] difference as an institution', and which has 'for ground and space the dispersion that is natural: space itself' (232). This commentary on Rousseau hinges on articulation as 'pure dispersion' and originary spacing. However, because Derrida must admit that in Rousseau '[t]he written sign is absent from the body' (234) and that '[w]riting is the eve of speech', this happy state of language as 'pure dispersion' is bound to suffer a rude awakening when the body comes into play. Language existing as natural condition and as 'pure dispersion' and 'spacing' must at some point encounter the body and this is where violence emerges. Rousseau describes the process:

> *The passions have their gestures, but they also have their accents*; and these accents, which thrill us, *these tones of voice that cannot fail to be heard, penetrate to the very depths of the heart, carrying there the emotions they wring from us, forcing us in spite of ourselves* to feel what we hear. *We conclude that while visible signs can render a more exact imitation, sounds more effectively arouse interest* [emphasis in original]. (in Derrida, 239–40)

The extract might be read as a passage that describes how the passions, embodied in 'gestures' and 'tones of voice', are more affecting than 'visible signs'; they arouse us and shake us out of our false sense of security. In other words, it can be read as a passage that describes how passions which are always regarded as being connected to the heart arouse, through their gestures and vocalized accents, emotions and feelings in a way that 'visible signs' do not. However, Derrida reads it differently. For Derrida, it describes how '[v]oice penetrates into me violently, it is the privileged route for forced entry and interiorization' (240). Derrida makes much of this extract that seems to suggest, for him, that the body somehow works against itself in suffering the voice. Rousseau tells us that it is the 'passions' – that have their 'tones of voice' – that really stir us up and 'wring' the emotions from us, whereas Derrida describes this simply as 'voice'. Is Derrida's deconstruction of Rousseau going too far? Is the passion that arouses people when they may not wish to be aroused, when they might prefer to be off doing something else, a 'violent' voice that brings embodiment to language as 'interiorization'? It raises the question of where Derrida's 'pure dispersion' and 'spacing', which he describes as representative of Rousseau's 'natural condition', take place? If this is writing before the body, then how and where is 'space' prior to the body understood? If a state of 'pure dispersion' prior to body is privileged, then it is no surprise that when the body comes along any version of language or writing it initiates is regarded as violent.

It is for this reason that the weakness and 'impotence' (227) that Derrida assigns to such elements of articulation and supplementarity as punctuation must be regarded as purely structural weaknesses removed from weakness as described in the other writers we have examined so far. Derrida makes this process perhaps more explicit when he describes how Rousseau is yet again giving in to Western metaphysics in his description of song and melody. Derrida argues that Rousseau believes that for song and melody there '*must (should) have* been plenitude and not lack, presence without difference. From then on the dangerous supplement, scale or harmony, *adds itself from the outside as evil and lack* to happy and innocent plenitude' (215). Because, for Derrida, Rousseau sets up the origin of song and melody as an 'innocent plenitude' that is attacked by the 'evil' and 'dangerous supplement' of scale and harmony, he is invested in 'classical ontology' instead of 'the logic of supplementarity' (215). For classical ontology the 'outside is outside', but Derrida's logic of supplementarity 'would have it that the outside be inside, that the other and the lack come to add themselves as a plus that replaces a minus, that what adds itself to something takes the place of a default in the thing, that the default, as the outside of the inside, should be already within the inside, etc.' (215). However, because Rousseau stubbornly insists on the outside as outside, the 'lack' 'breaks in as a dangerous supplement, as a *substitute* that *enfeebles, enslaves, effaces, separates,* and *falsifies*' (215). In other words, what '*enfeebles*' is what Derrida sets up as external to the privileged presence. However, because what has been external is always the writing that is 'absent from the body', what *enfeebles* here, or what weakens, is something other than the body. Weakness in Derrida must therefore be understood in a manner that is prior to the body; it must be understood apart from the weaknesses examined thus far and this is a difficult task.

If weakness in Derrida is 'purely' structural, we must then examine how writing and criticism exhibit what he describes as a 'force of weakness' in his essay 'Force and Signification'. Derrida has repeatedly challenged metaphors that relate to embodiment such as the 'linguistic incarnation' (Derrida, 1989, fn. 89) that he unravels in his introduction to Husserl's *Origin of Geometry*.[2] When Derrida writes about weakness in this essay he is examining criticism; however, it is an account of weakness that must also be regarded as important for his understanding of alterity and community. Derrida argues that criticism is 'impotent' in every age and that it is 'only now' becoming aware of this. For Derrida, 'form', which describes structuralism or criticism for him, 'fascinates when one no longer has the force to understand force from within itself. That is, to create' (2002, 3). Derrida suggests that because criticism feels removed from force it must inaugurate a 'separation' between 'the critical act and the creative force' (2002, 380 fn.). He argues that criticism feels that it must prove that this separation is then also a condition of the artwork (ibid. 3). Criticism has brought this

notion of separation to literature and, for Derrida, it implies that '[i]mpo-
tence, here, is a property not of the critic but of the criticism' (380 fn.).

Derrida then describes what he calls a 'force of weakness' in the roots of
'modern structuralism'. He argues that this weakness 'can only be articulated
in the language of form, through images of shadow and light' (2002, 32–3).
Derrida roots this 'force of weakness' in Husserl's problematic account of
genesis and language. He questions the appearance of this 'weakness' in
Husserl, because for him it sets up a dichotomy or 'oppositional couple'
(33) of force and weakness that will never properly explain force. However,
what is most interesting is Derrida's description of how criticism should
overcome the opposition integral to this 'force of weakness':

> Our discourse irreducibly belongs to the system of metaphysical oppo-
> sitions. The break with this structure of belonging can be announced
> only through a *certain* organization, a certain *strategic* arrangement which,
> within the field of metaphysical oppositions, uses the strengths of the
> field to turn its own stratagems against it, producing a force of dislocation
> that spreads itself throughout the entire system fissuring it in every direc-
> tion and thoroughly *delimiting* it. (Derrida, 2002, 22)

This is a violent process that Derrida is describing, one that can only then set
up another kind of opposition between this process and what it acts on.
However, there is a reluctance to fully embrace weakness for what it is by assigning to it a systemic deconstruction that would appear to work by brute force
alone. To think that a 'force of weakness' must be overcome through such a
violent process may only be a result of believing in a violence of the sign. We
recall Derrida's words in 'Violence and Metaphysics': 'even though language
in its "original possibility as offer [or gift]"' is non-violent, there is no phrase
which 'does not pass through the violence of the concept' (2001, 185).

Writers from outside the phenomenological circle have developed this
original, non-violent sense of language as 'offer' or gift. Giorgio Agamben
argues that a kind of weakness is central to humanity: 'Beings that exist in
the mode of potentiality *are capable of their own impotentiality*' (1999, 182).
Impotentiality, is therefore part of any creative force mediated by the body.
Agamben believes that there is a 'potentiality of saying' (2005, 136) which

> [I]n dwelling near the word not only exceeds all that is said, but also
> exceeds the act of saying itself, the performative power of language. This
> is the remnant of potentiality that is not consumed in the act, but is con-
> served in it each time and dwells there. If this remnant of potentiality

is thus weak, if it cannot be accumulated in any form of knowledge or dogma, and if it cannot impose itself as a law, it does not follow that it is passive or inert. To the contrary, it acts in its own weakness, rendering the word of law inoperative (2005, 137).

Potentiality then finds its 'telos in weakness' to such an extent that Agamben quotes from Paul, who writes *hē gar dynamis en astheneia teleitai*, 'power fulfills itself in weakness' (140). The question, then, is what is the form of this power?

In extending the close reading of Derrida's 'Force and Signification', keeping in mind Agamben's willingness to assign weakness and impotentiality to being as it is bound up with gift and giving, we may find a way forwards by using this metaphor of the gift to bring Derrida and Agamben together around a notion of 'giving flesh'. Even though Derrida owes much to structuralism, it is ultimately weakness that seems to enable him on this occasion to move beyond form in allowing greater scope for the political. He writes: 'Structure is perceived through the incidence of menace, at the moment when imminent danger concentrates our vision on the keystone of an institution' (*Writing and Difference*, 2002, 4). We are still focused on structures and institutions here and are far from human frailty and the body or flesh. Derrida writes that 'the force of our weakness is that impotence separates, disengages and emancipates' (4). Derrida will always be quick to extend this weakness to writing: 'that it can always fail is the mark of its pure finitude' (13). Derrida therefore looks for a way to describe this force of weakness in terms of form. He writes that structures must depend on an 'opening' that liberates time and genesis, and genesis is often the essence of force for Derrida. Derrida advises us on how to express something akin to force: one must 'refer to language's peculiar inability to emerge from itself in order to articulate its origin' and that we must not refer to the 'thought of force'. (Derrida (2002), p. 31).

It is therefore a weakness that is being highlighted once again. Derrida is again aligning the non-expressibility of force with what he refers to as the 'incarnation of telos'. He admits that 'one would seek in vain a concept in phenomenology which would permit the conceptualization of intensity or force' or that would describe an 'incarnation of telos' (2002, 32). He then admits that force, a force of weakness, cannot be conceived on 'the basis of an oppositional couple'. Perhaps it must then be conceived on the basis of a reciprocating couple. He says that we must phrase our move beyond this system of metaphysical oppositions in terms of a 'dream of emancipation' and it is noteworthy that one of the epigraphs to the second section of this essay is from Freud and reads: 'Valley is a common female dream symbol'. He is moving towards literary language and as he does so he tells us that literary criticism is a 'hopeful discourse for plotting this dream'. He advises criticism to exceed itself to the point of 'embracing force as desire for itself' (33). Are we, thus, to find the solution with weakness and female dream symbols and self-desire?

The final passages of 'Force and Signification' see Derrida coming out from behind other writers. It is when he is at his most lyrical. He recommends 'excavation within the other toward the other in which the same seeks its vein and the true gold of its phenomenon' (35). This 'fraternal other is not first in the peace of what is called intersubjectivity but in the peril of inter-rogation' (35). Derrida's reading drags up age-old metaphors. He describes a process of excavation that writing both enacts and is a metaphor for. The excavation might also be an evacuation, an emptying, and we would then be back with the kind of neutralization and emptiness that Derrida critiques in structuralism; however, he does acknowledge that 'the same is nothing, is not (it)self before taking the risk of losing (itself)' (35). But why is the solution to the elusive force found in an inter-rogation of the other? Derrida leaves us with the work of excavating and digging and with the female dream symbol of the valley and we would appear to be back with another well-worn 'oppositional couple'. In ending his excavation of the force of weakness, Derrida describes writing as the 'moment of the depth of decay', an image that would seem to neutralize the energy he has set up between the valley and the digging. But why has the self-givenness of life again returned to the gift of death and decay? The answer may be found in his closing epigraph, a piece from Nietzsche: 'Behold here is a new Table, but where are my brethren who will carry it with me to the valley and into the hearts of flesh'. Derrida, who typically flees the flesh, ends here with a description of a gift that is to be carried forth and delivered into the flesh. But what is a 'heart of flesh' and why does he end with the repetition of a plea to carry the Table into the flesh, what might be described as a 'graphic incarnation'? A heart of flesh is, of course, an impossibility; it is yet another male idealization of the flesh that might only lead to an arrest. However, it is when Derrida steps out from behind his commentary on other writers and engages with the lyricism of language, with the signification that drives his philosophy, that he ends, through Nietzsche, with a description of a fleshy gift describing an 'incarnation of sorts'. It is a gift that is dependant on a law and a giving flesh and on a covenant that is made with and through 'heart[s] of flesh'. It is clear, then, that weakness returns us to the gift and to the law that must be incorporated into 'hearts of flesh'; weakness returns us to a giving that only flesh can mediate.

Chapter 6

Is there a 'Weaker Vessel'? Reshaping 'Phallic Identity' with 'Womb Vision'

'Why shouldn't we be weak for once in our lives, Jug? It's quite excusable. Let's be weak – be weak, Jug. It's so much nicer to be weak than to be strong'.
Katherine Mansfield, 'The Daughters of the Late Colonel', 1966, p. 219

Have women writers been allowed the same opportunities for being weak in writing? Mansfield's words above have an eerie prescience to them. An elaborate philosophy of weakness is now evident in the different traditions we have read and the woman's voice is all too silent. Perhaps weak female experience in literature is missing because the 'strong' woman is also missing. Toril Moi reminds us that Elaine Showalter 'deplores' Virginia Woolf's 'lack of sensitivity to "the ways in which (female experience) had made (women) strong" [Moi's bracket insertions]' (Moi, 7). However, the problem may lie in the fact that the 'strong man' in fiction *is* fiction, both because of the very real historical dominance – for Moi, 'traditional humanism' is 'part of patriarchal ideology' (8) – and because modernism in particular has spent a great deal of its existence explaining how weak the 'strong man' is while still allowing him to sustain his voice. As Blake reminds us, 'without contraries is no progression'; the 'weak man' may now have grown so long in the tooth precisely because in retaining enough strength to let himself be heard, he has been deaf to advances made by women writers that can explain a great deal about the weakness he cannot resist, a weakness he may still be building up, somewhat like Thomas Mann's Gustav Aschenbach, into a "herosim of weakness" (1998, 205). There are a great number of phenomenologies of the body written by men, but has man ever learnt to write an *écriture masculine*? How many times have we been told that Austen's, Eliot's and even Woolf's heroines are 'untypical' in being rational and strong-willed, but where is the phenomenology of the woman's body that occupies an equivalent place in the canon or in course readers to the celebrated, male-dominated texts of twentieth-century phenomenology? To be given the space to reflect on weakness in writing may only exempt the writer from the still greater weakness of the voiceless or the silenced.

The 'vessel' metaphor has a long history in writing. Even Nietzsche, who is very often misogynistic, claims that 'significant women' must act as 'sacrificial animal[s]' for their husbands in 'becoming a vessel' for 'other people's general ill-will and occasional bad humour' (*Human*, 1984, 206–7). Carl Gustav Jung has also traced the 'origin of the vessel symbolism,' important for Biblical descriptions of Mary, to 'extra-Biblical source[s]' (18) and to 'Gnostic symbolism' (19). Antonia Fraser's *The Weaker Vessel* examines woman's lot in seventeenth-century England and the claims for woman's 'insatiably stronger' (1985, 4) sexual appetite and her 'frail nature' that may have allowed her to demand greater leniency in moral failings (we recall Emilia Lanier's reading of Eve in terms of '[w]hat weakness offered, strength might have refused'). She asks 'were these vessels all really so weak as society ostensibly supposed?' (6).

Sandra Gilbert has explored many aspects of the 'literary maternity' that the figure of the 'vessel' also connotes when applied to the 'womb vision' that women possess (2011, 342). In revisiting her classic essays in her recent collection *Rereading Women*, Gilbert argues that the 'old theme of literary maternity' has received 'radical variations' in recent poetry by women (343) because of the 'shift from a biomythology based on woman's powerlessness to one founded in a sense of her power' (306). Despite the fact that the 'metaphor of literary maternity' (307) has always been a 'problematic one for women', (307) Gilbert explores how twentieth-century women poets have transformed this 'vessel' figure through a process of 'gynandry' into a 'Great Vessel' that incorporates 'male power into female potency' (314) to invest the womb as vessel with a divine creative agency that can be offered up as a general metaphor for artistic creativity. Gynandry is a fantasy that explains how the 'male generative abilities' are 'subsumed into the Great Vessel of the goddess's womb' so that 'childbearing can become itself divine as well as a metaphor for the divine because it has been stripped of its literal associations with 'blood, mucus, discharge, purulent offensive discharge' (338). However, this is a figurative possibility that is, for Gilbert, only possible in poetry and not in the 'realistic' novel. One would imagine, then, that it is also beyond the possibilities of philosophy and gender theory to account for the potential of this figure. However, because it is derived from a 'biomythology' that is founded on woman's 'power' and because it is a figurative possibility that incorporates 'male power into female potency', it still makes much of the power/powerlessness opposition. In order to see a way beyond traditional expressions of this gendered biomythology so as to allow for the work of 'gynandry' to be felt within more 'realistic' genres, it is important to assess how weakness and powerlessness have been understood by some of the leading feminists of the twentieth century.

Many of the discourses we have examined privilege the body and what the body mediates, namely, impulses, appetites, desires and even sin in describing how the will or the self incorporates, embodies or incarnates strength and weakness; early scripts also suggest that strength and weakness, as inscriptions, had their origins in the observation of bodies in nature. The trace of this originary connection may be lost in the Indo-European scripts but, as we have seen in Chapter 2, the character for weakness in Chinese derives from a pictograph that is believed to be a representation of a young bird's wing. Since gender theory is always haunted by a sense of difference that returns us to sexual difference and the body, notions of strength and weakness are common in the discourse and they cover far more than the physical differences evident in any respective 'show of strength'. Shakespeare has Hamlet lament, 'frailty thy name is woman'; Mary Wollstonecraft explains how women of her day were advised that 'a little knowledge of human weakness, justly termed cunning', rightly deployed, should win the 'protection of a man' (1967, 49); De Beauvoir writes of 'the dominating affirmation of his [the male's] power over the female in coitus' (1976, 55); Germaine Greer writes of the 'impotence of feminine women, who submit to sex without desire' (1999, 72); Luce Irigaray writes of the 'male organ as signifier of omnipotence' (*Speculum*, 1985, 117); and recent newspaper headlines describe how women in 'high-powered' positions in society have had to 'man up'. Weakness and strength have a variety of meanings in the description of gender difference but many are grounded on a biomythology traced to the 'performance' of agents in the 'sex act' or to the 'role' of 'sex organs'.

Simone de Beauvoir's work marks a benchmark in the history of twentieth-century feminism. Her works respond to Sartre, Camus and Merleau-Ponty and their male-oriented treatment of the alienation and existential condition of the person in existentialism and phenomenology. Woman is 'weak', 'frail' and 'fragile' for de Beauvoir, not only in regard to her 'muscular inferiority' (1976, 67), for 'physiological fact[s]' simply demonstrate how 'biology becomes an abstract science' (66). Physiological facts are used to bolster more 'abstract' and unverified claims about dominance in society in general. De Beauvoir argues that once the 'physiological fact . . . takes on meaning, this meaning is at once seen as dependent on a whole context; the "weakness" is revealed as such only in the light of the ends man proposes'

(67). In other words, de Beauvoir is challenging any essentialist connection between physical might and philosophical and psychological dominance. She continues:

> If he [man, as opposed to woman] does not wish to seize the world, then the idea of a *grasp* on things has no sense; when in this seizure the full employment of bodily power is not required, above the available minimum, then the differences in strength are annulled; wherever violence is contrary to custom, muscular force cannot be basis for domination. In brief, the concept of *weakness* can be defined only with reference to existentialist, economic, and moral considerations [de Beauvoir's emphasis]. (1976, 67)

De Beauvoir is herself 'abstract[ing]' from biology here to make a profound comment about our general understanding of violence and weakness. Man's approach to the world is often duplicitous; a stated intention not to want to '*grasp*' the world conceals the fact that, with his physical superiority, man treats the world as he would any other object. He desires to take hold of it and exert a degree of 'muscular force' above the 'available minimum'. De Beauvoir is extrapolating from 'grasp' as a sign of greater 'muscular strength' (66), as a physical manoeuvre man can perform with greater strength, to 'grasp' as a philosophical conception of dominance in relation to 'the world' in general. The implication is that there is an alternative, a more equitable regard for 'the world' – one presumably associated with woman – that does not require grasping, seizure or any level of violence. However, because this existential regard for 'the world' or for being in general, despite claims to the contrary, is smothered beneath the typically 'male' regard for 'the world' in terms of grasping, seizure or a '*seize* the day' mentality, it is dismissed as simply a sign of 'weakness'. For this 'might is right' logic, the privileging of greater physical strength is creative of an unquestioned privileging, of a 'grasping' and reductive approach to 'the world' and to existence in general. If the alternative approach, the 'female' approach, to the world can be explored, then the true value of such '*weakness*' can be revealed. A regard for the philosophical approach to existence that arises from the woman's acceptance of greater physical weakness leads to a reappraisal of weakness in the ontological sense.

De Beauvoir's reading of '*weakness*' – what lies at the heart of her descriptions of the 'differences' between the sexes – can only be understood 'with reference to existentialist, economic, and moral considerations'. De Beauvoir is calling for an examination of weakness-as-regard-for-the-world as an alternative to the more 'grasping', reductive 'male' approach to being. Weakness has a distinct meaning in each 'existentialist, economic, and moral' context;[1] however, I want to examine here the kind of weakness she assigns to women and how she extrapolates from 'physiological fact' and 'historical materialism' in describing such weakness. De Beauvoir argues that the 'male principle', a principle mediated through his 'practical life' and 'his symbolic representations', has 'triumphed' in history in general (106):

> Spirit has prevailed over Life, transcendence over immanence, technique over magic, and reason over superstition. The devaluation of woman represents a necessary stage in the history of humanity, for it is not upon her positive value but upon man's weakness that her prestige is founded. In woman are incarnated the disturbing mysteries of nature, and man escapes her hold when he frees himself from nature. (1976, 106–7)

Once again, we are reminded that any committed engagement with the weakness that is unique to woman, and that can offer a glimpse of something beyond existential 'grasping', is also bound up with 'man's weakness'; woman has typically been granted 'prestige' only because she brings out the 'disturbing mysteries of nature' that are also 'man's weakness'.

De Beauvoir employs the word 'man' to refer to both the species in general and the 'male sex'. Since she argues that woman is made to suffer the domination of both, it is sometimes difficult to separate in her work the precise contours of species-domination from those of male-domination. She argues that woman is in 'bondage' to the species and must suffer the 'aggression' of the male not only in coitus. Woman is also alienated from herself in having her 'sexual life in opposition' (64) to her 'existence as a person' and in having her 'body' as 'something other than herself' (61). In other words, woman, for de Beauvoir, does not seem able to achieve her potential as an 'individual' because of a system of 'laws' and rights that is grounded on an essentialist connection between physical might and privilege. Man's 'transcendence' and 'self-fulfilment', in her description, seems to be rooted in his physical condition; one seems directly linked to the other. He can avoid a similar 'crisis' (59) to the woman because 'his sexual life is not in opposition to his existence as a person' and because he leads a 'more independent life' (56); he is 'permitted to express himself freely' since 'the energy of the species is well integrated into his own living activity' (57); in reproduction, 'he recovers his individuality intact at the moment when he transcends it' (54), and in penetration he 'finds self-fulfilment in activity' (53). But how do we know that man's 'sexual life' is not 'in opposition to his existence as a person' or that in penetration he 'finds self-fulfilment in activity'? Are we in danger here of equating man's sense of his own 'existence as a person' with a 'sexual life' that is often as alien to him as a woman's sexual life is to her? Are we presuming not only that 'muscular superiority' implies more fulfilling 'penetration', but also that 'muscular superiority' implies that the male is more likely to equate 'self-fulfilment in activity' as 'penetration' with 'existence as a person'? This is as dangerous as it is to presume that a woman's 'sexual life' must also be 'in opposition' to her 'existence as a person'. In other words, certain presumptions are being made here about the connection between physiological facts and psychological and philosophical states in regard to 'reproduction' and 'penetration', and these would only come to be addressed by the next wave of gender theorists. The 'reality' of man's sexual experience is underdeveloped here; any redressing of this 'reality' may only deny man de Beauvoir's idealized state without guaranteeing woman any greater agency since, as de Beauvoir argues, woman is also in 'bondage' to the species and it is the 'species' that 'takes residence in the female and absorbs most of her individual life' (56).

De Beauvoir treats psychoanalysis '[l]ike all religions'; it is the discourse most responsible for producing a dangerous symbolism in discussions that relate existence to sexuality. Words such as '*phallus*' are 'indefinitely expanded and take on symbolic meaning, the phallus now expressing the virile character and situation *in toto*' (70). A symbolism epitomized by what this 'weak little rod of flesh' (73) has been made to signify and symbolize is therefore responsible for what she describes as a 'will to power' in both Freudian and Adlerian accounts of the person. Despite the fact that Freud, for de Beauvoir, 'is ignorant regarding the origin of male supremacy', (81) existence-as-sexuality is still defined for psychoanalysis in terms of a 'will to power' where the play of weakness and strength is always grounded in the edifying symbol of phallus-as-power. In other words, the basis for such a reading has not been explained. However, even though she is correct to challenge how psychoanalysis-as-religion 'indefinitely expand[s]' words in constructing this dangerous symbolism, she does not go much further in explaining this 'origin of male supremacy' as mediated through the phallus-as-power. In describing a narrative and mythos of female sexuality, possibly for the first time, she also might be regarded as constructing a dangerous symbolism of her own that only serves to entrench further the symbolic value of weakness in regard to women. De Beauvoir's woman is regarded as 'Other'; she is alienated from herself in having her 'sexual life in opposition' to her 'existence as a person' (64) and in having her 'body' as 'something other than herself' (61). However, even though de Beauvoir is correct to challenge the complete identification of the male with the phallus by arguing that 'the penis is regarded by the subject as at once himself and other than himself' and as being 'set apart' (79), it is precisely this degree of separation and non-identification that, for de Beauvoir, allows 'man' to 'bring into integration with his subjective individuality the life that overflows from it' (79). In other words, separation from and non-identification with, one's sexuality, and with the fleshy mediators of one's sexuality, appear to have different psychological results for the man and the woman. When the woman's body appears to her as 'something other than herself' there is 'alienation', (83) but when the man regards his body as 'set apart' from him it is simply so it can be used for 'self-fulfilment in transcendence' (83). In other words, it would appear that de Beauvoir is applying a previously determined psychological dynamic to the relationship between the 'physiological fact' and the 'mysterious unconscious', (78) one that 'abstracts' from the 'physiological fact' a quasi-naturalistic power dynamic of its own. Man's regard for his penis, even if as a 'weak rod of flesh', or even if as 'set apart' and as 'other than himself', still results in less alienation and in 'self-fulfilment in transcendence' or in 'the incarnation of transcendence in the phallus' as 'a constant' (79).

While de Beauvoir is right to argue that Freud was unable to explain the origins of 'male supremacy', one might suggest that despite her redrafting of the phallogocentric description of sexuality and existence and her observation that all these accounts are 'dissertations which mingle a vague naturalism with a still more vague ethics or aesthetics' (66), she is also found wanting when it comes to explaining what we might describe as the origins of female weakness. The female, for de Beauvoir, is already (when de Beauvoir extrapolates from 'all animals' [54]) she who '*submits* to the coition, which invades her individuality' (54). Woman is therefore aligned with inwardness and a whole host of synonyms and metaphors, such as immanence and interiority, which exacerbate any sense of 'otherness' that she might have to navigate. In discussing 'animal reproduction', she writes that an 'alien element' is introduced through 'penetration' (54); the female is 'first violated', 'then alienated' and she 'becomes, in part, another than herself' (54). There is, in these descriptions of animal reproduction, a degree of highly charged symbolic language at play which recalls her dismissal of psychoanalysis and its tendency to 'indefinitely expand' words in constructing a dangerous symbolism. When she describes the female mammal in coition, the female is already a subject whose 'inwardness is violated' and the male 'finds self-fulfilment in activity' (53). Psychological states such as violation and 'self-fulfilment', states with weighty connotations in gender theory, are here applied to the actions of mammals in rut and coition. De Beauvoir is the first to note in this regard that 'allegory should not be pushed too far' (44), but even her remarkable work might be regarded as begging the question in relation to the play of weakness and strength in gender theory.

Later theorists, such as Luce Irigaray, Nancy Chodorow and Toril Moi, have been eager to build on de Beauvoir's work, but the alignment of woman with 'inwardness' and man with what is external and active has continued. These norms must be challenged and the examination of weakness, which de Beauvoir regards as a defining feature of woman, has great potential in this regard. De Beauvoir does acknowledge that this process needs to begin. In referring to a 'new form of eroticism' that is 'coming into being', she writes: '[w]hat must be hoped for is that the men for their part will unreseservedly accept the situation that is coming into existence; only then will women be able to live in that situation without anguish' (292). However, if men are to be equipped with the kind of sensitivity that is necessary to 'unreservedly accept' this new kind of eroticism, they would have to depart quite dramatically from the norms she has linked them with.

De Beauvoir's description of the opposition between immanence and transcendence in relation to what she describes as a non-existent 'masculine mystery' also demonstrates how studies of masculinity have been content to function behind a veil of ignorance. De Beauvoir writes that because the male genitalia and in particular the penis are 'outside' man, that man can objectify the penis to a certain extent because it is easy 'to see' – he can 'measure the length of the penis', the force of the urinary jet and 'the strength of the erection and the ejaculation' (79). This all implies, for de Beauvoir, that 'man can bring into integration with his subjective individuality the life that overflows from it'. In other words, as she describes later on, 'the incarnation of the transcendence of the phallus is a constant' (79). It would seem to be the case, then, that man has a more healthy relation with transcendence than the woman – who de Beauvoir reminds us many times is 'doomed to immanence' (105) – because he can objectify a certain part of himself that has become a symbol in society for male dominance. His ability to associate the objectivity of the penis's strength, breadth and power with his own subjectivity and his ability to regard these characteristics as attributes that are his by an almost divine right originate in his physicality. This difference is traced to the genital differences between the sexes and, in turn, to the realm of work and labour. Not only is the work of the man generally regarded as taking him 'outside', allowing him to communicate with 'the rest of the world', (314) but de Beauvoir also believes that this difference is incarnated 'in his penis' (299); the penis takes on the form of an *alter ego*. However, surely this is as problematic as Freud's suggestion that dolls are phallic substitutes for little girls. De Beauvoir tells us that the little boy, and presumably the man too, who seems on occasion to be only an overgrown little boy, 'sees himself' in his penis and can therefore 'boldly assume an attitude of subjectivity; the very object into which he projects himself becomes a symbol of autonomy, of transcendence, of power; he measures the length of his penis; he compares his urinary stream with that of his companions; later on, erection and ejaculation will become grounds for satisfaction and challenge' (306).

The little girl, on the other hand, and presumably the woman also, 'cannot incarnate herself in any part of herself' (306). She has no obvious physical appendage through which she can gain such a sense of agency, subjectivity or pleasure; her pleasure is internal and thus remains opaque to her. What does de Beauvoir mean by saying that woman 'cannot incarnate herself in any part of herself'? Gilbert has described, in reference to the 'Notes' of the poet H. D., the potential for recognizing writing and the poem in particular as 'an incarnation of the womb, the flesh *and* spirit of the female not unlike Christ himself' (342), but de Beauvoir is referring to a psychological state here. Man has typically aligned himself with a religious metaphysics of incarnation but de Beauvoir is speaking for something else; man's ability to reconcile general truths associated with strength, subjectivity and dominance with the aspects of these general truths that he persuades himself are also evident in his penis produces an 'incarnation' that brings feelings of authentic power and agency. The result is that the immanence that woman sees physiologically embodied in her own body as her sexual difference, her physiological self-contact and her manner of being self-enclosed, becomes something that cannot be readily accepted as an empowering sense of inwardness. However, we are then told that the woman also submits to her 'physiological nature' as something 'from outside'; the woman's 'physiological nature is very complex: she herself submits to it as to some rigmarole from outside; her body does not seem to her to be a clear expression of herself; within it she feels herself a stranger' (286). The fact that de Beauvoir writes that the man's 'sexual life is not in opposition to his existence as a person, and biologically it runs an even course, without crises and generally without mishap' (64) is again evidence for the fact that her sociological study was written at a time when men were even less open about their sexuality than they are today. The only reason men may appear as being at one with their bodies and with their sexual lives is because they have been willing to assume more completely and more convincingly the myths they have been fed about male identity from childhood. Even though the man, de Beauvoir suggests, can directly take pride in the exterior power that his penis is regarded as embodying for him, the woman cannot accept such a metaphorical arrangement 'from outside' as a feature of her own self-understanding of her body. Where should women turn in order to regain this ability to incarnate themselves in parts of their body? Gilbert's gynandry and its 'Great Vessel' offers a way forwards that is expressed in poetry. However, if it is not to be found internally in an immanence that de Beauvoir argues only further displays that women have less of an 'individual life' than men, and if it is not be found 'externally', then women are left confused. The elaborate and rhetorically inventive expressions of the 'liminal' states that later French writers produced offer a way forward.

Even though the woman, then, is doomed to immanence, it does not appear to be an understanding of immanence that enables her to feel at one with her body. De Beauvoir argues that nothing is 'more firmly anchored in masculine hearts than that of the feminine "mystery"' (285) and she may be right for reasons she does not intend or readily acknowledge. If woman can somewhat contradictorily be more tied to immanence and yet also, as de Beauvoir suggests, have less of an individual life, it is, at any rate, an individual life that enables her to recognize myths that have been developed about her sexual identity. Since feminism and its 'realistic' discourses have benefitted from advances in describing the relationship between self-understanding and the body, surely it is time to incorporate modernism's extensive exploration of the male body into the more 'realistic' discourses on masculinities. The narrative of masculinity that de Beauvoir charts from Plato to porno may now seem, in the wake of advances in gender theory, to have a predictable telos attached. The capacity within each male that de Beauvoir refers to in terms of a 'feminine "mystery"' is also integral to male immanence. The fact that feminism has made itself aware of this untapped resource in man reminds us that there is also a 'masculine "mystery"' integral to woman. However, de Beauvoir notes that literature and culture have always worked with the preconception that there is 'no such thing as a masculine mystery' (289). An engagement with weakness in literature, what I undertake in the next section, can help unravel this myth that there is no equivalent 'masculine mystery' in literature and culture.

Before we move to the work of Luce Irigaray, I want to briefly show how this depiction of man-as-phallus without any 'masculine mystery' has found its way into later gender theory. Toril Moi's *Sexual/Textual Politics* argues that 'patriarchal ideology' (8) has at its centre, what she calls, 'the seamlessly unified self – either individual or collective – which is commonly called "Man"'. While I am not suggesting that many male and female writers have not presented us with male heroes who meet the requirements of this 'unified' stereotype, what I do question is the easy correlation of humanism's 'unified self' with what Moi calls the 'phallic self'. The version of the male that such a history has given us, this 'phallic self', is constructed she tells us 'on the model of the self-contained, powerful phallus' (8). It is '[g]loriously autonomous' and 'it banishes from itself all conflict, contradiction and ambiguity. She continues:

> In this humanist ideology the self is the *sole author* of history and of the literary text: the humanist creator is potent, phallic and male-God in relation to his world, the author in relation to his text. History or the text become nothing but the 'expression' of this unique individual: all art becomes autobiography, a mere window on to the self and the world, with no reality of its own (Moi, 1985, 8).

While this myth of the potent, humanist creator that is inextricably linked to a 'phallic self' may still haunt all cultural manifestations, perhaps it is time to assess its potency. In a society where impotence is estimated to affect 2.3 million men in the UK alone, where a drug for male erectile dysfunction is a pharmaceutical best-seller, and where impotence is also often a result of unprecedented levels of prostate cancer[2], perhaps it is time to explore why literature and culture act, according to de Beauvoir, as if there is no such thing as a 'masculine mystery'.

Luce Irigaray has sought to re-imagine the female body's relation with the space exterior to it. The lips of the female sex are set up as a symbol for an identity that transcends traditional limitations of expression and embodiment:

> A remaking of immanence and transcendence, notably through this *threshold* which has never been examined as such: the female sex. The threshold that gives access to the *mucous*. Beyond classical oppositions of love and hate, liquid and ice-a threshold that is always *half open*. The threshold of the *lips*, which are strangers to dichotomy and opposition.

Gathered one against the other but without any possible suture, at least
of a real kind. (Irigaray, 2004, 17–18)

Irigaray recognizes that something has not been said and investigated in
relation to sexual difference, that something trapped inside humanity,
something akin to the 'feminine "mystery"' which de Beauvoir regards as
being anchored inside man, has been 'held in reserve' in relation to the
examination and understanding of sexual difference: 'Has something of
the achievement of sexual difference still not been said or transmitted? Has
something been held in reserve within the silence of a history of the feminine: an energy, a morphology, a growth and flourishing still to come from
the female realm?' (19). Irigaray does not refer to this untapped human
resource in terms of a 'feminine "mystery"' that is only trapped within man.
It is instead an 'energy' that has been hidden with a 'history of the feminine' and it is not specified where this feminine is located.

Irigaray has famously suggested that women are more 'in touch' with
their sexuality than men because '[w]oman "touches herself" all the time'
(1985, *This Sex*, 24); she argues that women's experience of sexuality is not
genitally centred, but spreads across their whole body as multiple and diffuse pleasure which is radically unlike men's (in Minsky, *Psychoanalysis and
Gender*, 195). The two lips of the woman's sex, in constantly touching each
other – 'woman is constantly touching herself' (1985, 29) – also allow the
woman to be more in touch with her self-representation of her body and
with what her body embodies for her. However, Irigaray's compelling and
novel model for examining how bodies inform and mediate sexuality has
been slow to infiltrate studies of masculinity. If there is such a relationship
between the physiology of the woman and the psychology or sense of self-
awareness of the woman, then it must surely beg the question: How is such
a relationship between the physical make-up of the male sex and male self-
perception or male psychology manifested in, or embodied by, the man?
What kind of sexual self-awareness does the male sex, a sex that may incidentally also be capable of self-touching if we consider the touching between
the foreskin and the glans of the penis, grant to the man? If lips that are
touching is creative of a sense of self that is more 'in touch' with the rhythms,
needs and urges of the body, what distinctive features of the male sex can
be re-imagined in order to reappraise how the male sex mediates sexual
awareness so that studies in masculinity can learn from these advances in
feminist writing?

As with de Beauvoir, Irigaray emphasizes the sense of exteriority peculiar
to the male genitalia; the male genitalia are therefore remote from the kind

of physical-psychological circuitry possessed by the woman. Such an emphasis on the external and exterior nature of the male genitalia – '[i]n order to touch himself, man needs an instrument' (1985, 24) – has contributed to notions of maleness as exhibitionist. This in turn informs descriptions of maleness that privilege voyeurism, whereby the male must employ a 'male gaze' to both concretize his understanding of sexuality as bound up with perception and objectification and which, in turn, leads to the 'grasping' that de Beauvoir highlights. If the sex can be described as external, then the implication is that there is some physical and psychological core that this sex is removed from, or in exile from. The suggestion would then be that man is exiled from himself in some way and with this come notions of return that are integral to the actions of so many archetypal male heroes in literature. Therefore, by emphasizing the exteriority of the male sex we run the risk of implicitly essentializing and reinforcing those traditional trappings of maleness that have, for feminist critics, contributed so much that is objectionable to the received understanding of maleness in literature. It would seem, then, that the male sex must be given a second look so that it can learn from the advances made in feminist writing.

The involuntary erection is a masculine experience the study of which can inform discourses that promote the phallus-as-power. Irigaray's 'two lips touching' may very well suffer a 'brutal separation of the two lips by a violating penis' (1985, 24), however, the penis is not always erect and violating; it is not always involved in 'sexual performance'. The important point for Irigaray's woman appears to be the self-touching that is prior to perception and violation; the touching is sensed by the woman, it is rarely perceived by her. This moment of potential and this touching prior to the perception of the erect 'hard penis' must also be described for the man. This moment occurs before and during the involuntary erection and there still may be no other kind of erection. These are moments prior to the perception and enacting of 'sexual performance'. The pulsations of blood and stirrings in the flesh might be regarded as offering a circuitry of sensation that privileges self-awareness and potentiality in the man in a similar manner to the means by which Irigaray's 'self-touching' in woman results in a heightened regard for touch.

When man does eventually, through perception, connect these stirrings with the rising penis, then an influential connection can be made between physical vigour, the physical 'show of strength' and sexuality. It is difficult to describe the physiology of the involuntary erection without connoting force and potency. The man who is very often supine and lethargic when the involuntary blood-pushing strikes is brought into contact with aspects of himself that connote force. It is an unwieldy weapon. He can feel external to his own body, like de Beauvoir's woman, when the moment strikes. But what the irruption also draws his attention to is the corollary of force and potency; namely, weakness and impotence. The involuntary erection brings home to the man both the indiscriminate and transitory nature of this force-as-sexuality, this phallus-as-power. It is a transitory force and it indirectly recalls states that are far more evident now in their absence. Irigaray suggests that 'the phallus loses its power' in homosexual relations because the 'penis becomes merely a means to pleasure' and this is 'outside the mechanisms of commerce' (1985, 193). However, even the commercial exchange that directs our designations of power can be re-imagined through an engagement with im-potentiality and weakness. Man may very well be more privy to the first-hand perception of the play of force and weakness.

This involuntary force raises questions of the kind of sensory circuitry implicit in Irigaray's description of the woman's 'two lips touching'. If two parts of our body or of our flesh must be touching in order for us to possess this authentic sense of ourselves, then can this be extended to cover an experience between the blood and the flesh or between the blood and our mental faculties? Irigaray explains that her sense of touching moves beyond touching as understood by Maurice Merleau-Ponty. In her reading of his work in the chapter 'The Invisible of the Flesh', she questions his reduction of touching to a form of perception. In her system '. . . I see only by the touch of the light, and my eyes are situated in my body. I am touched and enveloped by the felt even before seeing it' (2004, 138). And later, again in reference to Merleau-Ponty: 'Reduction of the tactile into the visible, to begin with. . . . A way of talking about the flesh that already cancels its most powerful components, those that are moreover creative in their power' (146). The involuntary erection, where the man is made to confront his potentiality and impotentiality, is also a moment of felt stirring where sexuality is not yet assigned to a 'diffuse pleasure' or a 'sexual performance'. The description of this male 'primal scene' is a description of male sexuality in terms of what it has not yet realized; potentiality and impotentiality are overlooked in studies of masculinity in favour of 'domination' and 'violence'. After all, it is as the 'limp father of thousands', the 'languid floating flower', (1992, 107) as James Joyce reminds us through Leopold Bloom, that man is most familiar with his sex.

Irigaray does comment on male impotence. She believes sexuality has always been examined in relation to a privileging of procreation, with fatherhood being regarded as a '*proof of his potency*' (2004, 54). She develops her understanding of the female sex, which designates 'the place of uselessness, at least as it is habitually understood' (18), in relation to male impotence. She says that she regards the 'sexual relation' as 'impossible'. However, for Irigaray, this realization of a general impotence has not led men to be more accepting of 'feminine pleasure': 'The problem is that they [men, epitomized in this instance as psychoanalysts] claim to make a law of this impotence itself, and continue to subject women to it' (1985, 105). Men are regarded as transferring the previously problematized logocentric performativity onto their appraisal of impotence, making a virtue of necessity while failing to examine the true nature of this 'lack'.

Giorgio Agamben's description of "im-potentiality", what he relates to Aristotle's notion of impotentiality that I examined in chapter one, is a political concept that can inform this exploration of potentiality in regard to male sexual awareness. In a section entitled "Potentiality and Law" from *Homo Sacer* Agamben explains:

> Potentiality (in its double appearance as potentiality to and as potentiality not to) is that through which Being founds itself *sovereignly*, which is to say, without anything preceding or determining it (*superiorem non recognoscens*) other than its own ability not to be (1998, 46).

Agamben reads potentiality as that which only founds itself '*sovereignly*' through its 'ability not to be' or through its 'im-potentiality, so as to return to man the ability to claim his own life'. An act is sovereign 'when it realizes itself by simply taking away its own potentiality not to be, letting itself be, *giving itself to itself* [my italics]' (1998: 46). This notion of 'im-potentiality' can be used to describe a move to recover for man an ability to admit to the loss of all presupposed relations to his sexual existence conceived as realized potential. But, in borrowing from Agamben's description of the sovereign act, how might sexuality be regarded as what is eternally 'giving itself to itself'? Agamben aligns impotentiality with another philosophical notion, that of immanence, which is also important for de Beauvoir. He reminds us that '[t]o be potential means: to be one's lack, *to be in relation to one own's incapacity*. Beings that exist in the mode of potentiality *are capable of their own impotentiality*; and only in this way do they become potential' (1999, 182). To be capable of our own impotentiality is a uniquely human attribute, since without it, 'potentiality would always already have passed into act and be indistinguishable from it' (215). In other words, it is the understanding of impotentiality that gives full meaning to potentiality; it is only through a proper understanding of our incapacity, our failure to always realize what we might, that the moments of realized potential are truly understood. Impotentiality enables the subject to understand potentiality as that which is '*giving itself to itself*'. Gender studies, philosophy and literature can help us understand how such philosophical concepts are also important for the description of sexual awareness and desire. It is perhaps foolhardy to imagine a figurative potential that does not borrow from features of sexual difference, from neither a 'womb vision' nor a 'phallic power'. The 'inadequacy of signification' and the 'rupture in the lines of communication' may be nowhere more evident than in the description of sexual difference; it is the language of the body that manifests such inadequacy by first engaging with physical weakness.

Part Two

Literature

Chapter 7

Recognizing Limits: Keats's 'Weak Mortality' and Wordsworth's 'Frailties of the World'

No man can think write or speak from his heart, but he must intend truth. Thus all sects of Philosophy are from the Poetic Genius adapted to the weaknesses of every individual

William Blake, 'All Religions are One', Principle 2ᵈ, The Complete Poems

In 1849, a year before the death of Wordsworth, Matthew Arnold published his poem 'Shakespeare'. Arnold describes Shakespeare as 'self-school'd, self-scann'd, self-honour'd' and finally as 'self-secure'. He marvels at how Shakespeare's self-sufficient and 'immortal spirit' walked 'on Earth unguess'd at'; his genius and curious transcendence of natural time as an 'immortal spirit' leads Arnold to suggest that '[a]ll pains the immortal spirit must endure'. Immortal spirits like Shakespeare must endure being regarded as considerably less than 'immortal' in their lives. Such 'spirit[s]' can therefore endure a kind of suffering unknown to the rest of us. Arnold then sums up Shakespeare's genius in terms of weakness: 'All weakness that impairs, all griefs that bow, Find their sole voice in that victorious brow' (1971, 25.13–14). Shakespeare's greatness for describing the human condition is chiefly an ability to understand man's weakness; he is the 'sole voice' for describing this 'weakness that impairs'.

The next year Arnold takes up the honorific tone again in 'Memorial Verses' as he remembers Wordsworth and other Romantic icons such as Goethe and Byron. He calls Goethe 'Europe's sagest head' (34.16) and he describes his work once again in terms of an ability to describe human weakness: 'He took the suffering human race,/He read each wound, each weakness clear-/And stuck his finger on the place/And said- Thou ailest here, and here.' (34.19–22). Goethe shares Shakespeare's capacity for alerting mankind to 'weakness' through art, which for Arnold 'still has truth' (34.28). He advises the reader to 'take refuge there'. He then moves to a description of Wordsworth and his work. He tells 'the shadowy world' to rejoice as it is now in the company of his 'soothing voice' (34.35–6). For Arnold, Wordsworth appeared in an age that was a 'wintry clime', an 'iron time/Of doubts, disputes, distractions, fears', an age perhaps not too unlike our own in that it 'had bound our souls in its benumbing round' (34.42–5). Wordsworth, for Arnold, has the ability to restore to humanity a vision of an earlier time, a time that Arnold compares to humankind's childhood in Eden: 'He laid us as we lay at birth/On the cool flowery lap of earth' (34–5.48–9). Arnold then explains how Wordsworth's special gift was his compassion and his deep understanding of frailty and vulnerability: 'Others will teach us how to dare,/And against fear our breast to steel: Others will strengthen us to bear-/But who, ah! who, will make us feel?/The cloud of mortal destiny,/Others will front it fearlessly-/But who, like him, will put it by?' (35.64–70). Unlike other writers who rouse the reader to feats of ambitious daring, Wordsworth asks us to put the 'cloud of mortal destiny' by so that we can *feel*. For Arnold, then, feeling is bound up not with 'steeling' the soul or the spirit, or with the fearless fronting of destiny, but with the tireless examination of those states that teach us to feel. For Arnold, Shakespeare, Goethe and Wordsworth can 'read' . . . each weakness clear' and, in doing so, they can offer a 'soothing voice' to the reader.

There are two kinds of weakness I wish to examine in this chapter that may well become central concerns for the first time with the Romantics. The first is authorial weakness and the second refers to the poet's representation of liminal characters and the 'weak' in order to tap into what Victor Turner calls 'secular weakness as sacred power' (1969, 125). Before I move to a reading of the poetry, it is important to acknowledge the special place the Romantic figure has in literary criticism in general. The exuberance of Romantic poetry and its figures very often struggles to stave off the confines of a negative epistemology that has descended on criticism in recent decades. The poetry might often seem redundant for contemporary readings raised on post-structuralism and deconstruction. However, Paul de Man's reappraisal of the rhetoric of romanticism by way of a 'power of negativity' in some of the poetry of the age seeks to revitalize the Romantic figure by giving it new life in a significantly altered field of representation (1989, 188). In doing so, de Man admits that 'our criticism of romanticism so often misses the mark' in an age when 'we are less than ever capable of philosophical generality rooted in genuine self-insight, while our sense of selfhood hardly ever rises above self-justification' (197). In such a climate, we are more likely to focus on those moments when there are kinks in the armour of selfhood and cracks in the ideology that supports it. In this regard, Jerome McGann argues in *The Romantic Ideology* that Wordsworth is the chief culprit in creating such a harmonizing ideology where 'an image and landscape of contradiction' is replaced with one 'dominated by "the power/Of harmony"' (1985, 86). Authorial weakness, as the presentation of an authorial 'self' that is described within the work as not up to the task in hand, is a technique that both foregrounds and unsettles the Romantic privileging of 'self'.

In this chapter I examine, first, how readings that privilege a 'power of negativity' in Keats can misrepresent what Keats refers to in his own work as 'weak mortality',[1] – Keats's speaker frequently intimates that he will expire before his pen 'has glean'd my teeming brain' – and, second, what Wordsworth's attention to the 'lowly' and the 'frailties of the world' reveals about his understanding of weakness. I examine Wordsworth's presentation of these 'frailties' through the sense of authorial weakness he also describes – his autobiographical speaker describes his 'weak hand' as he contemplates the work he sets himself in *The Prelude* – and through his representation of 'weak' and 'lowly' characters. How effective is Wordsworth's presentation of the poor in revealing, what Turner describes, as 'secular weakness as sacred power'? Wordsworth's presentation of authorial weakness is often duplicitous. Dorothy's notes on her brother suggest that he clearly had a sense that his work would commend him respectably well to posterity. As Andrew Bennett argues, his 'sense of his own greatness is truly remarkable' (1999, 45).[2] One might suggest that such duplicitous weakness anticipates modernist impersonality where the most poignant renditions of personal fragility are no longer assigned any authentic self and become grist for the mill of objectivity.

With Keats, as Bennett has demonstrated, authorial weakness has the added dimension of the 'failing body'. Bennett argues, in a persuasive reading of the sonnet 'This mortal body of a thousand days', that Keats's weak and sickly constitution, his particular 'physical organization', to use a phrase from Coventry Patmore (in Bennett, 1999, 156), creates a body of work where 'the uncanny presence of the written and writing body and its uncanny prescience, too' cohabit to a degree that is possibly overdetermined in Keats criticism. Keats is prescient because his written corpus proleptically figures the writer's future death by inscribing 'the living poet into a posthumous life' (155). Bennett argues that 'the death of John Keats, the dissolution of the poet's body, is an escapable element of any reading of his work' and that, in turn, Keats's literal body 'takes on the status of a signifier of dissolution' and that this dissolution 'affects or infects the distinction between body and writing, corpus and corpus' (156). Bennett's somewhat

Derridean reading – at one point he describes Keats as carrying out a 'deconstruction' – focuses on the deictic opacity of the sonnet: 'Inscription is *this*: *this* body, here, now, not here, not now'. He directs us to the 'instability of the referent of "this"' (1999, 250 fn.) in Hegel, Derrida and others, and one can only but recall another famous use of 'deictic opacity' in relation to a body; namely, Christ's 'This Is My Body'. It takes us back to Derrida's description of the 'vulgar' metaphoricity at the heart of language that I examined in Chapter 5. However, when the 'referent' of 'this' is a body then it will always seem to possess a little more 'instability' for a reading that must make a detour via the renunciation of phonocentrism. Keats did not live to see embodiment rephrased by way of a writing that disowns the voice, but it is undeniable that he was prescient in regard to where his ill-health might lead and he may even have possessed what Susan Wolfson describes as a 'weirdly prophetic intuition' (in Bennett, 144) in writing 'This mortal body of a thousand days' in the summer of 1818 at the birth-place of Robert Burns while 'staring at the prospect of his own death, less than three years ahead' (Aileen Ward in Bennett, 140).

Keats is aware of how his weak constitution has a strong influence on his writing. He writes to Fanny Brawne on 25 July 1819, 'I tremble at domestic cares ... I have two luxuries to brood over in my walks, your Loveliness and the hour of my death. O that I could have possession of them both in the same minute. I hate the world: it batters too much the wings of my self-will, and I would take a sweet poison from your lips to send me out of it' (1958, Vol. II, 133).[3] In a letter to J. H. Reynolds of 24 August 1819, Keats expresses quite clearly how his weakness is not only responsible for his writing and for the feeling that sparks his writing, but that such a state is 'the only state for the best sort of Poetry'. He writes:

> But I feel my Body too weak to support me to the height; I am obliged continually to check myself and strive to be nothing. It would be vain for me to endeavour after a more reasonable manner of writing to you: I have nothing to speak of but myself – and what can I say but what I feel? If you should have any reason to regret this state of excitement in me, I will turn the tide of your feelings in the right channel by mentioning that it is the only state for the best sort of Poetry – that is all I care for, all I live for. (1958, Vol. II, 147)

It is therefore the kind of poetry that is ever cognizant of limitations and that must consistently resist any reaching after fact and reason that is best; it is achieved only by the poet who is willing to 'continually' 'check [him]self and strive to be nothing'. It is bound up with a concern for the self and for the manner in which such self-restraint, while expressing the being-in-un-certainties endemic to possessors of negative capability, is creative of a heightened regard for how the self feels. In a letter to Taylor dated 5 September 1819, Keats again refers to himself as a 'weak one' (156) and he may even recognize how he is beginning to articulate this 'weak mortality' in his poetry since he refers to his own poem 'Isabella' as a '"weak-sided Poem"' (Letter of 21/22 September 1819 to Richard Woodhouse, Vol. II, 174).

However, with Keats we must be wary we do not overdetermine the 'fail-ing body' as figure for his written corpus despite the glorious posterity that it might ascribe to the afterlife of the poet. We may end up reductively fram-ing weakness as 'failing body' within a narrative of slow demise that, because of the deconstructive equivalence of corpus with corpus, also becomes a somewhat constricting guide for reading Keats's poetry. The 'failing body' does not only look to posterity; it must also grapple with the conditions and the phenomenology, if you like, of weakness in 'straining at particles of light in the midst of a great darkness – without knowing the bearing of any one assertion of any one opinion' (Letter to George and Georgiana, February–May 1819, Vol. II, 80), as Keats writes the following year. In the same letter, in reference to another sonnet, he asks his brother and sister: 'look over the last two pages and ask yourself whether I have not that in me which will bear the buffets of the world. It will be the best comment on my sonnet; it will show you that it was written with no Agony but that of igno-rance; with no thirst of any thing but knowledge when pushed to the point though the first steps to it were through my human passions' (81). Keats writes later that 'my hopes are very paramount to my despair' (to George and Georgiana, 18 September 1819, 189), and he describes this capacity for hope as a 'quiet power': 'Some think I have lost that poetic ardour and fire 't is said I once had – the fact is perhaps I have: but instead of that I hope I shall substitute a more thoughtful and quiet power' (to George and Georgiana, 21 September 1819, 209). Keats's 'weak mortality' was not always a being-towards-death. It is undoubtedly true that Keats's illness and 'weak mortality' informs his work, but to read his work as a figure for the 'failing body' and then to see in this work only 'the failure of desire, the failure of not achieving one's desire' (Bennett, 150), 'the wasting of the living', 'mor-tal fading' and 'bodily failure' (151) is to overdetermine one aspect of the corpus to the detriment of the 'particles of light' such weakness also grants. After his terrible hemorrhage of 3 February 1820, when he must have been particularly in touch with his own mortality, Keats suggests that he was more inclined to convey how illness had granted him an enlightening sense of perception: 'I must premise that illness as far as I can judge in so short a time had relieved my Mind of a load of deceptive thoughts and images and makes me perceive things in a truer light' (to James Rice, 14–16 February 1820, 260). It is important to examine a different aspect of Keats's 'failing body'. I want to explore how he mines it for experiences so that he is able to 'know' himself better – 'Give me this credit – Do you not think I strive-to know myself? Give me this credit' (to George and Georgiana, 19 March 1819, 81) – in meditating on the particular characteristics and illumina- tions of the poet's 'weak mortality'. Keats transforms his unique kind of experience into an aesthetic experience that strives, first, for complete transcendence from the body – he writes at one time of his desire for 'a direct communication of spirit' with his brother and sister (16 December 1819, 5) – and then for an openness to death that is stark in its resignation and courage.

Keats's famous description of negative capability describes a philosophy of art and life that must be content with being in uncertainties and offering these up as treasures of contemplation for the reader. In one of his earliest sonnets, 'On Seeing The Elgin Marbles For The First Time', Keats is already acknowledging his special kind of weakness not in terms of a 'failing body' but in terms of his 'spirit': 'My spirit is too weak; mortality/Weighs heavily on me like unwilling sleep/And each imagin'd pinnacle and steep/Of god- like hardship tells me I must die' (1951, 60.1–4). Paul de Man describes the 'pattern' of Keats's work in terms of 'anticipations of future power' (1989, 181). Keats clarifies the kind of weakness his frame and his love of indolence and sleep will draw him to for these 'anticipations'. To privilege being in uncertainties is to privilege the glorious moments of incapacity in decision- making, those boundary events, that lead on to greater self-awareness. It is worth recalling the famous Negative Capability letter of December 1817:

> [I]t struck me what quality went to form a Man of Achievement, espe- cially in Literature, and which Shakespeare possessed so enormously – I mean *Negative Capability*, that is, when a man is capable of being in uncer- tainties, mysteries, doubts, without any irritable reaching after fact and reason – Coleridge, for instance, would let go by a fine isolated verisimili- tude caught from the Penetralium of mystery, from being incapable of remaining content with half-knowledge. (Letter to George and Thomas Keats, 21 December 1817, Vol. 1, 193–4)

The 'man of Achievement' in Literature must not give himself up to an 'irritable reaching after fact and reason'. To do so, for Keats, would result in a Wordsworthian type of 'Egotistical Sublime' (to Richard Woodhouse, 27 October 1818, Vol. II, 227). Keats was not always complimentary of Wordsworth; he writes to Reynolds: 'It may be said that we ought to read our Contemporaries, that Wordsworth &c should have their due from us, but for the sake of a few fine imaginative or domestic passages, are we to be bullied into a certain Philosophy engendered in the whims of an Egoist?' (To J. H Reynolds, 3 February 1818, Vol. I, 223). However, Keats does admire 'half of Wordsworth'. In the famous 'Mansion-of-Life' letter, he writes that Wordsworth was come 'as far as I can conceive when he wrote "Tintern Abbey" and it seems to be that his Genius is explorative of those dark Passages' (3 May 1818, Vol. I, 280). The exploration of these 'dark Passages' is of the utmost importance for Keats; these 'dark Passages' are one with 'the Penetralium of mystery' that he believes Coleridge steers past in his inability to be content with 'half-knowledge'. The question, then, is how the writer is to explore these 'dark Passages' resolute in the knowledge that a philosophy of life lies therein while at the same time privileging the spirit of being-in-uncertainties? Keats's famous comparison of life to a 'large Mansion of Many Apartments' that moves the individual from 'the infant or thoughtless Chamber' to 'the Chamber of Maiden-Thought' might offer some clues. The progress through the Mansion necessitates the 'sharpening' of

[O]ne's vision into the < head > [heart] and nature of Man – of convincing ones nerves that the World is full of Misery and Heartbreak, Pain, Sickness and oppression – whereby This Chamber of Maiden Thought becomes gradually darken'd and at the same time on all sides of it many doors are set open – but all dark – all leading to dark passages – We see not the ballance of good and evil. We are in a Mist – *We* are now in that state – We feel the 'burden of the Mystery." (1958, Vol. I, 281)

We are beyond good and evil in these 'dark passages', as Nietzsche might suggest, and we must retain the 'burden of Mystery'[4] that sickness and misery afford so that by 'mak[ing] discoveries' we can 'shed a light in them'. It produces what Faulkner describes as 'the problems of the human heart in conflict with itself' (in Li, 133), or, as Keats's representation of this struggle in 'The Fall of Hyperion' makes clear when the poet has acknowledged that suffering must be intensely experienced in order to be transformed into tragic power: 'Without stay or prop/But my own weak mortality, I bore/The load of this eternal quietude' (1951, 'The Fall of Hyperion' I. 388–90). It gives the poet-dreamer the more 'quiet power' he desires. The poet then can spend longer illuminating the 'dark passages' because of this 'weak mortality'.

But what is the nature of the tragic power that the poet must reveal and how does the individual move from the second Chamber, the 'Chamber of Maiden-Thought' with its 'dark passages' to the 'third Chamber of Life' that is 'stored with the wine of love-and the Bread of Friendship'? The recasting of the Eucharistic elements here leads on to Keats's other great image for self-discovery, one that transforms the Christian 'vale of tears' into the 'The vale of Soul-making'. In the 'Vale of Soul-Making' letter, where Keats asks the most 'interesting question that can come before us' – 'How far by the persevering endeavours of a seldom appearing Socrates Mankind may be made happy'? – he says he can imagine such happiness 'carried to an extreme' but that it would still end in 'death'. However, since death must still await us all, such happiness would mean that the 'whole troubles of life . . . would the[n] be accumulated for the last days of a being who instead of hailing its approach, would leave this world as Eve left Paradise'. This leads Keats to write that he cannot believe in this 'sort of perfectibility' (Vol. II, 101). It is a stark rebuttal of much ethical theory and Christian morality; it consigns altruism and good-natured disinterest to a shadowy world. Keats's suggestion is to 'Call the world if you Please "The vale of Soul-making"' for then 'you will find out the use of the world'. In such a world souls are made out of 'Intelligences' that are 'sparks of the divinity', but these souls only gain 'any identity' or 'bliss peculiar to each one's individual existence' when 'each one is personally itself' (102). How does each one become 'personally itself'? It is only by being 'altered by the heart – or seat of the human Passions' (103). Man is formed by 'circumstances' that are 'touchstones of his heart' and these, in turn, are 'proovings of his heart' (103). These 'proovings' are 'fortifiers or alterers of his nature' and his altered nature is his 'Soul' (103). The 'Identity' is therefore made through 'the medium of the Heart' and the heart becomes this medium only 'in a world of Circumstances' (104). If we therefore try to follow the logic of this narrative without irritably reaching after fact and reason we can see that the circumstances of the heart mediate experiences so that each individual or identity can become 'personally itself'. Keats asks in the letter: 'Do you not see how necessary a World of Pains and troubles is to school an Intelligence and make it a soul?' (102). Since Keats's 'weak mortality' was driven by the 'circumstances' of his weak and sickly frame, it is these that have granted him the 'proovings' to illuminate those 'dark passages' that take us beyond 'where youth grows pale, and spectre-thin, and dies' and keep us focused on the 'beauty' that 'still will keep/a bower quiet for us' ('Endymion', 3–4) so that we 'yet have visions for the night' ('Ode on Indolence', 297.57). Lionel Trilling reminds us that 'the idea of soul-making, of souls creating themselves in their confrontation of circumstance, is available to Keats's conception only because he has remained with half-knowledge, with the double knowledge of the self and the world's evil' (in Li, 14). Even though the poet stares into an 'eternal fierce destruction' (Li, 119) it is only by going through what Ou Li describes as a 'shocking disparity between his self and the greater Other that he is delivered from his willful blindness' (Li, 106), and the greatest Other is surely the image we have of ourselves if we fail to let our identity become 'personally itself'.

Keats's notions of 'quiet power' and 'weak mortality' influenced many later poets. Over 200 years later, Charles Olson would draw inspiration from Keats in his Black Mountain lectures. In *The Special View of History* Olson strives to articulate a 'redefinition of humanism' (1970, 32). Olson claims that the age of Enlightenment or Modernity has been an 'AGE OF POWER' and he wants to 'spatialize or reify time or process' (in Spanos, 49). For Olson, all such endeavours in the 'Western philosophical/literary tradition' (49) are grounded in 'the logocentric human ego, which according to him has enjoyed an increasingly privileged status since Plato and Aristotle, culminating in the Industrial Revolution, that is, the age of technology, and takes the form of the Will to Power over being' (Spanos, 49). Olson writes: 'one can dub the period 1750 to 1945 the AGE OF POWER. And thus get another light on why Keats was on target in trying to extricate another sort of "Man" from the MAN OF POWER – what you will recall he called Wordsworth and Milton in literature and otherwise called those who have a "proper self" the "Egotistical Sublime"' (1970, 41). It is this other sort of '"Man" from the MAN OF POWER', the 'versifying Pet-lamb', that Keats would more and more find himself to be. It is a state and a 'metaphysical road' that he felt he had to navigate in order to put off the 'bitterness' of death:

> I wish for death every day and night to deliver me from these pains, and then I wish death away, for death would destroy even those pains which are better than nothing. Land and Sea, weakness and decline are great separators, but death is the great divorcer for ever. When the pang of this thought has passed through my mind, I may say the bitterness of death is passed. (*Letters*, Vol. II, 345)

The later poems reveal this progression in thought by way of 'weak mortality'. The 'Ode On Indolence' seeks a kind of indolence that is representative of a new and uniquely Romantic form of weakness. It describes a degree of lethargy that is beyond moral weakness, weakness of the will and any Christian weakness of the flesh. It speaks of a drowsy almost semi-conscious state that is content to be in the body even though the body's sensations and the mental faculties register very little, if anything. The speaker of the poem admits: 'For Poesy! –no,- she has not a joy, - /At least for me, - so sweet as drowsy noons,/And evenings steep'd in honied indolence;/O for an age so shelter'd from annoy,/That I may never know how change the moons,/Or hear the voice of busy common-sense!' (1951, 297.45–50). The human traces that prevent the speaker from realizing the state it pushes itself to, a state even beyond the claims of the speaker in 'Ode To A Nightingale', are Love, Ambition and Poesy. Even though the speaker bids them vanish 'from my idle spright,/Into the clouds, and never more return!' (1951, 298.59–60) the willed unshackling from the last traces of the human form is perhaps less successful than the more drowsy, unconscious movement away from human endeavour by way of 'fancy' in 'Ode to a Nightingale'. The voice of 'Ode On Indolence' ultimately leaves us with a sense of resignation and frustration.

Not content to make do with indolence and negative capability, Keats is eager in many of his later poems to explore the world that, for him, epitomizes weakness and the Fall – namely, the world occupied by the Titans after their 'golden age'; it is the world that Saturn and his siblings woke up to after their defeat at the hands of Zeus and the Olympians. Both 'Hyperion' the early work and the unfinished, later 'The Fall of Hyperion' explore both the visionary's ability to access this world because of his weaknesses as a human being and the godly experience of weakness in the 'fallen house' of Saturn after the 'golden age' of the Titans (1951, 376.284–5). Their fall being so great, the gods' experience of their new-found weakness is ever more poignant. The speaker-poet of 'The Fall of Hyperion' is, like Dante's speaker-poet in *The Divine Comedy*, a writer who is allowed to enter where few can because he is a 'dreamer' and 'visionary'. The guardian of the realm, Moneta, reveals his true self to the poet: 'Thou art a dreaming thing,/A fever of thy self – think of the earth;/What bliss, even in hope, is there for thee?/What haven? every creature hath its home;/Every sole man hath days of joy and pain,/Whether his labours be sublime or low -/The pain alone, the joy alone, distinct: Only the dreamer venoms all his days,/Bearing more woe than all his sins deserve' (374.168–75). The dreamer or visionary is therefore allowed privileged access to this realm that epitomizes weakness and the Fall. Moneta, the 'priestess of his [Saturn's] desolation' further clarifies why such a dreamer is capable of entering into this realm.

To his questions 'What am I that should so be saved from death?/What am I that another death come not/To choke my utterance, sacrilegious, here?', she replies: 'thou hast felt/what 'tis to die and live again before/Thy fated hour; that thou hadst power to do so/Is thy own safety; thou hast dated on/Thy doom' (373.138–45). The weakness of his human form and his ability to envenom all his human days because of the 'weak mortality' he experiences there has enabled him to have 'dated on' his doom. His desolation in life as a visionary meant for greater experiences has allowed him to experience what is comparable to death – 'thou hast felt/what 'tis to die' – and with this experience he can then evade the death others suffer when they enter the desolation of the Titans' abode where Saturn laments a state of weakness, a lamentation that would be too much for mortal man to endure: 'Moan and wail./Moan brethren, moan; for lo! The rebel spheres/Spin round, the stars their antient courses keep,/Clouds still with shadowy moisture haunt the earth,/. . . Moan, Cybele, moan, for thy pernicious babes/Have changed a god into a shaking Palsy./Moan, brethren, moan, for I have no strength left;/Weak as the reed[5] – weak – feeble as my voice -/O, O, the pain, the pain of feebleness' (379–80.417–29). For Titans, then, weakness is too much of a burden, but Keats's 'poet-dreamer' is no Titan. These are very different incarnations to those described in Chapter 3. The god is reduced to 'a shaking Palsy'. His discovery of his fallen, human-like state is described in terms of weakness and the majority of the poem is devoted to an exploration of this "pain of feebleness". It was composed between July and December of 1819, shortly before Keats experienced the life-threatening hemorrhage that would begin his own steady decline. Perhaps Keats had intimations of this final weakening and of his own 'weak mortality'. He could find no better expression for it than that experienced at the dawn of the universe when the first 'golden age' brought about the first deliberation on weakness.

Wordsworth's speaker-poet in *The Prelude* also puts the device of authorial weakness to good use. He doubts his own abilities and describes his ability to make contact with those 'Breathings for incommunicable powers' (*The Prelude*, III, 100: 190) that have nothing to do with 'outward things' such as 'words' and 'signs' in terms of his 'hand however weak' (III, 100: 186). Not only does he make an inner communication with himself, he also makes an 'intimate communion' through his heart with the 'minuter properties/Of objects which already are beloved' within 'Nature's finer influxes' (II, 80: 283–4). In speaking through his verse to his 'friend' Coleridge, Wordsworth's *alter ego* also explains that he begins his narrative journey of self-discovery 'early' because he is 'feeling' '[t]he weakness of a human love for days/

Disowned by memory' (I, 62: 613–15). This might describe the 'diligent indolence' Keats admired in Wordsworth. In the very first book of *The Prelude* the speaker describes how he yearns 'towards some philosophic song/Of truth that cherishes our daily life' but that he has 'no skill to part'; he writes that he possesses '[v]ague longing that is bred by want of power', a 'timorous capacity' and the habit of 'infinite delay'. However, it is his, the poet's, 'vacant musing' revealed to the public as 'wanting – so much wanting' where '[s]ome imperfection' is found in every 'chosen theme' so that he must 'recoil and droop, and seek repose/In indolence' that allows Wordsworth to reveal so much about weakness. The weakness enables him, like Keats, to refrain from chasing after fact and reason like a 'MAN OF POWER', and to understand that it is this very weakness that brings us the 'truth' of the contact with Nature that gives to our human nature (I, 40–2, 229–66).

When Wordsworth describes his motivations for writing and for choosing the profession of poet over other pursuits he also discusses how an early enchantment with philosophy and most particularly with logic and reason led him to misrepresent Nature and all that it stands for. In Book Eleven he describes how in his youth he fostered a strong love of reason; reason was regarded as 'nobility in man'. (420: 70). However, this privileging of reason led him to denigrate the 'passions' that he had previously connected with Nature:

Thus strangely did I war against myself;
A bigot to a new idolatry,
Did like a monk who hath forsworn the world
Zealously labour to cut off my heart
From all the sources of her former strength . . . so did I unsoul
As readily by syllogistic words . . . those mysteries of passion which
   have made,
And shall continue evermore to make-
In spite of all that reason hath performed,
And shall perform, to exalt and to refine-
One brotherhood of all the human race (XI, 420: 74–89).

This slavery to reason even led Wordsworth to see a 'sense of weakness or infirmity' (422: 113) in Nature because the 'visible universe was scanned/ with something' of the 'kindred spirit' that he had taken up from his privileging of reason. Wordsworth therefore reacts against the scientific and overly objective 'scanning' of Nature. He believes that Godwin was one of the leading proponents of this reason-centred approach to the world.

In Book Ten he gives an ironic treatment of the kind of salvation and the kind of freedom such philosophies preach: 'What delight!-/How glorious!-in self-knowledge and self-rule/To look through all the frailties of the world,/ And, with a resolute mastery shaking off/The accidents of nature, time and place,/That make up the weak being of the past' (X, 402: 818–23). Wordsworth does not believe that man should regard himself as self-sufficient and therefore capable of encountering nature with a cold objectivity. Weakness and the 'frailties of the world', which Arnold felt he had a gift for representing, must not be approached with a 'resolute mastery' driven by reason that shakes off 'the accidents of nature, time and place' for these are the details of the 'common' that reveal to Wordsworth the value of the 'lowly', which grants him his poetic voice.

Wordsworth also revolutionizes the voice of the epic poet in giving us an epic coming-of-age of the Romantic self in literature that is rife with passages that question the writer's abilities. Thinking back to his early twenties in France, the speaker-poet describes his artistic abilities: 'Mean as I was, and little graced with powers/Of eloquence even in my native speech,/And all unfit for tumult and intrigue' (X, 364: 131–4). He becomes conscious of his inexperience in confronting the horrors of the French Revolution and this grants him a poetic voice that convinces the reader of the worth of the journey back into self, no matter how weak, by way of the guiding spirit of Nature. On returning to Paris after the September massacres, Wordsworth experiences a moment somewhat similar to that of Leontius in Plato's dialogues, an influential moment, as we have seen, for Plato's tripartite division of the soul. Wordsworth sees the corpses of the revolutionaries and the Palace guards piled high in the Place de Carrousel and the scene haunts his thoughts later that evening. It prevents him from sleeping but it also sets off a recurring structural device in Wordsworth's work whereby the voice of the speaker reflects on some earlier defining moment, deliberating on the weaknesses it reveals and deriving sustenance for the future from the deliberation. The deliberation on the memory leads to an awareness of what must be learnt from the incongruity between his own inexperience and the stark social realism that the massacre symbolizes:

> I crossed-a black and empty area then-
> The square of the Carrousel, few weeks back
> Heaped up with dead and dying, upon these
> And other sights looking as doth a man
> Upon a volume whose contents he knows
> Are memorable but from him locked up,

Being written in a tongue he cannot read,
So that he questions the mute leaves with pain,
And half upbraids their silence. But that night
when on my bed I lay, I was most moved
And felt most deeply in what world I was;
. . . The fear gone by
Pressed on me almost like a fear to come.
I thought of those September massacres,
Divided from me by a little month,
And felt and touched them, a substantial dread . . . : 'The horse is taught
   his manage, and the wind
Of heaven wheels round and treads in his own steps;
Year follows year, the tide returns again,
Day follows day, all things have second birth;
The earthquake is not satisfied at once.' (X, 361–2: 54–74)

Wordsworth must experience his own 'black and empty area', as a 'fear to come'. He transforms the ghastly spectacle of the bodies slaughtered in the September massacres into a vision of a vast tome or body of work that is, as yet, 'locked up'. He not only discovers a personal philosophy that enables him to build on the personal inadequacy and the incongruity he experiences before the corpses, he also describes the philosophy of rebirth and second comings in an apocalyptic language that looks forwards to the writing of another poet of Nature and second comings, W. B. Yeats.

As a writer before the dead page, he also 'questions the mute leaves with pain,/And upbraids their silence'. He knows there is a fundamental lesson in what he sees, a lesson that will allow him to unlock the epic he is yet to write. This exploration of painful lessons from a personal history in terms of a body of work lying intact, but waiting to be deciphered and unravelled, provides Wordsworth with a template for his own epic of self-discovery in a similar manner to Keats, who has explained that each 'Identity' must become 'personally itself'. In the 'second birth' or the 'recollection' we can make sense of what has passed. Wordsworth transplants this approach to memorable events that deserve a 'second birth' onto the Romantic poet's crossing of his own 'black and empty area', his 'self'. In 'Tintern Abbey' the 'second birth' of the remembered influence of a favourite natural landscape in the mind of the speaker after a 'long absence' makes the speaker aware of how these 'forms of beauty' have been constantly revealing themselves to him in a consolatory manner so that 'sensations sweet' are '[f]elt in the blood'. It is now apparent that these 'forms' are found in a range of objects and situations; even the 'dead and dying' at the Place de Carrousel reveal some kind of truth in the shape of a 'memorable' 'volume' that must be unlocked. The 'forms' have an important 'influence' on the 'best portion of a good man's life' – namely, '[h]is little, nameless, unremembered, acts/Of kindness and of love' – and they grant a 'blessed mood' in which the 'burden of the mystery', the 'heavy and the weary weight/Of all this unintelligible world/Is lightened' so that the body is 'laid asleep' and we become a 'living sou' that can see into 'the life of things' (Wu, 266: 23–49).

A great deal, then, is gained from this process of revisiting and recollection so that poetry can be set up as 'emotion recollected in tranquility'. However, it is the admission of ignorance and incomprehension in the face of the large-scale 'frailties of the world', such as the events that led to the September massacres, that drives Wordsworth inwards to discover that the consolation for all that is 'unintelligible' lies in unravelling the connection between the recollected 'forms of beauty' and their influence on 'unremembered, acts/Of kindness and of love'. Since Wordsworth is less likely than Blake to describe the 'marks of weakness, marks of woe' of an external, political oppression, and since he is less likely than Keats to describe the influence of 'weak mortality', he must then create a form of weakness in his work to stand in for the 'frailties of the world' that must be described in the context of all the 'accidents of nature, time and place'. Wordsworth finds this necessary weakness in what he describes in his preface to the *Lyrical Ballads* as the 'low and rustic life' about him.

Gary Harrison has examined Wordsworth's treatment of the poor in terms of Victor Turner's descriptions of 'the weak' and the 'liminal'. Turner describes how the 'weak' in many communities possess a 'sacred power': '[i]n closed or structured societies, it is the marginal or "inferior" person or the outsider who often comes to symbolize . . . the sentiment of humanity' (Turner, 111). However, what I want to examine briefly here is how Wordsworth's willed separation from the 'heavy and the weary weight/ Of all this unintelligible world' might lead to a situation where the 'frailties of the world', as embodied by his descriptions of the 'weak' and of 'rustic life', end up playing a similar structural role in his poetry to the 'forms of beauty' he describes in Nature. The representation of each – the 'weak' and the 'forms of beauty' – seems to arouse both 'domestic feeling' (Harrison, 161) and 'affective power' (Harrison, 149). Is he a *spectator ab extra*, as Coleridge suggests, in his dealings with, and thinking on, the weak, or does he 'redeem the basic humanity of the beggar', as Harrison suggests (153)? For Harrison, Wordsworth negates the 'political and social determinants of being' by naturalizing poverty and assigning it to 'Nature's law'; poverty is neutralized behind this 'contemplation of a universalized transcendent order' (170). However, despite Wordsworth's 'Tory humanism', it is nevertheless the case that in poems such as 'The Old Cumberland Beggar' he 'attacks directly the proponents of those systems of relief that would dehumanize the poor' (171).

Wordsworth consistently describes the weakness of the common folk such as his 'Old Cumberland Beggar' in terms of the Nature that surrounds them. A passage from *The Prelude* allows us to see how 'man' can sometimes be one with the 'unassuming things' of Nature; Nature brings Wordsworth a mood that enables him to

> '[S]eek in man, and in the frame of life
> Social and individual, what there is
> Desirable, affecting, good or fair,
> Of kindred permanence, the gifts divine
> And universal, the pervading grace
> That hath been, is, and shall be'.

But Nature also brings more through the 'unassuming things':

> 'Above all/Did Nature bring again this wiser mood,
> More deeply reestablished in my soul,
> Which, seeing little worthy or sublime
> In what we blazon with the pompous names
> Of power and action, early tutored me
> To look with feelings of fraternal love
> Upon those unassuming things that hold
> A silent station in this beauteous world' (XII, 440: 39–53).

Once again, it is Nature and its 'forms of beauty' that has enabled him to 'seek in man' what is of 'kindred permanence' and to 'look', in particular, with 'fraternal love' upon those 'unassuming things' removed from 'power and action'. The question is, then, does this 'kindred permanence' that takes its cue from Nature and that seeks out a 'universal benevolence' in the deeds and actions of the beggar as 'silent monitor' (156) neglect what other writers such as Michael Hardt and Antonio Negri see in poverty when they describe it in terms of a 'biopolitical event' that 'comes from the outside insofar as it ruptures the continuity of history and the existing order' (2009, 59)? Of course, it may very well be true that in the 'vagrant' poems

Wordsworth is praising a 'gift economy' that challenges the existing dominance of the capitalist exchange economy; however, even Harrison, who puts forwards this notion, admits that the 'Cumberland Beggar does not return material gifts' (167). The Beggar's 'indigence' may very well provide 'an essential part of the collective exchange of *good* as well as goods' but this seems to stretch the definition of the 'gift economy' to encompass the exchange of metaphysical 'gifts'. If we are to use anthropological accounts of the gift economy or of secular and liminal weakness for Wordsworth's poetry, then we must examine the nature of his characters' 'liminality'. Do his beggars possess the 'sacred power' of the 'weak' and, if so, what is the nature of the 'humanity' that he reveals?

In his descriptions of such common country folk as the shepherd Michael and the old Cumberland beggar, Wordsworth is most eager to praise what is a form of meekness or silent power. In Book Twelve of the *Prelude* he contrasts these country people with 'men adroit/In speech and for communion with the world' (450: 255). He speaks for those 'men' of 'other mold', 'Meek men, whose very souls perhaps would sink/Beneath them, summoned to such intercourse:/Theirs is the language of the heavens'. For such people '[w]ords are but under-agents in their souls-/When they are grasping with their greatest strength/They do not breathe among them' (450: 270–4). He will later develop his theme of 'spiritual love', a love that is developed in man through a care for 'imagination' and 'intellectual love' (XIII, 468: 186). Whether such 'intellectual love' and hence such spiritual 'love' is accessible to the 'low and rustic life' of the country is unclear; however, such 'love' must be nurtured by each individual so as to 'complete the man' (470: 202). The soul of the man with such spiritual love will then have 'risen/Up to the height of the feeling intellect' and it 'shall want no humbler tenderness, his heart/Be tender as a nursing mother's heart;/Of female softness shall his life be full,/Of little loves and delicate desires,/Mild sentiments and gentlest sympathies' (204–10). Such a man of balanced mind and soul who is possessive of an 'intellectual love' that might elude the beggar and the shepherd becomes possessive of a 'feeling intellect' that opens him up to a life-long nurturing 'female softness'.

However, one might argue that Wordsworth's 'weak' are liminal precisely because they exist outside the norms of labour that drive our understanding of poverty today. Dickens's characters are perhaps the first truly industrial 'weak'. However, it is because Wordsworth's poor are naturalized and placed outside the work of the market economy as approximations of some humanized 'forms of beauty' that it is only death in Nature rather than, for example, a death similar to the one Stephen Blackpool suffers in the mine in *Hard Times*, that is ultimately seen as most threatening to them. In other words, they appear less weak than they might be; we are led to question whether they possess what Beckett will later describe as 'the authentic weakness of being'. The old Cumberland beggar, as the title of his poem suggests, suffers more from old age than from any privation resulting from his begging. In fact, his begging in Nature has preserved him to an extent that his age has 'no companion'. Wordsworth's speaker might urge the wind that 'sweeps the heath' to [b]eat his [the beggar's] grey locks against his withered face' (Hayden, 267.175–6) so that he dies in the 'eye of Nature' (268.196) – a phrase that puns the self-besotted 'I' whose presence sanitizes nature – but because the sustenance that his work as begging produces visits him as easily as the wind itself, he is not wholly convincing as a representative of those 'frailties of the world' that Wordsworth sought to speak for. Writing only a few decades later and during Wordsworth's lifetime, Dickens and Marx would forever transform the representation of the labouring 'weak' as proletarian labourers. Later political events, such as the famines in Ireland (both in the 1830s and 40s), events directly affected by the decisions of the Royal Commission on Poor Laws that Wordsworth challenged, would also demonstrate that being at the mercy of nature outside an organized labour market could produce greater hardships than Wordsworth had ever imagined for the subject dying in the 'eye of Nature'.

However, Wordsworth might still be regarded as setting up a spirit of charity that offered an alternative to the Reform Act and its instrumentalist programme for housing the poor in workhouses. In anticipation of Dickens's treatment of the poor in the next chapter, it is also important to note how contemporary theorists have described this change in society that occurred in moving from the Romantics to Dickens. Richard Sennet asks in *The Craftsman* whether the Romantic understanding of Nature as the 'common', which sets up Nature as our true home, runs the risk of 'leading us to seek escape in an idealized Nature, rather than confronting the self-destructive territory we have actually made' (2009, 13). Dickens will take us to the heart of this new industrialized destructiveness that brought with it a new form of weakness that had to deal with the transformation of the worker from *Homo faber* to *Animal laborans*.

Chapter 8

A Sentimental Man: Dickens, Involuntary Narration and the 'Experience of the Common'

Dickens moves us closer to the body of the weak and vulnerable. Despite Victorian standards of respectability and the fact that he may, as David Paroissien suggests, concern himself with an 'idealized truth about human experience', (1985, 291) no study of weakness and 'the weak' in literature is complete without him. The narrator of *The Old Curiosity Shop* reminds us that 'Nature often enshrines gallant and noble hearts in weak bosoms' (2000, 186). Dickens's description of the weakness of these 'bosoms' may well have a Christian feel to it, for his novels do, as Paroissien again suggests, hold to a 'belief that repentance is genuinely possible for all except those who will their destruction by refusing to change their hearts' (Paroissien, 297). Characters such as Ralph Nickleby, Paul Dombey or Louisa Gradgrind may not always 'change their hearts' in time precisely because they are unwilling to accept what often appear as Christian notions of humility and weakness. Louisa, raised as she is in the spirit of all that is 'sacred to fact' (2003, 28) and self-renunciation, realizes all too late the value of 'every natural prompting' (209) that she has strived to keep down her whole life. She groans aloud to her father as she falls at his feet, an 'insensible heap' (212): 'if you had known that there lingered in my breast sensibilities, affections, weaknesses capable of being cherished into strength, defying all the calculations ever made by man, and no more known to his arithmetic than his Creator is – would you have given me to the husband whom I am now sure that I hate?' (209). Dickens describes these 'weaknesses capable of being cherished into strength'. Not content solely to make do with traditional Christian virtues, he goes right back to when life is most weak and the body is beyond the 'voluntary exertion of the mind' (*Oliver*, 239). In this chapter, I want to examine how Dickens's fascination for the body close to death describes a taxonomy of weakness where the 'spark of life' dallies about the body, seemingly released from the confines of the character's agency. Dickens's work brings the Christian account of weakness into conversation with later philosophical notions that have been assigned to the 'spark of life' in his work, notions such as Henri Bergson's *élan vital* and Gilles Deleuze's account of immanence. His examination of this moment also leads to greater experimentation with the form of the narrative. By closely examining the body close to death, Dickens describes a new kind of narrative moment, what might be described as a moment of 'involuntary narration', where the instinct for narration is itself set up as a great 'current of life' that brings readers together as 'drops' in the 'great ocean of humanity'. As he writes of life itself: 'The more we see of life and its brevity, and the world and its varieties, the more we know that no exercise of our abilities in any art, but the addressing of it to the great ocean of humanity in which we are drops, and not to bye-ponds (very stagnant) here and there, ever or ever will lay the foundations of an endurable retrospect' (Letter to Macready; Paroissien, 350). Dickens's experiments with narration set up a similar dynamic of sharing between the reader and the intertext as collective conscience.

In *Oliver Twist* we get an early account of the body close to death:

> The boy stirred and smiled in his sleep, as though these marks of pity and compassion had awakened some pleasant dream of a love and affection he had never known; as a strain of gentle music, or the rippling of water in a silent place, or the colour of a flower, or even the mention of a familiar word, will sometimes call up sudden dim remembrances of scenes that never were in this life, which vanish like a breath, and which some brief memory of a happier existence, long/gone by, would seem to have awakened, for no voluntary exertion of the mind can ever recall them. (*Oliver Twist*, 238–9).

Oliver is unable to voluntarily recall those 'sudden dim remembrances of scenes that never were in this life'. The model of life described presupposes some continuity between lived experiences, brief memories of a happier existence long gone by and the 'dim remembrances of scenes' thrown up by these memories that belong to some larger current of experience beyond 'this life'. Oliver is awaking out of a prolonged battle with serious illness and the gestures of compassion serve as the catalyst on this occasion for these 'dim remembrances'. However, in describing such an involuntary memory, why does Dickens have the character 'recall' remembrances not from 'this life', and what, precisely, is being recalled? Dickens's later works frequently describe some exterior force that life lies open to at such moments when a body is close to death. He employs a range of motifs to describe this force; we recall the 'golden water' that Paul Dombey calls on, the image of the face of Florence that haunts and saves Mr Dombey and the 'shadow of advancing Death', the 'shadow of an actual presence' that is also a 'Light' that 'lay beyond Death' for the ever-weakening Betty Higden (*Our Mutual Friend*, 496). This involuntary connection with an exterior force that the individual life sustains at such times is described by means of rudimentary interior monologue[1] and involuntary narrative in Dickens's later work.[2] However, Dickens does not employ these techniques with the introspective dynamic of the later, modernist narratives of a Joyce or a Proust. The involuntary connection with a state beyond the individual life allows Dickens, even at such moments, to privilege a social thinking that brings out his belief in some universal current of life that binds all individuals.

The narrator's description above of how 'some brief memory of a happier existence, long gone by' (but yet experienced in this life) awakens 'dim remembrances' reminds us of Proust. As with Proust, the individual at this time would appear to be 'filled with the general essence common to these two' (*Remembrance of Things Past*, Moncrieff 1029) moments; however, Dickens does not consign the genesis of this involuntary force to a solely interior life. For Dickens, narrative becomes a vehicle for embodying a heightened social responsibility and interdependence when individual agency is on the cusp of being suspended. Bo Earle has explored how a kind of 'involuntary narration' exists in Proust's *Á la recherche* because Marcel's 'aesthetic subjectivity' is about 'abdicating rather than asserting agency' (2002, 957). As Dickens develops his narrative strategies throughout his novels, he may well be beginning to experiment with ways of describing such an abdication or renunciation of agency in the narration of a character's life. The narrator appears to stand back and the narrative impulse appears to flow on unchecked, free of its maker, just as the 'current of life' surrounding a Quilp or a Riderhood is also momentarily stalled and unattached as it hovers about the character's body or corpse. The narrative at these times of weakness embodies both a 'lifeworld' the characters inhabit and an intertext sustained by narration that Dickens suggests can be as involuntary as the life it details.

This way of understanding community also offers a new account of experience. Hans-Georg Gadamer has described how the understanding of experience, or *Erlebnis*, changed in the middle of the nineteenth century, influencing what he describes as the 'subjectivization of aesthetics'. The noun *Erlebnis* 'only became common in the 1870s' (60) but it introduces the idea that 'something becomes an "experience" not only insofar as it is experienced, but insofar as its being experienced makes a special impression that gives it lasting importance' (61). Dickens may well be using the narration describing the body close to death to elicit such an effect for the reader, enabling the reader to perceive how the experience of witnessing the passing of life or the struggle to sustain life gives the experience of life itself 'lasting importance' and formally advances Dickens's own social ideas that entail a close connection between the living and the dead.

There are a range of figures in Dickens's works that remind the reader of this great, cyclical current of life.[3] Dickens describes the involuntary[4] force within life, as a force that a character's weakness (be it moral or physical) will always bring to the surface and that appeals to life beyond the individual life and to social responsibility. It is an interest that enables him to experiment with the potential within narrative for rousing readers 'to a knowledge of their own relation' (*Dombey*, 739) to the world. Henri Bergson, whose notion of the vital impulse or *élan vital* has often been aligned with Dickens's treatment of life, also describes the vital impulse and life itself in terms of a 'current of life' (1944, 25). Bergson's evolutionist reading of this 'current' describes how it works in time traversing the bodies it has organized one after another, passing from generation to generation' (25); '*life is like a current passing from germ to germ through the medium of a developed organism* [Bergson's emphasis]' (26). Dickens extends this reading of the great current of life to the relationship between the living and the dead. As he writes in a letter to George Beadnell on 19 December 1839, '[i]t is impossible to separate the idea of the dead from the companionship of the living' (Paroissien, 49).

Dickens can also be read as prefiguring the work of later social theorists who describe how narration and community are interconnected. Dickens's notion of the 'current of life' is not out of place with Durkheim's notion of the 'collective consciousness', the 'collective person' and Habermas's notion of the 'lifeworld'. For Habermas, Durkheim's '"collective person"' is of 'such a nature that it reaches beyond the consciousness of the individual person and yet is at the same time immanent in him' (1989, 50). When Dickens is describing the body close to death, the individual life's connection to the greater 'current of life' sets up such a notion of a 'collective person'. Just as religious rites offer the community a special kind of 'intersubjectivity' (52) and, indeed, create community, narration sets up such a possibility for Dickens. Habermas explains how his own notion of the 'communicative act', a notion that also necessitates a level of 'narration', derives from '[r]itually generated solidarity' or 'obligations to the collectivity'. However, he points out, as Dickens appears to do in the famous Riderhood scene that I shall examine later, that '[s]pontaneous expressions linked to the body lose their involuntary character when they are replaced with or interpreted by linguistic utterances' (63). When language arrives, this involuntary character of life becomes lost. These two accounts of what we might call 'communicative action' attempt, then, to speak for the 'spontaneous expressions linked to the body' by accepting their involuntary nature, and these expressions are most urgently perceived for Dickens when the body is struggling to sustain life. Habermas also notes, however, that even though such spontaneous, involuntary or 'intuitive acts' are evidence for a 'reflective relation-to-self', where the reflective quality refers, once again, to a recognition of limitations – namely, 'knowing that one does not know' (75) – that these can also take place in the individual in the 'communicative practice of daily life'. In other words, Habermas does not follow phenomenology in exhaustively charting the interiority of these intuitions; he acknowledges that their examination must be accompanied by a deeper understanding of community and the 'common'. Habermas accepts that the 'intuitively accessible *concept of the sociocultural lifeworld*' is mediated by narration because it enables us to develop a '*cognitive reference system* [Habermas's emphasis]' for an 'everyday concept of the lifeworld' (136). In other words, narration appears to mediate the lifeworld for us and make it present and, I would argue that, Dickens, despite his very different artistic approach, accords narration a similar role in his fiction and it is the narration of the moment of weakness that is most enabling of this in narrative.

However, Dickens's emotive descriptions of the lifeworld, or the 'current of life', will always privilege need and weakness in a way that these later social theories may not. In this regard, Dickens may also have an important role to play in what Michael Hardt and Antonio Negri have recently described as the evolution of 'the common'. Hardt and Negri argue that a revised understanding of the common emerged in the nineteenth century 'that blurs the division between nature and culture'; it is a 'biopolitical' common, a more 'dynamic' concept, where the 'common is not only the earth we share but also the languages we create, the social practices we establish, the modes of sociality that define our relationships, and so forth' (2009, 139). Dickens's tireless presentation of such 'modes of sociality' in the metropolis of London, together with his interest in depicting a shared and unifying conception of life, provides an artistic backdrop for this modern form of the 'common'. Hardt and Negri's reading traces this notion of the 'common' and commonwealth back to Spinoza. In referring to Spinoza, they argue that 'the ignorance of children, for instance, or the weakness of our bodies or the brutality of the human social condition' always 'poses such states as poverty as the point of departure for a logic of transformation that moves out of the solitude and weakness by means of the construction of sociality and love' (53). They describe how the power derived from such weakness, which equates with Dickens's 'weaknesses capable of being cherished into strength', creates a 'quest for the common', and they argue that Spinoza seeks mechanisms whereby 'singular bodies can together compose a common power'. Dickens's treatment of weakness through his narration of the 'singular' body's struggle creates a similar 'common power'.

There is an important passage in *Dombey and Son* that examines how this 'current of life' and the life struggles it navigates must also be seen to affect all social classes. In Chapter 47 Dickens is describing the dinner scene between Edith, Dombey, Florence and Carker that leads to the eventual break up of the group forever. The narrator begins a lengthy diatribe on the social causes of the 'unnatural outcasts of society' (1985, 737); he argues that their unnatural behaviour is a result of an unnatural environment, of 'having been conceived, and born and bred, in Hell!' (737). He goes further by arguing that any 'moral pestilence' that rises with such people is also the result of the 'eternal laws of outraged Nature' (738). He scorns the fact that such people are then considered 'unnatural in losing and confounding all distinctions between good and evil' (737). At the heart of Dickens, then, is the redressing and confounding of what is accepted as good and evil. Where disease is generated there too is bred 'infancy that knows no innocence' (738); 'dainty delicacy living in the next street', in reviling such '[u]nnatural humanity!' (738), becomes similarly 'unnatural' in distancing itself from 'the spark of life' that it shares with such humanity. The narrator wants the 'dark shapes' that also 'issue from amidst' the homes of 'Christian people' to be made known so that they will be roused 'to a knowledge of their own relation' to the world. Dickens therefore takes us beyond the accepted 'Christian' worldview. The narrative aims to make such people 'acquainted with a perversion of nature in their own contracted sympathies and estimates; as great, and yet as natural in its development when once begun, as the lowest degradation known' (739). The battle of life that Dickens tirelessly describes is one that always forces a character to confront an impotence or weakness through which there is a heightened moment of self-regard. Characters and readers are granted the potential to view their own contracted 'sympathies and estimates' and their own 'perversion[s] of nature' and as the 'spark of life' does battle within them, its involuntary energy will reach out to, and involve itself in, the forces of life and death that are directly implicated in this 'unnatural humanity'.

The border point between life and death becomes a favourite moment for Dickens's exploration of how best to embody in narrative this shared humanity. Even in early episodes such as Quilp's death-scene from *The Old Curiosity Shop*, Dickens asks us to re-examine this boundary event as we cross surreptitiously the border between the representation of animated body and corpse in following the narrative of Quilp's drowning. Since neither the narrator nor the reader can know precisely when such a crossing-point is reached, there is a momentary hesitation in the narrative that describes the passing of life. Quilp is rushing in complete darkness to flee his pursuers. His final words to himself, given in reported speech, wish for complete darkness forever: 'If I had but that wish, it might, for anything I cared, never be day again' (510). He then slips into the river and is carried away. The omniscient voice takes up the thread of his final moments: 'For all his struggling and plashing, he could understand that they had lost their way, and had wandered back to the point from which they started; that they were all but looking on while he was drowned' (510). We move via a free indirect style from interior voice to omniscient voice; the passing of life is directing the form of the narrative. The narrative continues: 'Another mortal struggle, and he was up again, beating the water with his hands, and looking out with wild and glaring eyes that showed him some black object he was drifting close upon . . . One loud cry now – but the resistless water bore him down before he could give it utterance, and driving him under it, carried away a corpse' (512). Quilp has now truly passed on. The description of this moment of transition, from *Leib* to *Körper*, as phenomenology might suggest, is fascinating for Dickens. He presses the point home; the body is described as 'ghastly freight' that is carried along in such a way that it tarnishes everything natural it comes in contact with: 'now bruising it against the slimy piles, now hiding it in mud or long rank grass, now dragging it heavily over rough stones and gravel, now feigning to yield it to its own element, in the same action hurrying it away, until, tired of the ugly plaything, it flung it on a swamp' (512). There are few corpses that get such treatment in Dickens. Dickens is clearly exploring how the narration of the moment of life's flickering can grant new potential for bringing readers together around narrative.

However, Dickens is not yet finished with Quilp's corpse; he describes how the dying body maintains a spark of life that marks the natural world in its passing: 'And there it lay, alone. The sky was red with flame, and the water that bore it there had been tinged with the sullen light as it flowed along. The place the deserted carcase had left so recently, a living man, was now a blazing ruin. There was something of the glare upon its face' (512).

The death is described in terms of a 'deserted carcase' leaving a 'living man' and the 'living man' at the point of death is a 'place' from which the 'carcase' departs so as to leave a 'blazing ruin' behind. How are we to understand this departure of the 'carcase' from the 'living man'? Life does not 'leave' the 'carcase' easily; the 'carcase' is yet 'blazing' and there is still something of the 'glare' of life on its face just as there is a 'glare' of life in the form of the narrative that describes this passing. Dickens is clearly examining how the struggle of life and the 'trace' of life can mark both a natural environment and a narrative community.

The Riderhood scene from *Our Mutual Friend* is a more famous instance in Dickens that describes a more successful 'battle' to sustain life. Dickens again alerts the reader to the involuntary power or immanence that manifests itself when the body is somewhere between life and death. Yet the 'spark of life' that is in Riderhood, who has always been an 'object of avoidance' to those who will now rush to help him is, at this point, 'curiously separable from himself now, and they have a deep interest in it, probably because it *is* life, and they are living and must die' (439). The involuntary sense of life resuscitating itself here also works through the form of the narrative. Since Riderhood is struggling in some *lieu vague* and his life is momentarily neither here nor there, Dickens decides not to give us a third-person voice in detailing the work of the doctor and the 'four rough fellows' to resuscitate this life:

> Stay! Did that eyelid tremble? So the doctor, breathing low, and closely watching, asks himself.
> No.
> Did that nostril twitch?
> No.
> This artificial respiration ceasing, do I feel any faint flutter under my hand upon the chest?
> No.
> Over and over again No. No. But try over and over again, nevertheless. See! A token of life! An indubitable token of life! The spark may smoulder and go out, or it may glow and expand, but see! The four rough fellows, seeing, shed tears. Neither Riderhood in this world, nor Riderhood in the other, could draw tears from them; but a striving human soul between the two can do it easily (*Our Mutual Friend*, 440).

The free indirect discourse gives way to what appears to be a rudimentary passage of interior monologue on the part of the doctor. The word 'artificial', however, puts us in mind of the character before our eyes and we then read the section as the musings of the author, Dickens, over whether this character should be killed off. The voice begins like Dickens's customary omniscient voice, which is always slightly moralistic: 'If you are not gone for good, Mr. Riderhood, it would be something to know where you are hiding at present' (439). However, the involuntary nature of the struggle taking place within the 'spark of life' that flickers within the body of Riderhood, brings out in Dickens's narrative a section that resembles an onlooker's interior monologue, its thoughts strung together in seemingly involuntary fashion. In the interior monologue, which typically 'lacks all signs of a narrator's control' (W. J. Lillyman, 47), Dickens is attempting to mirror the involuntary struggle his characters are witnessing: 'This fallby lump of mortality that we work so hard at with such patient perseverance, yields no sign of you' (439). And later: 'This artificial respiration ceasing, do I feel any faint flutter under my hand upon the chest?' Who is speaking here? Is it the doctor, Dickens the author or the universal reader? Is Dickens giving us the author's involuntary thoughts about the pen in 'my hand' upon the desk with its 'chests' of drawers? Dickens may be trying to capture the involuntary narratives of all readers who are so engaged with the struggle at this point that they picture themselves beside the body, pressing its chest. Such a bringing together of interior narratives could then be regarded as an attempt to capture the collective capacity for narration that flows through us all, like life itself, its different strands involuntarily rushing in, losing themselves in the effort to understand how a life can be sustained. The narrative will very quickly take up the third-person voice again when it seems Riderhood is coming to: 'He is struggling to come back'. At this point a sense of omniscience returns to the voice and we have left behind the involuntary energy that it seemed might have taken us anywhere as Riderhood swooned between life and death: 'Now he is struggling harder to get back. And yet – like us all, when we swoon – like us all, every day of our lives when we wake – he is instinctively unwilling to be restored to the consciousness of this existence, and would be left dormant if he could' (440).

Gilles Deleuze's reading of the Riderhood section searches for evidence of 'impersonal life' and immanence in the 'spark of life'. The seed of life he strives to describe must be distinct from 'individual life' that 'remains inseparable from empirical determinations' (2005, 30). Deleuze redefines sensation for his reading as 'only a break within the flow of absolute consciousness' (25); the 'passage' from one sensation to another is described as 'becoming' (25). For Giorgio Agamben, Deleuze wants to see evidence in the episode of a 'state of suspension' which 'cannot be attributed to any subject' (1999, 229). However, Agamben's commentary on Deleuze's reading reminds us that Dickens preferred to refer to the state in question as a state of 'abeyance', a word that originates in legal parlance and 'that indicates the suspension of rules or rights between validity and abrogation' (229). Both writers agree that some essence or spark of life is suddenly 'incarnated' in the battle of life by assuming the mark of a personality. However, whereas Deleuze's and Agamben's philosophical readings focus on '*a* life', Dickens privileges how such a 'spark' is reanimated through a connection with community and with the greater forces of life beyond 'this life'. Deleuze's reading ends with him offering the 'wound' as one of the 'virtuals that define the immanence of the transcendental field' (2001, 32). He focuses on 'virtuals' because, he argues, these are all that '[a] life contains' (31).

However, as we have seen with the description of Quilp's death, and as we know from the various other wounds that weaken other Dickens characters such as John Harmon, Nancy and Stephen Blackpool, it is precisely their 'particular reality' and not their virtuality, even when the life seems unattached and agent-less, that incites the social thinking of Dickens. While Deleuze is right to suggest that Dickens privileges 'the simple moment in which individual life confronts universal death', Dickens also emphasizes how the 'individual life' can find itself involuntarily sustained by a greater current of life. Characters such as Paul and Florence Dombey and Little Nell[5] are connected with this 'river of life'. The battle of life, for Dickens, never seems to lie on 'a threshold beyond good and evil' as Deleuze suggests. Dickens's characters reveal their nature even in their final moments. Each of his characters has a personal history, a history that is grounded on the universality of necessity and responsibility. While Riderhood's 'spark of life' might appear separated from 'good and evil' it is part of a social context, it is a pure expression of need and weakness that calls on a giving from elsewhere. Even though Riderhood may be lost to himself, his spark's struggle with life creates a scene of communal endeavour that strives desperately for the resuscitation of that life.[6] Deleuze argues that his reading 'reintroduces Spinozism into the heart of the philosophical process' (28). However, if we return to Spinoza's *Ethics*, a book that is central for Hardt and Negri's understanding of the 'common', we read that 'power which ordinary people factiously ascribe to God is not only human ... but also involves lack of power' (1996, 34). It is this recognition of 'lack of power' or weakness that, I believe, Dickens never wholly divorces his characters from and it is why, again to use the words of Spinoza, the 'weakness of our bodies or the brutality of the human social condition' require 'sociality and love' for their transformation.

However, many of Dickens's 'death-scenes' describe a death *in* life, what one might refer to as a social death. Characters such as Mr Dombey and Ralph Nickleby turn their backs on a human capacity for goodness and fellow feeling that Dickens at times seems to present as equivalent to the 'breath of life' that leaves a body at death; they become walking dead. In *Dombey and Son* we see how virtue or goodness can provide such a 'spark of life'. An involuntary sense reveals itself to characters at those moments of weakness when the life within them is severely threatened and when fellow feeling is making one last appeal to their vanquished humanity. Mr Dombey's life reveals such a struggle. The scene that describes his train journey with Major Blagstock merges the omniscient description of a character's thoughts with a haunting first-person, involuntary voice. Dombey has just met Mr Toodle and he becomes annoyed at what he perceives as Toodle's presumptuousness in relation to his very private bereavement over his son: 'To think of this presumptuous raker among coals and ashes going on before there, with his sign of mourning! To think that he dared to enter, even by a common show like that, into the trial and disappointment of a proud gentleman's heart!' (*Dombey*, 353). We are very close here to an interior monologue even though the extract's punctuation and slightly mocking tone retains the tinge of an omniscience focalized through a semblance of an interior, untagged voice. However, as Dickens develops the powerful metaphor that relates the indomitable force of death to that of the train and the railway industry in general, Dombey is visited by a series of seemingly involuntary memories that spark a morbid contemplation of death and the future. Once again, the omniscient voice appears to know far too much about Dombey's inner demons to be regarded as an impartial, objective third-person observer: 'The very speed at which the train was whirled along, mocked the swift course of the young life that had been borne away so steadily and so inexorably to its foredoomed end' (354). This sounds very much like the train of Dombey's own inner thoughts. He has become deluded through his grief to the extent that he begins to see the very landscape itself and the course of the train through it as merely a reminder of that other great power that also 'forced itself upon its iron way' (354); namely, 'Death'.

In those episodes where life's struggle to sustain itself is paramount, an involuntary energy manifests itself in the form of the narrative as it tries to mimic either the experience of involuntary memory or an involuntary force of narration that merges the omniscient voice with a character's interior thoughts. Dickens is eager to create for the reader the experience of being completely absorbed by what might be described as an 'involuntary power instinct'. In the passage that describes Dombey's thoughts on the train, the presentation of the struggle requires a seamless merging of tenor and vehicle for the metaphor that relates the progress of the train to death:

> There are jagged walls and falling houses close at hand, and through the battered roofs and broken windows, wretched rooms are seen . . . and deformity of brick and mortar penning up deformity of mind and body, choke the murky distance. As Mr. Dombey looks out of his carriage window, it is never in his thoughts that the monster who has brought him there has let the light of day in on these things: not made or caused them. It was the journey's fitting end, and might have been the end of everything; it was so ruinous and dreary (*Dombey*, 355).

The closing sentences of this extract remind us, in case we have forgotten, that the destructive journey of the railway through the landscape, a journey of death, is a figure for the relentless, by now almost involuntary, journey of ruin and decay through the self-preserving and life-affirming instincts of Mr Dombey. By drawing attention to the shape and design of his own narrative, by explaining for the reader how 'it is never in his thoughts that the monster who has brought him there has let the light of day in on these things', Dickens is also perhaps recognizing the limitations of omniscient and focalized narration for representing an overwhelming involuntary energy in the character. The narrative voice reminds us that 'it is never in his thoughts' that the 'monster' – which the reader must take as representative of the forces of death aligned with the train and now with aspects of Dombey himself – has 'let the light of day in' on how these destructive forces are linked. In other words, Dickens wants to convey how Dombey has begun to embody this realization; he has moved beyond merely acknowledging how the two forces are linked. Dombey's continued efforts to restrain and curtail the forces of love and empathic life within him create an ash-strewn involuntary force that threatens to kill off these preservative forces for good.

The narrative continues to describe Dombey's thoughts: 'All things looked black, and cold, and deadly upon him. He found a likeness to his misfortune everywhere' (355). It is at this point of despair for Dombey, at this point of weakness, when the battle of life is well and truly underway within him, albeit in a very different fashion to that experienced by his son, Riderhood, and Oliver, but in no less a vital fashion, that Dombey's admission that he is finding his own self reflected 'everywhere' throws him into a memory of a vision from the previous night. Dickens is recording in great detail the motivations for a moment of involuntary memory in the character. Just as Dombey begins to 'read his soul' in the blackened and death-stricken landscape surrounding him, he recalls the face of another who had also 'read his soul', the face of his daughter Florence: 'There was a face – he had looked upon it, on the previous night, and it on him with eyes that read his soul, though they were dim with tears, and hidden soon behind two quivering hands – that often had attended him in fancy, on this ride' (355–6). The face of Florence becomes distorted by Dombey since he is giving in to the forces of death within him. The battle of life unleashes an involuntary power within Dombey that is potentially a more destructive force than that which threatened Oliver and Riderhood, since it leads to death in life. The close detailing of the transition taking place within Dombey enables the reader to throw off the impression that he or she is only getting his thoughts secondhand. The movement from the realization that the blackened landscape is a reflection of the self to the setting up of Florence's face as the symbol for all this destructive energy describes a personal journey that the reader now feels only Dombey could truly know. The reader becomes alert to the involuntary power of narrative itself to mediate personal experience and to instantiate the potential for empathy[7] and fellow feeling. Dombey's refusal to give in to what the involuntary forces from within are telling him – namely, that the face that now 'was abroad', the face of Florence, the face that has usurped the 'likeness to his misfortune' which he found 'everywhere', is a face of love and not a face of destruction – speaks for the perils of misreading how narrative can reconnect us with the social context through a careful reflection on the relevance of the signs and symbols we find in the landscape and even in the face of the other.

We then return to an omniscient voice: 'Because he knew full well, in his own breast, as he stood there, tinging the scene of transition before him with the morbid colours of his own mind, and making it a picture of decay, instead of hopeful change, and promise of better things, that life had quite as much do with his complainings as death' (356). Dombey's morbid thoughts have run roughshod over his contemplation of life and death. The influence of his 'complainings' have become larger than the forces of death themselves, and the narrative integral to 'complainings' brings with it a *telos* of decay rather than any prospect of 'hopeful change'. Dombey is fragile here but life's core struggle within him has not taken him to the confessional state of Paul Dombey or Oliver Twist. He has retained too much of his former self, a former self that is possibly only ever fully thrown off when, like Paul and Oliver, we are at death's door, both physically and mentally, and when the habits of life have not yet marked us indelibly.

Dombey is unwilling to get to the bottom of the visions of death that surround him or to understand the 'expression of defeat and persecution that seemed to encircle him like the air' (356). His worldview is unwilling to admit to any kind of defeat. The feeling of darkness and urgency rising within him is 'too strong for his composure', and with the involuntary forces that then overtake him he searches desperately for something that 'he could interpose between himself and it' (356). In his despair the involuntary powers of life point him in the right direction. They direct him to the vision of the one face that can restore the powers of life to him in the form of 'hopeful change, and promise of better things' and he uses the face, the face of Florence, as a battering ram to charge down the remaining elements of life within him, rather than as a springboard to an engagement with the 'spark of life' doing battle within.

It is the vision of this face that haunts Dombey throughout the remainder of the narrative. Frequently, when Dombey's most destitute moments are being described, an omniscient voice, like the voice of some universal narrative presence or a Greek chorus, interrupts with the refrain: 'Let him remember it in that room, years to come!' (934). It refers to the moment in Dombey's study when, after Paul's death, Florence 'urged on by the love within her' (327) approached him to console him and to seek some sign of love from him. Dombey does not give in to the forces of life within him; he cannot accept his human frailty so he clings to his floundering worldview and rejects the love expressed in his daughter's face. The reader now has the sense that the narrative is describing an involuntary energy that narration can sustain, an energy made manifest on occasion in the novel through the vision of the golden ripples of running water seen by Paul at his death and in the voices from the 'mighty sea' and the 'swift river' of life at the end of the novel, which are echoed by James Joyce's own descriptions of life at the end of the *Wake*. It is an involuntary energy that acts as a preservative for the life forces Dickens rarely extinguishes completely in his novels. The refrain 'let him remember' and the involuntary current it embodies returns when Dombey's life has become inanimate to the narrator and Dombey contemplates putting an end to what remains. Catching his 'haggard, wasted likeness' in a mirror, Dombey becomes obsessed by the image, which goes on to haunt his actions. From this point until his resurrection in the arms of Florence, Dombey has died to the narrator who describes him as an 'it': 'It was quiet and unmindful, and sat thinking. Suddenly it rose, with a terrible face, and that guilty hand grasping what was in its breast' (939). In a supreme act of subjugation, Dickens appears to rescue a character intent on his own destruction with what he presents as the involuntary force of the narrative of life. Dombey has become the agent-less energy Deleuze assigns to the immanence of '*a* life', but his desperate struggle reveals how consciousness itself may incur a worse death than any 'virtual' wound might. Florence, who embodies the involuntary restorative force in the novel, is the medium for reanimating the character: 'Unchanged still. Of all the world, unchanged. Raising the same face to his, as on that miserable night. Asking *his* forgiveness!' (939). The face that the narrative has warned he will remember against all odds is the embodiment of a life force that Dickens foregrounds in the novel and it is the life force of narration itself.

While Dickens's representation of the involuntary charges implicit in narrative is bound up with the return to community and with the responsibilities even a 'spark of life' can elicit, the later modernist narratives of Proust, on the other hand, will channel these forces inwards, enabling the reader to get at the roots of an involuntary energy that transcends time. Proust enables the 'spark of life' of a community of readers to be reanimated through life as memory, while Dickens never lets the spark forget the 'unnatural humanity' and the 'common' about him. If narrative is still regarded as enabling of greater ethical awareness by granting readers a 'knowledge of their own relation' (*Dombey*, 739) to the world, then it is the involuntary energies that Dickens records which most evocatively describe this relation with the 'common' in nineteenth-century narrative.

Chapter 9

'Words of Silent Power': Joyce, Kindness and 'Life's High Carnage of Semperidentity'

Margot Norris, one of the most distinguished readers of *Finnegans Wake*, recognized nearly forty years ago that the 'conservative, novelistic approach' to the *Wake* which had 'dominated *Wake* criticism' for the previous 'thirty years' had a serious 'limitation'; this 'limitation . . . is most evident in its lack of progress toward establishing clearly the intellectual orientation of the work' ('The Consequences of Deconstruction', 1974, 131). In order to offer a way forward, Norris chooses to align Joyce's work with that of Jacques Derrida, whose work was only then being incorporated into literary studies. Both Joyce and Derrida, Norris argues, put forward 'destructive discourses of the twentieth century which are engaged in the destruction of the history of metaphysics' (144). This 'destruction' 'breaks down language' by a 'mode of literary violence'; Joyce is an artist who works by 'deconstructing the language and literary traditions', (147) by making presence 'unlocatable' and by 'severing words from their referents' (138) which 'marks the disjunction of word from meaning' (139). The 'fall of the father' – HCE's fall – is the event which sets off this destructive and violent process of deconstruction and 'severing' in the *Wake*. The theme of 'the fallen father', Norris argues, has significant psychological and 'linguistic repercussions' (137).

The psychological motif of the 'fall of the father' is often regarded as epitomizing human weakening. Norris argues that the fall announces the 'severing of word from referent'; 'the Wakean proposition' holds 'that the voice of God, the voice of the father . . . is the sound of thunder, and that the thunder announces the father's fall with noise'. We are left, then, with a kind of babbling, but these babbles are symbolic: 'Both babble, the first speech of the infant man, and thunder, the first word of God to postlapsarian man, represent sound without meaning or signification' (139). In other words, the destruction and violence give way to a new dawn for language where the 'infant man' and 'the first word of God to postlapsarian man' are 'without meaning'. The creator of a 'destructive discourse' can imitate this process by recognizing that even though 'he cannot do without . . . his debt to language and literature' – which 'he seeks to oppose' – he must present the reader with a stream of cacophonous verbiage that is without 'significa-tion' and that lets 'the staleness out of' language (146), to borrow a quota-tion from William Carlos Williams. For Norris, the 'theme of the fallen father' is paralleled in the work by a process that 'calls for phonological and syntactical deviations from the norm of standard English' (141). As we look back now on Norris's reading, one of the first to describe a 'deconstructive Joyce', which would become an influential version of Joyce for Joyce Studies in general, it is important to reappraise the claims being made for Joyce's *Wake*. With the full weight of the Derridean scholarship produced in the interim now in our critical armory, I want to examine how we can distance 'the orientation of the work [the *Wake*]' from the 'violence' and 'destruc-tion' Norris foregrounds.

The *Wake* may well be full of linguistic 'junk' that is washed away in the 'liffeyism' (614.25)[1] of Joyce's words, but the 'destructive' work that is seen by Norris and others to work by way of 'literary violence' (147) is only part of what the *Wake* describes and is not expressive of the 'intellectual orienta-tion of the work'. The closing sections of the *Wake* privilege a feminine 'flesh-without-word' (468.6) that provides motivation for the future of lan-guage. Joyce also suggests that his language works by way of 'words of silent power' (345.19) that are not caught up with noise and violence but, instead, accommodate the falls and weaknesses of man while moving ever closer as the work progresses to the workaday tasks of a feminist and feminizing 'liffeyism' as presence.

Joyce does not give us any typical 'heroes'. However, Joyce's examination of human weakness is often difficult to swallow. It's far easier to build his formal and technical 'mastery' into a structural, post-structural or decon-structive android where the machinations of form and structure fill the void created by his 'words of silent power'. *Ulysses* gives us Leopold Bloom, a cuckold made to come to grips with impotence and inadequacy. These con-cerns are developed in the *Wake* where character is essentially killed off and where writing itself, or the Word, must be made to exhibit its weakness or 'silent power'. If Joyce was concerned with showing up human frailties and weaknesses, then what might it mean for him to assign such attributes to language? Following the era of the 'violence of the sign', what might it mean for signification or the word to be weak? Gilles Deleuze argues that 'truth is never the product of a preliminary goodwill, but a result of a vio-lence in thought',[2] and elsewhere that 'thought is primarily trespass and violence'.[3] However, the earlier explorations of weakness have shown that an ability to abide by the weak in the full acceptance of human fragility lies at the heart of any violence we might perceive in sign or system.

It is easy to be a bully when one has no chance of getting hurt and in the same way it is easy to privilege a violent sign when it has no chance of bruising flesh. As W. B. Yeats, Joyce's one time moneylender, reminds us: 'Labour is blossoming or dancing when the Body is not bruised to pleasure soul'; the true labour of sign-making does not need to bruise the 'body', and what kind of violence do we have without the body? Joyce speaks for such sign-making in the *Wake*, his 'tetradomational gazebocroticon'. The emotional and physiological weakness that writing mediates in the era of the 'rupture in the lines of communication' is not only the result of a 'destructive discourse'. As we have seen, Derrida also speaks of his own 'destructive discourse' in terms of a 'break' that 'uses the strengths of the field to turn its own stratagems against it, producing a force of dislocation that spreads itself throughout the entire system fissuring it in every direction and thoroughly *delimiting* it [Derrida's emphasis]' (*Writing and Difference*, 2002, 22). However, the break, rupture or destructive discourse is a symptom of a general perception that received styles are inadequate for describing and enlivening further truths about experience. Any psychology that teaches a primary 'fall of the father' acknowledges that destruction, self-harm or trauma are the result of repressions that we have not counselled into expression. Even the piercing primal scream announces our originary inadequacy for a life of myths. Is it possible to understand the destruction, the self-harm, the body trauma – even for the body without organs – without unweaving the waves of emotional and physiological struggle that the destruction speaks for and veils?

To think that a 'force of weakness' must be overcome and confronted through violence may only be a result of believing in a violence of the sign. Derrida again tells us in 'Violence and Metaphysics' that 'even though language in its "original possibility as offer [or gift]" is non-violent', there is no phrase which 'does not pass through the violence of the concept' (2001, 185). I want to look further into Joyce's gift of weakness that also merges non-violence, silent power and a degree of kindness. If weakness, as we have seen, is revealing of an affirmative potential or energy that might commonly be regarded as a 'strength', then the dialectical or reciprocal nature of the metaphysical opposition strength/weakness is made ever more apparent. However, since this dialectic is typically engaged with in writing through a system of representation that is already perceived by influential Western theories of signification as 'violent', then it is already too late for the representation of weakness.

Even though Joyce begins the *Wake* with a thunderous 'fall of the father' that strives to wash away all that the Law of the Father or the phallogocentric tradition has erected, it is the 'plainplanned liffeyism', those eternally lapping waters that wash around the man-made constructs, including language, that the book's closing sections privilege because they will 'carry on my hearz'waves my still waters reflections in words' (460.25–6). Joyce looks forward to a 'flesh-without-word', (468.6) a word untainted by a mythic male fall or sacrifice that has been buoyed up by a 'tootoological' (468.8) male 'soapbox speech' (469.30) approach to language that has misunderstood the 'flesh' and misrepresented the body. The fall is only so catastrophic because man has built himself up to such a state; he has made a song and dance out of his weakness because he has misunderstood the body in the first place. Joyce wants HCE to start 'self-righting the balance of his corporeity' (471.5–6) and to make a 'brand-new start for himself' (471.10–11)

Even at the level of thought-characters, Joyce can be regarded as sharing with Dickens a desire to speak for the downtrodden in society. From the washerwomen who cry '[s]corching my hand and starving my famine to make his private linen public' (196.15–16) to the Christ-like HCE who claims '[t]hough I heave a coald on my bauck and am could up to my eres hoven sametimes I used alltides to be aswarmer for *the meekest* and the graced [my emphasis]' (365.12–15), there is the sense that overlooked toil and effort is being acknowledged and that the one-time saviour HCE attempts to become weak like his disciples. We are reminded of Paul's first letter to the Corinthians: 'to the weak I became weak, to win the weak'. (1 Corinthians 9:22). In some of the more autobiographical sections, the voice of Shaun as Yawn also details the 'respectable' and weaker members of society the writer and the 'carrier of the word' hopes to speak for: 'as respectable as respectable can respectable be, . . . all, let them all come, they are my villeins [veins/villains], with chartularies I have talledged [puns tillaged] them. Hereto my vouchers, knive and snuff buchs. Fee for farm. Enwreak us wrecks' (545.11–23). There is almost a plea here for all to share in this 'enwreak[ing]' so all can be weak or become 'wrecks'. Joyce as Shaun and then Yawn lists the 'wrecks' he is writing for. They include:

[W]hole family attends mass and is dead sick of bread and butter, . . . wageearner freshly shaven from prison . . . house lost in dirt and blocked with refuse . . . slovenly wife active with the jug . . . bangs kept woman's head against wall thereby disturbing neighbours . . . eccentric navel officer not quite steady enjoys weekly churchwarden and laugh while reading foreign pictorials on clumpstump before door, . . . widow rheumatic . . .

serious student is eating his last dinners . . . man has not had boots off for twelvemonths, infant being taught to hammer flat piano . . . wife cleans stools . . . ottawark and regular loafer . . . harmless imbecile supposedly weakminded . . . . (*Wake*, 543.15–544.28)

But what is the motivation for Joyce the artist and the Christ-like HCE to speak for such people? For Joyce the word is heavily involved with the body. It is now a given of Joyce scholarship that he privileges embodiment; Frank Budgen reminds us how Joyce described *Ulysses* as '[a]mong other things . . . the epic of the human body . . . In my book the body lives in and moves through space and is the home of a full human personality' (1960, 21). As we know from his letters, Joyce also referred to himself and Nora as 'one flesh'; and in the *Wake* Nora is his '*life in death companion* [Joyce's italics]' (201.8). The frailty he explores allows for a giving that results in a potential for a more wholesome union. HCE recalls the love for ALP: 'And I cast my tenspan joys on her . . . so streng we were in one, malestream in shegulf' (547.30–3). Because the giving between the two parties is so mutual, any loss that is suffered is also a greater loss for the unit. HCE is also well aware that one must prepare oneself for disappointments and for the 'agenbite of inwit' of self-doubt and self-recrimination; but Joyce confronts the origins and metaphysics of weakness and self-reproach head on so as to learn from the experience:

> 'We have to had them whether we'll like it or not. . . . Scant hope their or ours to escape life's high carnage of semperidentity by subsisting pease-meal upon variables. Bloody certainly have we got to see to it ere smellful demise surprends us on this concrete that down the gullies of the eras we may catch ourselves looking forward to what will in no time be staring you larrikins on the postface in that multimirror megaron of returningties, whirled without end to end' (582.13–21).

In fact HCE and ALP and the Everyman and Everywoman they represent are so intertwined and so 'co-mixed' that HCE pleads with readers to listen to his 'better half': 'All that is still life with death inyeborn, all verbumsaps yet bound to be, to do and to suffer, every creature, everywhere, if you please, kindly feel for her! While the dapplegray dawn drags nearing nigh for to wake all droners that drowse in Dublin' (585.17–21).

But how does this thematic weakness extend to a weak language or a weakness of the word? Writing in the *Wake* itself is very often described in terms of the weakening of the body. The voice of the *Wake* opines: 'I will write down all your names in my gold pen and ink. Everyday, precious,

while m'n'ry's leaves are falling deeply on my Jungfraud's Messongebook I
will dream telepath posts dulcets on this isinglass stream . . . 'twill carry on
my hearz'waves my still waters reflections in words' (460.18–26). And later
we hear of 'the leabhour of my generations ['leabhour' connotes both
labour and *leabhar*, the Irish for 'book']' (484.29–30). But perhaps most
dramatic is a passage very close to the end where writing is portrayed in
terms of the bodily process Clive Hart describes by way of anastomosis:

> Our wholemole millwheel vicociclometer, a tetradomational gazebocroti-
> con . . . receives through a portal vein the dialytically separated elements
> of precedent decomposition for the verypetpurpose of subsequent recom-
> bination so that heroticisms, catastrophes and eccentricities transmitted
> by the ancient legacy / of the past, type by tope, letter from litter, word at
> ward . . . , all, anastomosically assimilated and preteridentified paraidioti-
> cally, . . . , may be there for you. (*Wake*, 614.27–615.8)

The passage describes how the Joycean intertext, the 'vicociclometer', or
the *Wake* itself is like a body in receiving 'through a portal vein' the archive's
decomposed elements. These elements then, in the shape of 'heroticisms,
catastrophes and eccentricities', aspects that privilege a body's desires and
weaknesses, are once again offered up in the intertext to the next reader.

Joyce describes the gains to be made from an acknowledgement and
engagement with weakness. ALP, Joyce's Everywoman, is first seen in a traditional role as encourager and supporter (as Virginia Woolf might suggest,
ALP is part of a tradition in which '[w]omen have served all these centuries
as looking-glasses possessing the magic and delicious power of reflecting
the figure of man as twice its natural size' [1996, 33]): 'Away! Rise up, man
of the hooths [sounds very like 'house' in a Dublin accent], you have slept
so long!' (619.25–6) . . . Rise up now and aruse! . . . I am leafy, your golden,
so you called me, may me life, yea your golden, silve me solve, . . . But there's
a great poet in you too. (619.28–32) . . . And stand up tall! Straight. I want
to see you looking fine for me. With your brandnew big green belt and all.
Blooming in the very lotust and second to nill, Budd!' (620.1–3). We see
how the husband and wife confidences reveal a concern for shared admissions of weakness that recalls the maternal, the first salvage for many weaknesses. ALP is willing to ignore faults and again she assumes a somewhat
traditional gendered pose. She tells HCE:

> I always know by your brights and shades. Reach down. A lil mo. So. Draw
> back your glave [glove]. Hot and hairy, hugon, is your hand! Here's where

the falskin [foreskin/false-skin – is Joyce intimating here that falsity – the 'falskin' – begins with a sexual life built on 'Hot and hairy, hugon[s]'?]. Smoos as an infams. One time you told you'd been burnt in ice. And one time it was chemicalled after you taking a lifeness. Maybe that's why you hold your hodd [head] as if. (*Wake*, 621.23–8)

ALP sees the weakness beneath the 'hugon'. She then reveals that HCE may not have fallen because he 'missed the scaffold'; it was not the scaffold that was of 'fell design', but rather HCE himself:

And people thinks you missed the scaffold. Of fell design. I'll close my eyes. So not to see [she is willingly blind to his weaknesses]. Or see only a youth in his florizel, a boy in innocence, peeling a twig, a child beside a weenywhite steed. The child we all love to place our hope in for ever. All men has done something. Be the time they've come to the weight of old flesch. We'll lave it. (*Wake*, 621.28–33)

Joyce acknowledges that all men have 'done something' by the time 'they've come to the weight of old flesch' but he gives us room for hoping that it does not need to be recognized as 'something' only by first announcing itself as a catastrophic fall.

In the closing sections, both ALP's and HCE's voices seem to be drowned out by a more elemental voice that embeds them both in its 'silent power' and that tries to speak for the weakness in all and for the shared natural inclination to fall: 'Be happy, dear ones! May I be wrong! For she'll be sweet for you as I was sweet when I came down out of me mother. . . . It's something fails us. First we feel. Then we fall. [627.7–11] How small it's all! And me letting on to meself always. And lilting on all the time. . . . I thought you the great in all things, in guilt and in glory. You're but a puny. Home! [627.21–5] Loonely in my loneless. For all their faults. I am passing out' [627.34]. The voice that announces 'First we feel. Then we fall' is once again mistaken; it presumes HCE would be 'great in all things' but he has proved 'but a puny'.

The voice that swirls around ALP will ultimately become a voice that succumbs to a metaphorics of weakness before the male presence that she asks to 'carry me along'. She describes the second coming of this fraught hero saying that she would do the same again so they could both fall together 'humbly dumbly' in a process of self-giving: 'If I seen him bearing down on me now under whitespread wings like he'd come from Arkangels, I sink I'd die down over his feet, humbly dumbly, only to washup. Yes, tid. Whish! A gull. Gulls. Far calls. Coming, far! End here. Us then. Finn again! Take. Bussoftlhee, mememormee! Till thousandsthee. Lps. The keys to. Given!' (628.9–15). Language is asked to bear the burden of a 'silent' and non-violent power in Joyce. By formally combining a thematic concern for weakness and a polyglossic subtlety of expression that recognizes that no language is autonomous, Joyce seeks to restore this 'silent power' to language. At times he seems to yearn for a writing that would leave no trace whatsoever behind – 'Leave the letter that never begins to go find the latter that ever comes to end, written in smoke and blurred by mist and signed of solitude, sealed at night' (337.11–14) – and it is a writing that is all the richer for its silent power.

There is another sense of weakness that Joyce might also be regarded as responding to in *Finnegans Wake*. In their book *On Kindness* Adam Phillips and Barbara Taylor chart a history of kindness. They explain that 'modern kindness' must be about being 'able to imaginatively identify with other people, and allow them to identify with us' (2009, 97). Even though Phillips and Taylor acknowledge that 'real kindness' is 'the ability to bear the vulnerability of others, and therefore of oneself', they also recognize that shows of such kindness are now regarded as 'a sign of weakness' (6). They argue that '[i]t is now generally assumed that people are basically selfish, and that fellow feeling is either a weakness or a luxury' (50). What happens, then, is that kindness, as we shall see in Joyce, becomes unreal, it becomes 'something that we are nostalgic about'; we have a longing for 'something that we fear may not really exist'. We even see kindness now as a 'cover story' 'for an ingeniously ruthless self-interest' (51).

Joyce, famous for his 'scrupulous meanness', avoids repetition at all costs in this sprawling, polyglossic work and yet his emotions may have got the better of him on at least one occasion. In Book II Joyce repeats, almost verbatim, in the space of eleven pages, a five-word phrase that hinges on the word 'kind'. In a section that satirizes the evangelical style of passing on life-stories, Joyce's revitalized evangelists Luke Tarpey, Marcus Lyons, Matt Gregory and Johnny MacDougall are reminiscing on 'bygone times'. However, in being Joycean evangelists they are also connected with the very beginning of language and 'the word' since in their 'bygone days' they were one with 'Nush, the carrier of the word, and with Mesh, the cutter of the reed [Nush and Mesh may be Joycean archetypes for the first oral poets and the first writers]' (385.6). A yearning for the origins of language and for youthful days that have passed are interlinked in this section. Joyce is deliberately conflating kindness and nostalgia; he is implying that real kindness, the kindness that can be passed on in story, should not become bound up with nostalgia and with the kind of nostalgic narratives of his revitalized evangelists. The underlying meaning may be that the real Evangelists' story of divine kindness as sacrifice in the scriptures has unleashed an equally nostalgic regard for kindness in narrative in general. By formally moving away from his evangelists' style of storytelling to that of the monologues of HCE and ALP in the final sections of *Finnegans Wake*, Joyce is attempting to throw off the influences of this powerful Christian narrative of kindness, sacrifice and redemption.

The human attribute that is most yearned for from this time of origins is kindness. The omniscient narrative voice that begins the section by describing the 'four' relates how they yearn for 'a cup of kindness yet' (386.9) associated with these times. The phrase 'a cup of kindness yet' comes from the Robert Burns song of 1788 'auld Lang Syne' ('we'll tak a cup o' kindness yet,/for auld lang syne'). Joyce aligns the nostalgia associated with drinking to old acquaintances and bygone times with his evangelists' reminiscing on days of their youth before language had been assigned to a Christian narrative and before the Word had become Flesh; the old stories and the fog of nostalgia that quickly surrounds them are always liable to become archetypes for a kindness that is forever lodged in the past. Joyce's monologues will shake us out of this 'sentimental' regard for kindness. Kindness has become representative of what their nostalgia for past times rekindles. They remember back to times of 'kindness' when the 'heart knew no care' (387.21–2).

After the four Joycean evangelists have finished making their reports, the omniscient voice returns to comment on their work: 'they were always counting and contradicting every night' (393.19–20); their gossip on the exploits of HCE and ALP has them 'hacking away at a parchment pied' (395.4). The voice begins to try to extricate itself from the authority that it traces to the Evangelists so that HCE and ALP can go on and speak for themselves in the following books and perhaps regain once more that 'cup of kindness yet' in the present. The evangelists eventually morph into ALP and HCE and we are caught up in a reminiscing on married life that is also a reminiscing on the Word and all words before language was made Flesh in the way that the Evangelists helped propagate. The reconciliation of the evangelists then begins to sound like the reconciliation of old lovers and HCE asks this time 'for a cup of kindest yet',[4] returning again to a nostalgia that is now almost synonymous with what is kind.

Towards the end of the evangelists' section we eavesdrop on a love-scene between a 'modern old ancient Irish prisscess' (396.7–8) and a somewhat worse for wear lover. The *Wake* is now seen to be revealing of what is described here as 'joysis crisis'. We recall Leopold Bloom and his own 'limp father of thousands' or his 'languid floating flower' (*Ulysses*, 107). We also recall how with his impotence he is envious of possessors '[o]f a bodily and mental male organism specially adapted for the superincumbent posture of energetic human copulation and energetic piston and cylinder movement necessary for the complete satisfaction of a constant but not acute concupiscence resident in a bodily and mental female organism, passive but not obtuse' (864). This concern is returned to in the *Wake*, and on this instance the passage describes a love scene between an older male lover, possibly HCE, and 'this, wellyoumaycallher, a strapping modernold ancient Irish prisscess' (396.7–8). She appears to be leading proceedings and the man is made to realize that his 'wildy' days are long behind him. The 'prisscess' is 'so and so hands high, such and such paddock weight, in her madapolam smock, nothing under her hat but red hair and solid ivory (now you know it's true in your hardup hearts!)' (396.8–11) and she possesses a 'firstclass pair of bedroom eyes, of most unhomy blue, (*how weak we are, one and all!*) [my emphasis]' (396.11–12). It is during this love scene that the voice alerts us to 'how weak we are, one and all'. The weakness of the older male lover is described in great detail: 'Could you blame her, we're saying, for one psocoldlogical moment! What would Ewe do? With that so tiresome old milkless a ram, with his tiresome duty peck and his bronchial tubes, the tiresome old hairyg orangogran beaver, in his tiresome old twennysixandpenny sheopards plods drowsers and his thirtybobandninepenny tails plus toop!' (396.13–18).

One begins to understand why the scribes are yearning for 'bygone times' and a 'cup of kindness'. When the narrative voice can take no more of this secondhand reportage of the second-rate evangelists, it bids them adieu and moves on to the monologues of HCE and ALP: 'The way is free. Their lot is cast. So, to john for a johnajeams [John-a-dreams (*Hamlet*, II.2.295): generic for a 'dreamy fellow'], led it be!' (399.35–6).[5] These recollections and calls for kindness satirize exegesis and the formal techniques of the real Evangelists. Each Joycean evangelist can be regarded as revealing different aspects of HCE. Unlike scripture's record of Jesus's life, any report on HCE always possesses an autobiographical strain – one also found in Shem's portrait – that makes him out to be less of a preacher than a poet.

What is the nature of the kindness then that lies in the 'bygone times' of the Joycean narrative? If literature can teach kindness and virtue as writers such as Martha Nussbaum and Alasdair McIntyre suggest, why does Joyce have the evangelists, the first and most influential Christian writers, lamenting that their own reports on HCE have distanced them from kindness? Is

Joyce implying that narrative authority as inherited from the evangelists has instituted a form of writing that cannot describe the 'cup of kindness/kindest' that is now as remote as the origins of language itself or as distant as the days of early childhood? Joyce may be suggesting that religion has corrupted the original acts of kindness described by the evangelists even though they sought to share the kindness of Jesus with others. Phillips and Taylor would support such a view. They argue that 'post-Augustinian Christianity' suppressed the 'joyous element in pro-kindness' and that kindness then became 'disastrously' linked 'to self-sacrifice'; 'Christian morality had long been at odds with natural human impulses' (2009, 26). Joyce's satirical treatment of Christian kindness leads him to a concern for kindness that only polyglossia, protmanteau words and monologue can ultimately describe, a form unavailable to the evangelists.

Phillips and Taylor argue for an 'unromantic kindness' that 'encourages a feeling of aliveness as compatible with, indeed integral to, a feeling of vulnerability' (116). Joyce's kindness is similar; however, as with most themes in *Finnegans Wake*, kindness, giving and the vulnerabilities they draw from and reveal are described in such mock-heroic terms that they are sometimes difficult to disentangle from the swirl of 'jetsam litterage of convolvuli' (292.16). HCE is conscious of being kind to ALP. He is even the one to teach her, albeit in a Dublin accent, the lovers' alphabet: 'I did learn my little ana countrymouse in alphabeater cameltemper, from alderbirk to tannenyou, with myraw rattan atter dundrum; ooah, oyir, oyir, oyir' (553.2–4). The passing on of language is the most enduring act of kindness. The extent of HCE's kindness, incorporating an autobiographical trace, expands into a ridiculous and all-encompassing giving: 'I laid down before the trotters [at her feet] to my eblantine [the eglantine rose or honeysuckle is often regarded as a symbol for generosity] my stony battered waggonways, my nordsoud circulums [Stonybatter Street and North Circular Road are Dublin street names], my eastmoreland and westlandmore [Eastmoreland and Westmoreland Street are also Dublin street names]' (553.28–31). Joyce therefore describes a kindness between lovers that gives from all sides of the known universe; Dublin street names denote the cardinal directions. Such kindness seems eager to give up even boundary markers since the gifts that mark the four corners of the earth are 'laid down' at her feet or 'trotters'. Joyce exaggerates kindness beyond all recognition before introducing an enduring version of interpersonal kindness in the later sections of *Finnegans Wake*. Such kindness confounds all estimations of ownership and personal property.

Joyce gives us moments from everyday life that remind us to acknowledge our vulnerabilities. His heroes have all seen better days: 'How he used to

hold his head as high as a howeth, the famous eld duke alien, with a hump
of grandeur like a walking wiesel rat' (197.2–4). Joyce is also aware that by
sharing vulnerabilities and weaknesses in this monologic, semi-autobiographical yet polyglossic text, by 'contemplating of myself' for 'relieving
purposes', as he puts it, that the historically and typically manly, phallogocentric or virile statement of self, what he describes as a 'trurally virvir
vergitable (garden)', can be disowned. There is the sense here that the
typically manly confessional exercise connoted by 'virvir' (*vir* is Latin for
man) and 'vergitable' (*verge* is French for penis) can be thrown off through
a painful internal struggle:

> [A]m entrenched up contemplating of myself, wiz my naked I, for reliev-
> ing purposes in our trurally virvir vergitable (garden) I sometimes, . . . a
> wake from this or huntsfurwards, with some shock (shell I so render it?)
> have (when I ope my shylight window and I see coocoo) a notion quiet
> involuptary of that I am cadging hapsnots as at murmurrandoms of dis-
> tend renations from ficsimilar phases or dugouts in the behindscenes of
> our earthwork. (*Wake*, 357–8.33–4)

One of the possible readings here is that the voice's contemplation of its
'naked I', something that it does through a 'shylight', or shyly, suddenly
feels that it is being connected seemingly involuntarily but sensually with
snapshots and memories or memorandums ('murmurrandoms') of similar
'phases' of half-fictional 'distant renations' (which puns nationals, relations
and the bodily [through 'renal']). In other words, the narrative voice
describes, in great detail, new dimensions of embodied vulnerability (he is
'naked' and peering through a 'shylight') thereby expanding the range of
what can be shared. There is also a thematics of warfare running through
this section on self-contemplation, signalling how difficult the process of
sharing is, a process that may even lead to hatred in the form of self-loathing.
The washerwomen in the *Wake* also talk about the pain of revealing all:
'Scorching my hand and starving my famine to make his private linen public' (196.16–17). In the above section, we have the theme of mental warfare
revealed through 'trenches', 'dugouts', the notion of hunting forwards –
'huntsfurwards' – and also the section 'shock [shell' which puts us in mind
of shellshock and trauma.

The effort to reveal all and admit to weakness in a supreme act of self-
giving that provides a ground for further acts of kindness is also connected
with the painful reliving of memories. Joyce nicely puns the pain of memory
in the book by referring to memories as 'maimeries [memories that maim]'

(348.7)[6] and by describing the lessons of experience as the 'lessions of expe-rience [lesson/lesion]' (436.20–1). In a section on the pain of acknowledg-ing what memories reveal, the narrative voice describes how '[b]etween me rassociations in the postleadeny [*postleden* is Pan-Slavonic for 'last'; also 'lead' suggests weighty][7] past and me disconnections with aplompervious futules [*plombe* is French for 'lead', again suggesting weighty; futures] I've a boodle ['lot' and 'book'] full of maimeries in me buzzim [bosom] and medears [puns 'mothers' and 'murders'] runs sloze [*sloze* is Serbian for 'agree'; also puns 'sleaze' and 'slows'] bleime [blimey!], as I now with pla-toonic leave recoil [recall] in (how the thickens they come back to one to rust! [roost])' (348.5–9). Joyce may be ironically quipping here how con-temporary psychoanalytic theories of memory grant him a 'platonic leave' to 'recoil' from as well as to recall memories involving loved ones ('medears'). However, the voice acknowledges how difficult it is to keep the nostalgia of the autobiographical at bay in this monologic narrative; the 'maimeries' keep coming 'home to rust! [puns 'roost']'. The narrative voice explains on one occasion that it does hope that the *Work in Progress* will be read widely and that it will serve an 'edifying' mission: the voice 'augur[s] in the hurry of the times that it will cocommend the widest circulation and a reputation coextensive with its merits when inthrusted into safe and pious hands upon so edifying a mission as it, I can see, as is his' (356.27–30).

In a late section where we have HCE speaking through a character called Yawn, we also hear HCE describing his charitable actions: 'In the humanity of my heart I sent out heyweywomen [highwaywoman] to refresh/the ball-wearied [puns a Sisyphean struggle men promote and sexual intercourse] and then, . . . my great great greatest of these charities, devaleurised the base fellows for the curtailment of their lower man' (542.35–543.3). The 'lower man', then, must be respected and must not be curtailed. This is what HCE describes as his greatest charity or kindness. In what sounds like a prayer to humanity, to all and sundry, the section ends with the plea 'Enwreak us wrecks'. It seems to be asking that all must be enwreaked or enlivened in some way to a new level of 'wreckage' or vulnerability; 'us wrecks' have to be enwreaked so that we fully acknowledge our 'lower man', experience our wrecked state and share it with 'heirs'.

ALP's monologue describes the value of vulnerability for story: 'Humbly to fall and cheaply to rise, exposition of failures. . . . As on one generation tells another' (589.17). The writer imparts him- or herself to this genera-tional retelling by allowing readers to share in the 'exposition of failures'. And in returning to that late section on anastomosis, it can be read as describing a self-giving in narrative grounded on an acknowledgement of vulnerability. We read how life lived as a 'plainplanned liffeyism [both a common life and a life beside the River Liffey in Dublin]' recognizes the pain of remembering from 'ever sides' so that '[o]ur wholemole millwheel vicociclometer [Joyce has a strong interest in Vico's notion of the recurring cycle of history], . . . receives through a portal vein the dialytically separated elements of precedent decomposition for the verypetpurpose of subsequent recombination so that heroticisms, catastrophes and eccentricities transmitted by the ancient legacy/of the past, type by tope, letter from litter, word at ward . . . may be there for you' (614–15.27–8). Joyce recognizes that the writer has a unique responsibility to transmit the whole human cycle of 'heroticisms, catastrophes and eccentricities' to the reader without sentimentality so there can be a spirit of 'intercommunication' that sustains kindness.

Chapter 10

Beckett and the 'Authentic Weakness of Being'[1]

Samuel Beckett once told Lawrence Harvey that, for him, 'art had commonly been thought of as a sign of strength'; he said that in his art he wanted to explore what he called 'the authentic weakness of being' (Knowlson & Haynes, 2003, 16). Harvey also recounts in *Samuel Beckett: Poet and Critic* how Beckett regarded French as representing '*a form of weakness*' compared with his mother tongue (1970, 196). Pascale Casanova's more recent study, *Samuel Beckett: Anatomy of a Literary Revolution*, explores what she describes as a 'syntax of weakness' (2006, 95) in Beckett, and Steven Connor finds a similar 'fragility of language' (1989, 41) at work in Beckett's *oeuvre* in the space between his 'French originals' and the English self-translations. Connor argues that each version of his translations 'becomes merely a version of the other, and is apprehensible as itself only by virtue of *its* differences from the other text' (36). This play of supplementarity reminds us that '*Le langage n'est qu'une fiction, une traduction sans original*' (44). Connor notes that the disparity between the different versions is often quite large and suggests that many of the changes are due to 'Beckett's deepening pessimism and bitterness' (30–1). However, the physical degeneration his characters suffer, in moving from impeded cyclists to mud-dwellers, describes a gradual physical weakening that is not necessarily a slide into pessimism and bitterness. The deepening engagement with the dimensions of this 'authentic weakness' reveals, on the contrary, how a voice and a practice of living can be discerned, negotiated and even affirmed in the most desperate of states. In his early letters, Beckett explains how the interest in a 'syntax of weakness' emerged. He describes his thrill at 'being allowed to violate a foreign language as involuntarily as, with knowledge and intention, I would like to do against my own language, and – Deo juvante – shall do' (Fehsenfeld and Overbeck, 2009, 520). But how is this 'syntax of weakness' related to Beckett's desire to describe the 'authentic weakness of being'? The former relates to a style of representation or to a linguistic capacity while the latter describes a broader assessment of the human condition. In this chapter, I want to explore how the two kinds of weakness are related in Beckett's work.

Pascale Casanova relates Beckett's notion of weakness to what she describes as his 'particular view of the world', one that, she argues, reveals a 'conviction of a beneficial, necessary division between the corporeal order and the intellectual order' (74). How important is such a 'division' for Beckett in his descriptions of 'authentic weakness' and, since his characters' various states of degeneracy must also bring a degree of pain, how does this division relate to a notion of 'doubleness' or 'dividedness' that Elaine Scarry has recently employed to describe the experience of pain? Scarry has written of the problems that can be encountered in language when one is trying to describe and accommodate pain. She argues that:

> The problems that come from the language of agency, then, come from the ease with which it can be separated from the sufferer; and the benign potential comes by holding the referent steady and not letting the spatial separation take place. The problems that come from the langauge of the body damage are exactly the opposite; the image of the body damage often sits on top of and blocks our access to the person in pain. (in Coakley, 2007, 284)

Beckett's representation of 'authentic weakness' and of physical deformity and suffering never quite assumes the proportions of a body damage that 'blocks our access to the person in pain'. His characters do not seem to experience the pain they should. However, he would appear in presenting physical degeneracy in an exaggerated manner, to want us to acknowledge its unique dimensions and this is achieved because he never severs 'the obscene spectacle of body damage [or physical degeneracy in Beckett's case] from the site of personhood', as Scarry suggests so many artists do (in Coakley, 304). His body damage victims are characters after all, and their personhood is important for their plight. Because the monologues gain much of their power from the physical nature of their speakers, it is sometimes difficult to read into the works what Casanova sees as Beckett's 'necessary division between the corporeal order and the intellectual order'.

Beckett's early study of Proust may show us where an interest in the inadequacy of signification originated for him. He describes how, for Proust, the 'baffled ecstasy' experienced before 'the inscrutable superficies of a cloud, a triangle, a spire, a flower, a pebble' can only be deciphered in the 'brightness of art' (*Proust*, 1999, 76). But this art originates through an encounter between 'matter' and 'the Idea': 'the mystery, the essence, the Idea, imprisoned in matter, had solicited the bounty of a subject passing by within the shell of his impurity, and tendered . . . at least an incorruptible beauty' (76). Beckett might be regarded as exploring this engagement between the matter-embedded Idea and the impurity of the subject that tenders an 'incorruptible beauty' in his own work that strives to represent the 'authentic weakness of being'.

That other weakness, 'the syntax of weakness' inherent in his language, works, for Ann Banfield, through his 'minimalist style' that is the result of his use of 'the lexicon's nonproductive grammatical function words' (6). However, it also emerges from his two-way struggle with his mother tongue. Banfield explains how the artist's own personal 'attack on the mother tongue' is further complicated in Beckett because of the 'Irish crisis of the mother tongue' (2003, 8). One might suggest that the artist's struggle with the mother tongue is forever parodied by Beckett's suspending of his mother-tongue-as-lack, his self-alienating Hiberno English, behind a veil of self-translation. His self-translation from what Vladimir Nabokov described as his 'schoolmaster's French' (Taylor-Batty, 163) gives the impression of cleansing this non-standard language, this dialect that is always in the background, of its impurities, while also revealing a greater authorial 'truth' that has been stripped of its subjective baggage. However, such an impression is only a distraction. If we fall for it, it is ever more revealing of a need to believe in the self-fulfilling prophecy that sees artistic communication as an idealization of a possibly phonocentric communicative act. This *lieu vague*, where meaning seems to be lodged between languages, draws from Joycean polyglossia and looks forward to the Derridean 'impossibility' of translation; Derrida reminds us in '*Des Tours de babel*' that any attempt to create a tower or figure to house even the meaning lost in crossing between two languages only returns us to 'translation inadequate to compensate for that which multiplicity denies us' (Acts of Religion, 2002, 104). Beckett's syntax of weakness may well emerge from his foregrounding of this inadequacy since there are meanings that are doubly lost in his work as they move from mother-tongue-as-lack to schoolmaster's French and back again.

However, any concentration on the syntax to the exclusion of what the syntax relates runs the risk of bringing us back to structuralism and forces of 'dislocation'. Beckett's semantic excursion into a 'syntax of weakness' also gives a 'voice' to what Richard Ellmann describes as 'the decrepit and maimed and inarticulate' (in Schendler, 1989, 1) so that we have a multilayered articulation of weakness that, as Pinter suggests, 'grinds my nose in the shit'.[2] The voice is the last sign of life for Beckett's characters; in *How It Is* 'my life a voice' (2001, 175.230) strains to sustain itself by being heard through the 'ear' that 'conditions the gift of understanding the care for us' (177.237). The speaker is troubled because he finds his 'words' are 'not weak enough' (165.185). The 'immemorial imperishable' 'unchanging drone' of the voice as life through the 'untiring listening' of the ear must be 'of the fragile kind made for the blackbirds when to the day the long night yields at last' (177.236). Even though the voice screams 'I SHALL DIE' when the body is 'flat on my belly' in the mud, the intention for the words of the voice to be 'weak enough' and 'fragile' is not given up.

However, there has been far too much celebration of the depravity of this aesthetic of weakness; the affirmative potential and 'authentic weakness' of this depravity is also an important feature and it is one of the aspects that brings out the humour in Beckett. Recent philosophical studies of Beckett have related his work to abstract notions such as the 'image'. Anthony Uhlmann regards Beckett as understanding the 'image' as what acts as 'a bridge between those objectively existing things and our thoughts' (2006, 8) and Casanova argues that the 'more or less figurative "images" structure what are virtually abstract stories' and that Beckett works to 'invent literary images freed from figurative norms and prescriptions, including the intuitive obviousness of psychological interiority' (11). However, this concentration on the disembodied head as primary instance of an image that produces 'abstract stories' and that 'bridges' a gap between 'things' and 'thoughts' or a 'necessary division' between the intellectual and the corporeal would only then set up more pronounced 'figurative norms' where the image, removed from the 'interiority' of bodily experience, reins supreme like an age-old ideal or perfect form. In *How It Is*, when the voice seeks an 'image' for itself it is at the mercy of the body and those brief reprieves when its 'panting stops'; it is only when 'I hear me again murmur me in the mud [that I] am again'. What kind of weakness remains when the embodiment that allows us to bring the syntax and the 'being' together confronts this 'division' Casanova describes?

Beckett's desire to give voice to the suffering that haunts weakness is rather playfully lampooned in the later fiction that details his art of 'impoverishment': 'All lies. I have nothing to do, that is to say nothing in particular . . . Labyrinthine torment that can't be grasped, or limited, or felt, or suffered, no not even suffered, I suffer all wrong too, even that I do all wrong too, like an old turkey-hen dying on her feet, her back covered with chickens and the rats spying on her' (*Trilogy*, 316). This may seem a far cry from Beckett, the critic, who describes Proust as being 'romantic in his substitution of affectivity for intelligence' (*Proust*, 81). However, Beckett also notes that, for Proust, 'the quality of language is more important than any system of ethics or aesthetics' (88). Through his early criticism and poetry Beckett works out that it is only a careful attention to the syntax of language and to the type of language self-translation produces that anything like the weakness, suffering or the 'bodily need' he later describes in *Molloy*, can be adequately expressed.

James Reid's *Proust, Beckett and Narration* gives a reading of the two writers that privileges the 'difference' in their work. He argues that in the *Recherche* and the *Trilogy* 'first-person narration takes the form of an interplay between the tropes of irony and allegory' and he describes Beckett's 'irony' as 'the apparent mark of Beckett's literary historical difference' (2003, 10). However, it is not so easy to align Beckett's language with a language of difference, aporia and absence? In *The Unnamable* we hear, very early on: 'I should mention before going any further, any further on, that I say aporia without knowing what it means' (*Trilogy*, 293). However, Reid's study does demonstrate how a mind/body connection drives the narrative. For Reid, Beckettian forgetting is 'this mental loss of the ability to perceive or represent temporal or historical difference as the gradual handicapping and decomposing of his narrators' bodies'.[3] However, James Knowlson reminds us that Beckett's aesthetic may focus on a moment of such 'bodies' that is very different to any such abstract notion as 'temporal or historical difference'. Knowlson writes: 'it was one of the key features of Beckett's aesthetic that what he once described . . . as "the cold eye" had to be brought to bear on a personal experience before it could be used in a work of art' (Knowlson, 1997, 347). We can see something of Beckett's 'cold eye', and what contributes to his own aesthetic practice, in the words of his protagonists. In *Malone Dies*, Malone ponders the 'outer world':

> And as if that were not enough to satisfy me it is the outer world, the other world, suddenly the window across the way lights up, or suddenly I realize it is lit up, for I am not one of those people who can take in everything at a single glance, but I have to look long and fixedly and give things time to travel the long road that lies between me and them. (*Trilogy*, 238)

The 'cold eye' that is brought to bear on a personal experience before such an experience can be included in the artwork is also an eye that recognizes the 'long road' between it and these 'things'. It recalls Casanova's claim that Beckett describes a 'necessary division between the corporeal order and the intellectual order'. However, Beckett himself suggests in his letters that it is less of a 'division' than a 'discrepancy': 'The discrepancy between mind and body is terrible' (Letter to McGreevy, Fehsenfeld, 273). The terrible beauty the representation of the limits of this discrepancy reveals for Beckett is found through an engagement with the weakness and suffering that always calls it into question. Beckett's understanding of weakness might then be regarded as a description of the human tendency to become fascinated and hoodwinked by the experience of travelling this 'long' but 'necessary' road between things and whatever self-consciousness we are granted. Even though Beckett satirizes both Joycean epiphanic awareness and Proustian memory – it is Madeleine who rids 'I' of his 'paltry excrements every Sunday' in *The Unnamable* – Malone does come to a rather symbolic realization in the passage above after travelling his own long road along this 'necessary division'. The possibility therefore remains that Beckettian weakness is all about becoming absorbed and somewhat 'surprised' along this fruitless 'long road'.

Beckett's own trajectory along the 'long road' away from his literary precursors Joyce and Proust is important for understanding the weakness he describes. James Knowlson describes the writing of the *Trilogy* as the result of a 'writing frenzy' that ran from 'May 1947 until January 1950' (1997, 336). Beckett finally admitted to Knowlson that there is indeed much of him in the *Trilogy*. The voice of the *Trilogy* displays an almost devotional approach to the contemplation of objects and to work that Knowlson relates to Beckett's farm work during the war. Beckett's syntax acts as a counterweight to the sprawling memory-scapes of the young Marcel. However, both Marcel and Macmann [or son of man] are writing as they ruminate on their writing. Even though the voice of Beckett's *Trilogy* may possess the irony, readerly 'demystification' and the 'self-deception' unique to autobiographical writing, which James Reid sees Beckett as inheriting from Proust and then transforming, the first-person narrative excerpts in the *Trilogy* that speak of work, care and weakness are difficult to align with what Reid describes as 'an ironical revelation of the materiality of language as a relation between words that are as indistinguishable as pebbles on a beach' (94). Words, for Beckett, are never as indistinguishable as pebbles on a beach, and the model for their mode of 'circulation' and use is more exhaustively worked out than Molloy's stone-sucking. In the stone-sucking episode from *Molloy*, Molloy is desperately attempting to find some way to tell his stones apart so that the order of his stone-sucking will no longer be left to chance. The process leaves Molloy with the realization that 'I had to seek elsewhere than in the mode of circulation'. In abandoning the hope for a system that always had a 'kind of equilibrium' in which each stone is forever sucked in its turn, he admits that he 'preferred to make the best of the comparative peace of mind I enjoyed within each cycle taken separately' (*Trilogy*, 73). And even with this relative peace, Molloy ends his investigation on stone-sucking by realizing that in abandoning his desire for continuous perfect equilibrium, or his 'principle of trim', he is also abandoning 'something more than a principle' – namely, a 'bodily need' (74). Trim can also refer to 'material for ornament' and this puts us in mind of the subtext here; namely, the broader discussion of aesthetic form. It is perhaps no surprise that the protagonist, as a kind of alterego of the writer who made so much of 'the rupture in the lines of communication', is keen to dispense with unnecessary style and elaborate aesthetic models. Beckett is both disrupting any easy application of a transparent overarching artistic model to his work and describing how he has possibly moved on from some of his most influential literary precursors. The multilayered, cyclical form of a Joyce disrupts the 'peace of mind I enjoyed within each cycle taken separately'. We recall 'the commodius vicus of recirculation' that opens *Finnegans Wake* and also Proust's sprawling narrative which is' for Beckett, 'a monument to involuntary memory and the epic of its action' (*Proust*, 34). However, the important admission in this veiled discussion of aesthetic form is that the desire to stick to the 'principle of trim' and the desire to give it up are each linked to a 'bodily need': 'Here then were two incompatible bodily needs, at loggerheads' (74). Form and syntax, as pillars for any aesthetic 'principle of trim', speak directly for bodily needs and the slightest alteration in form will reveal a different bodily need. Beckett engages with those unique individual degeneracies and physical wounds and ruptures that are the sole support for the 'peace of mind' that is only found in 'each cycle taken separately'.

Beckett also throws off the 'Proustian equation' and Proust's 'myth of interiority' by creating space in the artwork for what he describes, reprinted in James Knowlson's latest work, as the 'moment between' willing and doing. This is another important moment in his aesthetic that again arises from the fact that he allows himself the time to take each cycle of physical failing or weakness separately. Knowlson believes that Peter Bowles's article on Beckett, published in the *PN Review* in the 1950s, has been neglected by Beckett scholarship. It is an article that makes much of this 'moment between' willing and doing. Bowles records that Beckett described the essential moment that 'breaks the circle' as follows: 'It is as if there were a little animal inside one's head, for which one tried to find a voice; to which one tries to give a voice. That is the *real* thing. The rest is a game' (Knowlson, 2006, 111). The voice in Molloy's head, which leads him to this moment of revelation where he is willing to accept how chance and the 'moment between' disrupt any preconditions he might have for his art as stone-sucking, may echo Beckett's own reaction to the famous revelation for his work that he has admitted to experiencing in his 'mother's room' in 1945. The revelation described later in Krapp's *Last Tape* may describe a similar moment of aesthetic insight, a moment where Beckett is seen to discover that 'the dark' was his 'most precious ally' (Knowlson 1996, 319). [James Knowlson 1996]:

> Spiritually a year of profound gloom and indigence until that memorable night in March, at the end of the jetty, in the howling wind, never to be forgotten, when suddenly I saw the whole thing. The vision at last. This I fancy is what I have chiefly to record this evening . . . What I suddenly saw then was this, that the belief I had been going on all my life [Krapp moves to switch off the tape] great granite rocks the foam flying up in the light of the lighthouse and wind-gauge spinning like a propeller, clear to me at last that the dark I have always struggled to keep under is in reality my most [Krapp switches tape again] unshatterable association until my dissolution of storm and night with the light of the understanding of the fire. (Beckett, 1990, 220)

Beckett later explained this revelation to Knowlson in terms of the differences between him and his greatest artistic influence at the time, Joyce:

> I realised that Joyce had gone as far as one could in the direction of knowing more, [being] in control of one's material. He was always adding to it; you only have to look at his proofs to see that. I realised that my own way was an impoverishment, in lack of knowledge and in taking away, in subtracting rather than in adding. (Knowlson, 1997, 319)

Molloy and Beckett then 'seek elsewhere than in the mode of circulation'. Molloy's contemplation of the 16 stones might also be an ironic take on Beckett's laborious contemplation and translation of much of the 16 or 17 episodes of *Finnegans Wake*, a task that influenced much of his early work and that might be seen to come to the surface a few pages earlier in Molloy's recollections of the mysterious Lousse. Lousse sounds very much like an allegorical merging of Lucia and Joyce, that emotionally fraught coupling so influential for Beckett's artistic coming of age. Knowlson describes how Beckett had to continually explain to the impressionable Lucia that his visits to the Joyce household were for the company of her father. In his letters, Joyce also blames himself for Lucia's condition. If the figure of Lousse does stand in for something of Joyce, then the passage in which Molloy describes his time at Lousse's house is revealing of his rejuvenated artistic temperament:

> For that is the conclusion I would come to, fatally. I who loved the image of Geulincx [the Belgian Cartesian Beckett also spent a great deal of time translating from the Latin without, in his words, 'knowing why' (Knowlson, 207)] dead young, who left me free, on the black boat of Ulysses, to crawl towards the East, along the deck. That is a great measure of freedom, for him who has not the pioneering spirit. And from the poop, poring upon the wave, a sadly rejoicing slave, I follow with my eyes the proud and futile wake. Which, as it bears me from no fatherland away, bears me onward to no shipwreck. A good while then with Lousse. (*Trilogy*, 51)

It is evident, then, through these obscure references to *Ulysses* and 'the proud and futile *wake* [my emphasis]', that Beckett has seen a way beyond the works of Joyce and Proust.

But what are we to make of Beckett's fascination for weakness? It is the charting of the long road along the 'necessary division' between intellectual experience and corporeal experience that appears to shape his protagonists' experiences of weakness. The representation of weakness begs the question in terms of how corporeal experiences are to be 'embodied' in language when such a division is upheld. If Beckett strictly upholds the division between intellectual and corporeal experience, as Casanova suggests, but is yet committed to the representation of 'authentic weakness' through a 'syntax of weakness', then how is this physiological, corporeal and even spiritual attribute to be represented? Beckett was enough of a philosopher to know that the proof for the clear form of dualism Casanova's 'division' presumes is impossible. He was possibly familiar with what earlier phenomenological mutations in the shape of Heidegger had had to say on this matter. Beckett may have studied some of Heidegger's *Sein und Zeit*, published in 1927, or of the English translation that appeared in 1962.[4] Heidegger formulates cleary the 'problem of Reality' that a division between intellectual and corporeal experience throws up:

> The 'problem of Reality' in the sense of the question whether such a world can be proved, turns out to be an impossible one, not because its consequences lead to inextricable impasses, but because the very entity which serves as its theme, is one which, as it were, repudiates any such formulation of the question. Our task is not to prove that an 'external world' is present-at-hand or to show how it is present-at-hand, but to point out

why Dasein, as Being-in-the-world, has the tendency to bury the 'external world' in nullity 'epistemologically' before going on to prove it. (Heidegger, 1997, 250)

Now this sounds very much like the task Beckett sets aesthetically with his statement of the problem. He buries us all in the 'nullity' of an '"epistemologically"' worked out elaboration of weakness – what shows up the futility of clinging to proofs of dualism – before going on to prove that the experience of this 'long road' of weakness is entirely necessary. Like Heidegger, he is eager to show that any proof for a world 'out there' distinctly separate from our 'inner' wranglings is impossible, despite making such a proof appear as a kind of aesthetic ideal that must be approached in order to make the futility of the approach appear so beautiful. Perhaps this is as close as we can come to some philosophical estimation of the weakness that Beckett was so eager to depict. In taking the parallel with Heidegger a little further, it is interesting to note that Heidegger believed, too, that the '"problem of Reality"' had to be faced in a new way. Heidegger saw the root of the problem in the fact that 'the primary understanding of Being has been diverted to Being as presence-at-hand' (250). The problem is that if the question is posed like this, then all one finds 'present-at-hand as proximally and solely certain, is something merely "inner"'. For Heidegger, as soon as the 'primordial phenomenon of Being-in-the-world has been shattered, the isolated subject is all that remains, and this becomes the basis on which it gets joined together with a "world"' (250). It is surely something akin to this 'primordial phenomenon of Being-in-the-world' that Beckett strives to reconstruct by taking us right back down to our own 'isolated subject' and our own 'ends and odds'. Beckett presents us, or so it seems, with so many 'isolated subjects', yet it is impossible for them to rely on anything that might be solely 'inner' since their physical weakness, their decrepit conditions, keep calling their wandering monologues back to a desperate and painful physicality that prevents anything, be it mental or physical, from ever being wholly 'inner'; he grounds the reader and the viewer in a shared physicality where the degree of aspiration is directly proportional to the degree of physical limitation. Beckett depicts various characters' states of almost unsurpassable weakness as he also consistently takes us on the futile 'long road' from the intellectual to the corporeal in his literary attempt to refashion our 'primordial phenomenon'. The elaborate description and detailing of weakness allows us to glimpse the 'moment between' willing and doing. This drawing out of this 'moment between' in the shape of a detailing of weakness produces the sense of invigorating tension in

Beckett's work. In *The Unnamable*, 'I' describes this peculiar predicament: 'What is more important is that I should know what is going on now, in order to announce it, as my function requires. . . . Do they believe I believe it is I who am speaking? That's theirs too. To make me believe I have an ego all my own, and can speak of it, as they of theirs. Another trap to snap me up among the living. It's how to fall into it they can't have explained to me sufficiently' (*Trilogy*, 348). So 'I' does not believe he has an 'ego all my own'. And yet what he laments is not that they erroneously believe that he believes in an ego 'all my own', but that they had not explained to him 'sufficiently' 'how to fall into [believing] it'. Beckett's characters need to know how to fail better in order to prolong the experience along the futile road from what is 'inner' and what is of the ego to what lies beyond in the shape of traps and stones.

I now want to take a closer look at two of Beckett's works – 'Enueg I' and *How It Is* – in light of what the recently published letters reveal about his motivations for an 'authentic weakness' that envisages some kind of bridging of the 'terrible' disparity between mind and body. These works are written thirty years apart and they therefore demonstrate how his understanding of the 'authentic weakness of being' evolves. 'Enueg I' was written while Beckett was lecturing in Trinity College. An 'enueg', as Raymond Thompson Hill explains, 'designates a poem that treats the annoyances of life from mere trifles to serious insults'. Such poems also typically exhibit, for Thompson, the 'entire absence' of 'continuity of thought' (1912, 265). Beckett's enuegs are addressed to the suffering and the melancholy evident in his early letters. Beckett's letters speak regularly of art and the problems it raises as being related to the pus and abscesses of the body, what may remind us of a medieval interest in alchemy and such bodily emanations as phlegm and bile. He explores a kind of transmutation of an aesthetic of weakness and suffering.

This peripatetic style of bearing witness to a kind of suffering is extended beyond the self in the earlier poetry. In 'Enueg I' the speaker is on a journey from the hospital after seeing his 'darling' suffering from tuberculosis. The speaker, 'his head', 'clot of anger', is 'skewered along strangled in the cang of the wind'. 'Cang' or 'cangue' can refer to 'a broad heavy wooden frame or board worn round the neck like a kind of portable pillory (*OED*)'. The wind is therefore a medium through which to pass, and one to pass along with, or accompany, in moving from a terrible moment of witness *to* suffering, as well as being a sometimes restraining and punitive force. Beckett makes the body share in some of what the spirit produces. In his letters, Beckett describes the physical trials that accompanied him through the writing of the 'Alba & the long Enueg & Dortmunder'. The spirit is attacked for being so remote from the ills of the body yet Beckett recognizes that these poems 'have something that distinguishes them from the others': they are 'written above an abscess and not out of a cavity, a statement and not a description of heat in the spirit to compensate for pus in the spirit' (Fehsenfeld, 134). And later in the same letter he asks for some kind of forgiveness for his analysis of suffering and pain: 'Forgive all this? Why is the spirit so pus-proof and the wind so avaricious of its grit' (135). The lines blur any clear divide between the primordial pus and juices of the body and the behaviour of the elemental forces housing it. The speaker in the early poetry is typically subjected to the actions of verbs assigned to the elements and seems to rely for his existence on physical realities of the geographical and natural environment.

The speaker is '[t]ired of my darling's red sputum' and there is a movement of 'toil to the crest of the surge' that must 'lapse down blankly under the scream of the hoarding/round the bright stiff banner of the hoarding/ into a black west throttled with clouds' (*Collected Poems*, 10). There is no direct subject or predicate and no direct action attributed to the voice. All is verb use and image that calls up the actions of elements that trouble our understanding of what is physical and what is extra-physical: 'My skull sullenly/clot of anger/skewered aloft/strangled in the cang of the wind/bites like a dog against its chastisement' (10). Beckett animates the sometimes seemingly dead parts of the body such as bone and skull and even blood by granting them an emotional life. By way of a rhyme that almost sounds like a repetition, the skull becomes sullen and then, as a perturbation of the blood in the form of clot, it is angry. The defining feature of vertebrate life, the spine, becomes a source of suffering as it 'skewers aloft' this angry skull. This angry seat of the intellect and imagination is skewered and strangled. The environment provides no respite for the voice, since the wind itself is a 'cang' or punitive imprisonment that is more biting than the innocuous retaliations of the speaker against his 'chastisement'. Beckett's animation of the not-so-distinct features of the body, skeleton and environment leaves the reader in a momentary state of suspension over the grey hinterland that emerges when the discrepancy between mind and body is explored.

What might typically prove fundamental to such a peripatetic speaker – namely, his feet – also proves ineffective: 'I trundle along rapidly now on my ruined feet/flush with the livid canal'; 'flush' can describe both a physical location in relation to something else but also a physical sensation. All that is typically described in terms of exterior Nature or elemental forces from without is employed as an energy from within that first surfaces in the most neglected and pestilent deposits of the body. Later in the poem barges also die, and in the 'cloister of the lock' we see a barge carrying instruments for a crucifixion; the barge 'rocks itself softly' like a cradle, and the retelling of this mythic account of life, incarnation and death becomes embroiled in the visions of life and death that the speaker may have entertained with his 'darling'.

Later in the poem we again have the merging of the living flesh with the dead flesh of welts and weals and the wind: 'Then for miles only wind/and the weals creeping alongside on the water/and the world opening up to the south/across a lamentable parody of champaign land to the/mountains' (*Collected Poems*, 11). Weal describes a welt or skin abrasion. Different to an abscess, it is a 'ridge on the flesh raised by a blow; a hard, raised white patch on the skin'(*OED*). Beckett describes the aesthetic aspects of these poems in his letters in terms of the flesh, the pus and the wind. The poems are, we recall, 'written above an abscess and not out of a cavity, a statement and not a description of heat in the spirit to compensate for pus in the spirit' (Fehsenfeld, 134). There would appear to be some elemental connection, then, between the spirit, which Beckett wants his poems to consume, and the wind that swirls around the speaker blowing dead thoughts to life. Beckett has assigned aspects of decay and physical detritus to the wind-as-inspiration. The wind in 'Enueg I' plays havoc with a mind that is interfered with and driven on by a new kind of suffering of the flesh: 'and the stillborn evening turning a filthy green/manuring the night fungus/and the mind annulled/ wrecked in wind'. Death still nurtures life and the 'night fungus' may once again connote the poem-as-abscess with its pus that is 'manuring' overnight when the mind is 'annulled' or declared invalid by a heart that is 'wrecked'.

Despite the fact that his poetry is 'a statement and not a description of heat in the spirit to compensate for pus in the spirit' (Fehsenfeld, 135), Beckett laments the fact that more of his writing is not 'the spontaneous combustion of the spirit to compensate the pus and the pain that threaten its economy'. In the same letter, he describes his writing as 'fraudulent manoeuvres to make the cavity do what it can't do – the work of the abscess' (134). The cavity, the emptiness, cannot do the work of the abscess, the work of pus and pain; this is a physical and mental result the cavity cannot produce. The cavity is of the body and it houses the pus and pain and creates them. It is the body attacking itself as the simplistic medical prognosis might suggest. The sense seems to be that the cavity cannot be made to do the work of the abscess, or in the jargon of deconstruction or authenticity, the absence cannot do the work of the abscess. The bodily frame cannot be made to do the work of the pus and the pain for, if it does, it is then only engaged in 'fraudulent manoeuvres'. Beckett is voicing Scarry's concern that the description of 'body damage' alerts us to 'the problems that come from the language of agency' and 'the ease with which it can be separated from the sufferer' (in Coakley, 284); it is sometimes all too easy to represent a suffering so that the description becomes 'fraudulent' in its attempts to communicate a pain and a pus. It is the 'spontaneous combustion of the spirit', a spirit that lies beyond the body, yet somewhere in the emptiness of the cavity, that Beckett wants his poetry to be. In other words, the 'work of the abscess', what is both the product and cause of suffering that leads to the 'spontaneous combustion of the spirit', must 'compensate the pus and pain that threaten its economy'. Spirit and body must be responsibly aligned through that which connects them; namely, suffering, weakness and pain.

How It Is, written thirty years later in French and then self-translated into English in 1964, is possibly more pared down but not necessarily more 'pessimistic'. The speaker, in the mud, is often 'too weak' even to entertain the question 'how I got here if it's me' (23). However, the work, in describing severe physical limitations, demonstrates that Beckett has developed a philosophy of weakness around his characters in the intervening years that still might be regarded as compensating for the 'pus and pain' that threaten the spirit's economy in those early letters. The titles of the work in its respective French and English translations – *How It Is* and *Comment c'est* – embody the parallel evident in his philosophy of existence; life is very much a getting to grips with the reality of one's condition, with 'how it is', and each stage along this continual process is also a beginning of a kind (the *commencer* punned by the French title). The speaker and Pim lie together in the mud; the speaker hears voices that on occasion sound like memories; he says that 'I murmur in the mud what I hear in me when the panting stops bits and scraps' (103).

However, when the speaker describes his and Pim's physical proximity it is both revealing of a human aspiration and fellow feeling that is all the stronger precisely because of the extreme weakness of the couple. We read that they are 'together like two old jades harnessed together no but mine my head its face in the mud and his its right cheek in the mud his mouth against my ear our hairs entangled together' (119). Later, the voice describes how, in a quasi-incarnational mode, and despite the 'rupture in the lines of communication', 'we are one and all from the unthinkable first to the no less unthinkable last glued together in a vast imbrication of the flesh without breach or fissure' (2001, 185.264). The speaker can only hear the 'voice' that is 'in me' when the toil of panting stops; it is a 'voice' that comes from 'in me' only because Pim's lips are eternally pressed to the ear of his speaker/partner. The stripped down fellow feeling he entertains when speculating on how the seemingly lifeless Pim survives, a Pim whose lips to the ear of the speaker may well be the source of the speaker's life-as-voice, describes how even the weakest possess an empathy that strives to know how the other can survive:

> And Pim all this time vast stretch of time not a movement apart from the lips . . . to be sure by me imparted Pim has not eaten . . . and far too much I have eaten/offered him to eat crushed against his mouth lost in the hairs the mud my palm dripping with cod's liver or such like rubbed it in labour lost if he's still nourished it's on mud if that's what is is I always said so this mud by osmosis long run fullness of time by capillarity. (2001, 83)

The speaker is made to meditate on his own plight by imagining how one in a similar situation survives and therefore the question about sustenance contributes to his own awareness about his own survival. Because of this imagined empathetic excursion, the voice is later able to imagine the plight of someone in a worse state: 'the paltry need of a life a voice of one who has neither' (159.141). He realizes that 'the mud I always said so it keeps a man going' (83). Both of them survive then through osmosis of nutrients from the mud either 'by the tongue when it sticks out the mouth when the lips part the nostrils the eyes when the lids part the anus no it's high and dry the ears no' (83). Having ruled out osmosis by the anus, his enquiry into self-preservation alights on the urethra: 'the urethra perhaps after piss the last drop the bladder sucking in a second after all the pumping out certain pores too the urethra perhaps a certain number of pores' (83). We are again at a ground zero of survival and weakness that leads to an intense speculation on empathy and nurturing. As with Wordsworth's beggars and vagrants, where those 'forms created the most vile and brute,/The dullest or most noxious' should not exist '[d]ivorced from good', (1981, 265.75-7) so would it appear to be for Beckett. The speculation leads the speaker to realize that 'it is not aimless that is evident this creature is too intelligent to demand what is beyond my powers what then is not beyond my powers to sing to weep what else can I do could I do if I were put to the pin of my collar/think perhaps at a pinch it's possible what else am I doing at this moment and bless my soul there it comes again' (87.105). Some kind of revelation visits the speaker; he is at his wit's end in his self-examination about how he could help in a way that is not 'beyond my powers'. It is only then, through the admission of his weakened state, that he opens up to the plight of another, to what, through the 'ear', is described as 'a means of noting a care for us' (177.233) and in so doing is led to discover that one still has a degree of power and that one must go right back to the most basic kind of question, to the question 'what else am I doing at this moment', to discover the degree of power that sustains the weakening voice.

The syntactic implosion or 'syntax of weakness' in Beckett is the result of an initial wrestling with the proper precinct of suffering in terms of how the body affects the mind. 'Enueg I' describes a visceral examination of the 'long road' or 'discrepancy between mind and body' that the early Beckett finds so 'terrible' and that continues on into new heights (not only new lows) in *How It Is*. His refusal to give up on the problem first described in the early poems leads ineluctably to the later narrative and dramatic voices that forever defamiliarize our suffering and weakness.

Chapter 11

Vulnerability, Narrative Authority and 'the Animal' in the Work of J. M. Coetzee

Jacques Derrida argues that the shadow of death hangs over animals. He writes that 'a thinking of the human subject' that has for so long situated 'the possibility and necessity of sacrifice at the heart of its ethics, fails to feel concerned . . . by the *animot* [*animot* is his neologism for what metaphysics has failed to conceptualize in relation to 'the animal']' (2008, 106). The encounter with animals alerts us to an ever-present potential for violence and suffering. Because animals also traditionally embody a 'weakening' (96), the encounter with them allows 'humans' to revisit moments of weakness and may engender a unique sense of compassion for the other, perhaps a uniquely human sensation (along with the capacity to be 'beastly'). In this final chapter, I examine animal vulnerability in the work of J. M. Coetzee. I follow Derrida, however, in seeing no 'homogenous continuity between what calls *itself* man and what *he* calls the "animal" for the "sinister" reasons a history of atrocity gives us' (30). I do not follow Derrida in employing the neologism '*animot*' over 'the animal', since despite Derrida's suggestion that this word may help us think 'the absence of the name and of the word otherwise' (48), for me, it smacks too much of the referentiality it is attempting to unthink. This chapter explores moments of encounter between humanized and animalized fictional protagonists in Coetzee, and briefly in Kafka, and in so doing, questions the 'ontological difference' (Derrida 2008, 160) the encounter throws up; it explores a spirit of compassion invoked by the encounter that leads to a giving up of control and a revaluation of weakness that allows for 'the relation to what is inasmuch as one lets it be what it is' (2008, 160).

Recent studies in ethology and neuroscience differentiate between primary consciousness and secondary consciousness in animals; 'primary consciousness' entails 'the ability to create a scene in the "remembered present" in the absence of language' (Edelman and Seth, 2009, 476). This marks a move in animal consciousness studies away from a privileging of a direct analogy with humans, something that fiction on animal encounters, such as that of Coetzee, also sets up. The possibility of consciousness without language is being explored here. Derrida's recently published seminars chart similar ground by unsettling an age-old distinction between man and animal in philosophy that rests on the distinction between the symbolic and the imaginary. Derrida describes this opposition in his recently translated seminars *The Beast & the Sovereign* in terms of 'the specular capture of which the animal is capable and the symbolic order of the signifier to which it does not have access' (2009, 120). He deconstructs this opposition because he suggests that our approach to the animal should be one of 'wondering whether what one calls man has the right, for his own part, to attribute in all rigor to man, to attribute to himself, then, what he refuses to the animal, and whether he ever has a concept of it that is *pure, rigorous, indivisible, as such*' (130). Derrida suggests that writers such as Kafka 'understood this better than philosophers or theorists did' (127). Such studies in science and philosophy can therefore work in conjunction with literary narratives that strive to enter into the 'mind' of animals; they raise questions in relation to the linguistic representation of animal consciousness and allow us to reappraise the human weakness we often ground on an objectification of the animal as beastly other.

The 'reflections' published alongside J. M. Coetzee's novella *The Lives of Animals* by, among others, Peter Singer and Barbara Smuts, challenge attitudes to animals that deny them consciousness, awareness and the potential for friendship with humans. Barbara Smuts's anthropological 'reflection' argues that humans must privilege the notion of 'social subjectivity' in dealings with animals. In failing to honour the personhood of animals, she argues, it is humans who are diminished (2001, 114). She offers useful advice for scientific and fictional investigations of animals: 'relating to other beings as persons has nothing to do with whether or not we attribute human characteristics to them' (118). She argues that '[t]he possibility of voluntary, mutual surrender to the dictates of intersubjectivity constitutes the common ground' that philosophers have ignored. For Smuts, such surrender can be experienced only by 'giving up control of them and how they relate to us. We fear such loss of control but the gifts we receive in return make it a small price to pay' (118). She also questions the capacity of literature to grant access to 'the animal': 'encounters with animals have less to do with the poetic imagination and more to do with real-life encounters with other animals' (120). This chapter examines whether Coetzee and Kafka convey a sense of 'giving up control' when they describe animal experience, and it investigates how important narrative authority is for this feigning of 'the animal'.

Responses to the animal characters in Kafka very often privilege the 'suffering' or 'sacrificial nature' of the animal. Chris Danta's recent study of 'the animal' in Kafka argues that Kafka asks the reader to 'inhabit a wounded or a sacrificial body' (2007, 729). For Danta, Coetzee uses the Kafkan inheritance to examine how 'the "disgrace of dying" truly merges human and animal suffering' (734) to the extent that Coetzee's *alter ego* Elizabeth Costello must 'ground identification with animals in the possibility of imagining one's own death' (731); in the relation with animals one is made to confront one's complete weakening through the engagement with the 'weakening' and shadow of death that haunts the other as animal. However, if we are trying to get into the 'mind' of 'the animal' this way of reading the experience with animals may only further an anthropomorphism of sorts that presumes that animals care about the death whose 'shadow' we say they are in. What is so belittling and yet so intoxicating about the experience with animals is that they handle this shadow of death incredibly well, so well, in fact, that they seem, for the most part, completely oblivious to it. Barbara Smuts's anthropological accounts of living with chimpanzees also privilege animal joy over suffering; she speaks of a 'joyful intersubjectivity that transcends species boundaries' and she echoes Coetzee's *alter ego* Costello in saying that to be an animal is to be 'full of "joy"' (2001, 110). In consistently aligning the animal, and our relation to the animal, with the sacrifice, a sacrifice that was only ever a human invention, we may only be willingly blinding ourselves to a greater sacrifice of the 'animal' in man as we sublimate our obsession with death and with being-towards-death onto a regard for the animal and animal encounter in terms of sacrifice.

Martin Heidegger's description of human care and being in terms of the uniquely human capacity for being that is 'ahead-of-itself', 'Being-already-in' and even 'Being-towards-death' (1997, 293) reminds us that death for us '*is something that stands before us – something impending*' (294). Coetzee's attention to one of Kafka's aphorisms reminds us of how both writers search in the animal for a new state of being-for-the-animal that can describe care and existence differently. Kafka's aphorism reads: 'From a certain point on, there is no more turning back. This is the point to be reached. The decisive moment of human development is everlasting. Therefore those revolutionary spiritual movements that declare everything before themselves null are right, in that nothing has yet happened' (in Coetzee, 1981, 578). Coetzee and Kafka explore animal interaction and animal awareness in describing moments when human protagonists briefly experience the thrill of shaking off this living 'ahead-of-itself' for the 'decisive moment of human development' that is 'everlasting'.

Coetzee explores interaction with 'the animal' through protagonists who lead the reader to imagine empathically the death of another. This opening out of death through animal encounter sparks a giving up of control in regard to this living 'ahead-of-itself'. It helps us do away with what Derrida describes as 'an artificial monstrosity of the animal' (*The animal that therefore I am*, 2008, 25). Derrida goes so far, in his seminar readings of Lacan, to suggest that the animal 'is deemed . . . incapable of an authentic relation to death' (2009, 122); the 'animal does not die' (2009, 123). It is this kind of 'everlasting' hope and 'feigning' of 'immortality' that the animal can grant man in helping the animal in man to live less 'ahead-of-itself'. Judith Butler has also demonstrated how this rethinking of the animal in terms of 'weakening' and in terms of 'precariousness' can enliven political debate. She argues that there must be a 'more egalitarian way of recognizing precariousness, and that this should take form as concrete social policy regarding such issues as shelter, work, food' (2009, 13). However, in order for this sense of precariousness to be properly understood as a 'shared condition of human life' it must be seen as a condition that 'links human and non-human animals' (13).

A second, related issue that is important for Coetzee's description of the animal is narrative authority. This is a formal device that is traditionally central to an author's attempts to assert control; however, for Coetzee it is made to mediate the 'giving up of control' that dealings with animals necessitate. Coetzee's *alter ego* Elizabeth Costello argues that there is 'no limit to the extent to which we can think ourselves into the being of another' and the exploration of animal encounter brings an awareness of this capacity (2001, 120). However, does Coetzee's narrative experimentation exhibit the 'giving up' of control that Smuts believes is essential for understanding the animal? Since it is now 'well established' that 'the critic anthropomorphizes Kafka's animals at his or her own risk' (Danta, 2007, 722), Kafka's and Coetzee's animals can give the non-scientist some understanding of what Hanno Würbel describes as the long scientific effort to overcome 'earlier anthropocentric approaches where animals were protected to preserve human morality' (2009, 121). Kafka's and Coetzee's experiments with narrative authority in describing animal experience grant readers a greater access not only to the animal, but to a revised expression of the human; their presentations of the human in the animal by way of a complex defamiliarization – the animal as the human in 'sheep's clothing' – alert us to a lost humanity as well as a neglected animal.

The reasons for Coetzee's sustained interest in experimenting with narrative authority may well be expressed through Señor C in *Diary of a Bad Year*. Señor C, the protagonist of *Diary*, a seventy-two-year-old author from South Africa, who, like Coetzee, now lives in Australia and has written a book entitled *Waiting for the Barbarians*, questions 'what sort of art' he has devoted himself to. He laments the fact that his art 'fails to celebrate life' and 'lacks love' (2007, 170). Señor C (hereafter C) argues that since the 'dust has settled' (150) on the heated debates on authority sparked by the Russian formalists and the post-structuralists, the 'mystery of Tolstoy's authority, and of the authority of other great authors, remains untouched' (150). Great authors, therefore, are those who possess authority. C suggests that the claims of Barthes and Foucault on authority 'a quarter of a century ago' suggesting that authority 'never amounted to anything more than a bagful of rhetorical tricks' (149) may not have gone far enough. Coetzee not only problematizes the relationship between implied author and *alter ego* as never before, he also wants narrative authority to embody aspects of animal vulnerability.

C is a 'literary man', who is completing a book, tentatively entitled '*Strong Opinions*'. Even though Coetzee splices C's and Anya's different voices into distinct sections on the page, the reader of *Diary* never knows for sure what kind of authority will be forthcoming in C's own book. Anya, the 'book editor' and the inspiration for much of C's most personal ruminations, is the only character apart from C to cast her eyes over the finished volume, and she cannot read German, the language in which it will be published. We do not even learn the final title of the book that will contain C's 'Strong Opinions', since his wish to call the collection *Harte Ansichten* is, the last we hear, being considered by his publisher Bruno.

One must finally ask whether C is being a little disingenuous in reducing 'authority' in Barthes and Foucault to no more than a 'bagful of rhetorical tricks'. Foucault acknowledges in 'What is an Author?' that the author function allows readings that acknowledge several selves of the same author, framed by processes of 'evolution, maturation or influence' (1977, 111), and it is a practice that Coetzee, at any rate, would seem to have taken to heart. In his essay, Foucault does not write of the disappearance of the author and of the new textual 'indifference' in relation to 'who's speaking?' in terms of 'rhetorical tricks', but as something that reveals the 'fundamental ethical principles of contemporary writing' (116). This new understanding of writing is 'primarily concerned with creating an opening where the writing subject endlessly disappears' (116). Coetzee's representation of the animal encounter strives to introduce this endlessly disappearing subject to overlooked features of the animal.

In 'What is an Author?', Foucault describes this writing subject in terms of the 'kinship between writing and death', a kinship Coetzee develops most poignantly through an exploration of animal death. Even though Coetzee's privileging of the framing of authority may not leave the reader with the impression that the 'writing subject' is endlessly disappearing, his later works are most successful at dispensing with the framing of authority, or with what I call 'narrative control', when an imagined death is being contemplated, be it the death of an author-protagonist or the death of animals. Foucault reminds us that writing is now, unlike in earlier times, 'linked to sacrifice and to the sacrifice of life itself; it is a voluntary obliteration of the self that does not require representation in books because it takes place in the everyday existence of the writer' (1977, 117). For Foucault, 'the link between writing and death [is] manifested in the total effacement of the individual characteristics of the writer; the quibbling and confrontations that a writer generates between himself and his text cancel out the signs of his particular individuality' (117). Coetzee moves from the writer-as-sacrifice to an imaginative exploration of the animal and vulnerability that takes fiction beyond this confrontational 'quibbling'; he employs the relation between the representation of impending death, animal encounter and authority to imaginatively explore his own struggle with authority.

C reminds us that 'great authors are masters of authority', and it is important to ask, with C, what is the 'source of authority' (2007, 151)? C suggests that if authority 'could be achieved simply by tricks of rhetoric' then Plato 'was surely justified in expelling poets from his ideal republic' (151). The great author, then, the master of authority, must perhaps justify claims to authority by recourse to more than 'tricks of rhetoric': 'what if authority can be attained only by opening the poet-self to some higher force, by ceasing to be oneself and beginning to speak vatically?' (2007, 151). The great author must speak like a prophet and invoke the gods; he must speak in tongues. In aligning the mystery of authority with the greatest of authors and with the ability to speak vatically, or as a prophet or visionary, C then calls on that other great illusionist or philosopher-ventriloquist, Søren Kierkegaard, the philosopher who leaves many of his greatest theses to the 'left hand' or to alter-egos.

C reminds us that Kierkegaard advises us to '[l]earn *to speak without authority*', since 'god can be invoked, but does not necessarily come'

(2007, 151). However, C then succumbs to the mystery and paradox of authority. By striving to speak without authority, by 'copying Kierkegaard's words here', C argues that he 'makes Kierkegaard into an authority. Authority cannot be taught, cannot be learned. The paradox is a true one' (151). Kierkegaard's own philosophical struggles with 'signed' authorship will end with an important admission in *Two Discourses at the Communion on Fridays*, his penultimate published work before his three-year silent period. He says that he 'has wanted once again to read through, if possible in a more inward way, the original text of individual human existence-relationships, the old familiar text handed down from the fathers' (1985, 165). However, since John Berger reminds us that animals act as an '*intercession* between man and his origin', (2009, 15) it is likely that 'the animal' will never be far away for Kierkegaard in his reading of this 'old familiar text'. C acknowledges that authority has to be 'earned', and he considers how it might require the author to sound vatic, what Coetzee will mediate through his representation of the relation with the animal. Kierkegaard recognizes in *Two Discourses*, as perhaps Coetzee does for C, that the reader is inclined to 'like to hear the poet talk like this, "Oh, I wish I were a bird, or I wish I were like a bird, like the free bird that, delighting in travel, flies far, far away over land and sea, high in the sky, to lands far, far off"' (1985, 7). However, he reminds us that the poet is eternally frustrated in his wishes and must 'feel this cleft of the human heart also in my heart, neither able selfishly to break with everything nor able lovingly to sacrifice everything!' (7). Berger has traced this idea back to Descartes, who, he says, 'internalized, *within man*, the dualism implicit in the human relation to animals' (21). Giorgio Agamben's philosophy of the animal describes a similar kind of 'cleft of the human heart' within man in relation to the animal. Agamben challenges our ready acceptance of what he calls the 'anthropological machine'. He argues that the modern understanding of the animal is destructive because the 'anthropological machine' functions by 'excluding as not (yet) human an already human being from itself, that is, by animalizing the human' (2004, 37). This hiatus or 'cleft' within is most keenly felt when it enables man to face up to a truer understanding of human nature. Both Kierkegaard and C speak of the 'heartfelt' in describing the relationship with the animal. Kierkegaard continues: 'But it is, of course, an impossibility that I would be able to become like them, and for this very reason the wish to be like them is so heartfelt, so sad, and yet so ardent within me' (1985, 8).

The fictional construction of animal experience reconfigures authority and the reader's preconceptions of the differences between man and animal. As Leonard Lawlor argues in a recent essay on the animal: 'With the other in me, however, I am not substituting myself for another; the structure of becoming is not reciprocal. It is a zigzag in which *I become other so that the other may become something else* [my emphasis]' (2008, 170). The emphasis here is on a shared, creative encounter where control over the 'other' is given up. But how does the desire to speak for the animal in fiction extend our understanding of authority? Authority should describe the means through which an author creates storytelling that seems 'so natural' and that conceals its 'rhetorical artistry', to use the words of C; authority is then bound up with masks and disguises. If the notion of authority presumes some observable and identifiable distinction between a fictional construction and the 'real thing', then how is the reader to locate an authority, fictional or otherwise, that can identify where the animal begins and the human ends?

C recognizes contemporary theory's weakness in describing the animal and it becomes a benchmark for his own struggles with authority: 'What Cartesian nonsense to think of birdsong as pre-programmed cries uttered by birds to advertise their presence to the opposite sex, and so forth! Each bird-cry is a full-hearted release of the self into the air, accompanied by such joy as we can barely comprehend. *I!* says each cry: *I! What a miracle!*' (2007, 132). Elizabeth Costello notes that philosophy has at times proved unwilling to re-evaluate instinct and the animal. Descartes sees them as 'thinglike' (1999, 23), Aquinas regards 'how we treat animals' as being of 'no significance' because they are not made 'in the image of God' (1999, 22) and Thomas Nagel's famous article 'What Is It Like To Be a Bat?' argues that it is impossible for us to know what it is like to be a bat because of the difficulty of tapping into the subjective and 'objective character' of its experience (1974, fn. 450). Coetzee's representations of animals enable us to explore in narrative animals' 'embodied knowledge' (1999, 110).

Coetzee's 1981 essay, 'Time, Tense and Aspect in Kafka's "The Burrow"', an essay on one of Kafka's final unfinished stories ('The Burrow'), describes how Kafka's creature, which Verne P. Snyder refers to as the 'last of Kafka's humanized animals', (1981, 113) creates a 'time of crisis' that is 'incommensurable with human time'. The story describes an unnamed creature's attempts to find security and comfort in its burrow, away from the incessant whistling of what it imagines to be some larger burrowing creature. Because the creature is unnamed, its dilemma can appear ever more human, especially as the burrow assumes a grand metaphorical power, an 'all-embracing' power, that even refers back to its own representation and to the tasks of the writer as creator. Coetzee's chief objective in the essay is to explain how the jarring narrative time in the story, while not doing away completely with the distinction between 'repetitious and singular events' or between 'durative-iterative tenses' and 'singulative tenses', (565) does set up the sense of an eternal present that is realized partially because of the ease of gliding from tense to aspect in German. The story's privileging, for Coetzee, of the fact that 'there is only what is happening now, and this is always crucial' accords well with the popular belief that instinct compels animals to live 'for the moment', or in the moment. Coetzee continues:

> What we have in 'The Burrow', rather, is a struggle – not only the representation of the struggle but the struggle itself – with time experienced as continual crisis, and experienced at a pitch of/anxiety that leads to attempts to tame it with whatever means language offers. The entire linguistic construct called 'The Burrow' represents the stilling of this anxiety; the major metaphor for the linguistic construct is the burrow itself, built by the labors of the forehead. (1981, 576–7)

One must wonder, however, how animal time is 'time experienced as continual crisis'. Kafka's more 'humanized' characters, such as Gregor Samsa, the messenger in 'An Imperial Message', and the prisoner in 'The Penal Colony', already inhabit a very human 'time of crisis'. It is therefore more likely that this sense of urgency has merely been carried over into the stories with more explicitly 'animalised' protagonists. Earlier in his essay, Coetzee critiques Heinrich Henel's reading of tense in the story as 'generalizations rather than laws' (fn. 567). Coetzee suggests that any critical reading of the story should not be content with 'statistical generalizations' – that is, what amounts to 'generalizing from the totality of data' (567) – but with 'laws that explain detailed variations, laws whose models would be rules of grammar' (567). But how do we assign such 'laws' based on grammar that mediate an 'intentional unity' to a writer, whom for Rodolphe Gasché, consigns the 'concept of the law' in all its 'cloudiness' to a 'state of murkiness' populated by 'ambiguous combinations' (2002, 990)? And, in doing so, what happens to the animal, which, as we have seen, must be approached by giving up the sense of control and authority that language grants us?

There are other reasons why this 'time of crisis' may seem so human; Coetzee links it to an appreciation of death that regards death as part of every moment. Coetzee's reading of time and tense in the story recognizes the importance authority plays in the narrative. He argues that he does not deny the 'total implication of Kafka in the story' (577) and he does ultimately, towards the end of the essay, refer to Kafka's notebooks to understand the '"illogical" nature of its [the story's] temporal structure' (577). Coetzee pays particular attention to Kafka's notebook of October 1917 and to the aphorism I looked at earlier: 'From a certain point on, there is no more turning back. This is the point to be reached. The decisive moment of human development is everlasting. Therefore those revolutionary spiritual movements that declare everything before themselves null are right, in that nothing has yet happened' (in Coetzee, 578). Even though Coetzee references the 'literary-biographical problem of relating the journal entry to a story written some six years later' and Maurice Blanchot's reading of Kafka's journals that suggests, for Coetzee, that one cannot abstract 'Kafka's thought from the particular density of the experience it reflects on' (fn. 578), Coetzee must conclude his argument with reference to the aphorism, leaving the last word to the authority of Kafka, the writer. In giving in to the authority of the writer here and to the very human time of that writer, Coetzee allows us to see how Kafka may have transplanted his unique human experience of 'time as crisis', especially in relation to death, onto his animals.

Coetzee argues that 'there are no "crucial events" as opposed to other events: there is only what is happening now, and this is always crucial' (578). For Coetzee, the 'everlasting present' of the story is 'nothing but the moment of narration itself' (579); the 'construct of narrative time has collapsed' and there is only the 'time of narration left' (579). However, the problem of authority returns when we are left with nothing but the 'moment of narration itself'. Is it not now even more important to discern *who* is narrating, or is the suggestion that the collapsing in of all the possible times implies the collapsing in of all identities, including those of Kafka, the narrator, the nameless creature and possibly even the whistling beast? This parallel between the animal 'time of crisis' and the 'time of narration itself' is also at odds with what John Berger describes as the kind of seeing and awareness that the encounter with plant and animal life grants humans. Berger writes about the experience of staring at a field in *Why Look at Animals?*: 'By this time you are within the experience. Yet saying this implies narrative time and the essence of the experience is that it takes place outside such time' (74). As 'critic', Coetzee assumes an authority we rarely find in his fiction; he recognizes that the time in the story is 'incommensurable with human time' (574) and also that it is 'consciousness' (572) that keeps the creature from his burrow, or that alienates the narrator from his being-as-burrow.

Kafka's creature of 'The Burrow' gives us little sense of the 'joy' Barbara Smuts assigns to animals, and any animal ability 'to create a scene in the "remembered present" in the absence of language' (Edelman, 476) is hidden behind a very human-like 'capacity for accurate report of conscious contents' (2009, 476). The creature-speaker in 'The Burrow' describes itself as 'hypersensitive' (348), prone to 'self-deception' and at liberty to contemplate '*a priori* assumptions' (353) and the desire 'for reason to be reinstated on the throne' (349). In being advised by criticism not to fall prey to anthropomorphizing Kafka's creatures, such grand human diversions on the part of the creature still leave us searching for the animal inside the burrow. Kafka's diaries are riddled with entries that echo many of the creature's own admissions. He writes in 1911: 'I too have a pronounced talent for metamorphosing myself, which no one notices. . . . The alien being must be in me, then, as distinctly and invisibly as the hidden object in a picture-puzzle, where, too, one would never find anything if one did not know that it is there' (1975, 58). The beast the creature obsesses over in his burrow also ultimately becomes a beast within. The references to 'passages' and 'work' also serve to present the dilemma as an explicit description of the writer's struggle:

> But quite incomprehensible remains the beast's capacity to work without stopping . . . but apparently the beast has never yet allowed itself a really long rest, day and night it goes on burrowing, always with the same freshness and vigor, always thinking of its object, which must be achieved with the utmost expedition, and which it has the ability to achieve with ease. (1988, 354)

Kafka's diaries sound a similar note in describing his own inner battle, perhaps between the beast and the sovereign-as-artist. He speaks of 'two beings that fight each other within himself'; he says that 'he *is* their fight and will perish in their struggle' (53). He is also conscious of two different times struggling within him, and we recall that Coetzee assigns a similar struggle to 'The Burrow'. These parallels between the diary entries, the earlier more humanized characters and the voice of the creature in 'The Burrow', make it difficult for the reader to forget the authority of Kafka, the obsessive writer, behind the voice of his creature. In the end, Coetzee's early conversation as 'critic' with Kafka in this 'academic' essay may simply be a means for throwing off Kafka's controlling influence on his own literary work. The control that the 'anxiety of influence' exerts may be far more menacing than any 'whistling' creature and far more attentive to the marking of terrain.

Coetzee allows the themes of authority and the animal to converge in *Disgrace*. David Lurie, a university professor and possible alter-ego, who has had to resign from his teaching position because of an affair with a student, finds some kind of solace working in a dog clinic, putting dogs to sleep. Coetzee does not, like Kafka, present us with the 'mind' of a dog or burrowing creature. He concentrates on seemingly human deliberations that interactions with animals can spark. Both sections of the novel – the first section on the lecturer-student affair and the second section that describes his move to live near his daughter Lucy – offer further insights into how humans manage instinct in communities that are expected to work according to the linguistic parameters of entrenched legalistic and moralistic discourses. In the end it is only through the interaction with animals, an interaction that necessitates the daily killing of these animals, that Lurie can consciously discover a deep-seated reason for his actions.

The first section deals with the societal and legal repercussions of Lurie's submission to sexual impulses, or to instinct, in his affair with his student Melanie Isaacs. Coetzee demonstrates how the language of the law becomes inadequate when we are attempting to reconcile instinct with how the law must phrase admissions of guilt. Lurie is asked to make a statement before an academic board of enquiry that is investigating his misdemeanour. Lurie pleads guilty to the charges he faces, but this is inadequate for the board. They state that they wish to discover whether his statement 'comes from his heart', whether he is willing to 'express contrition' and whether his statement reflects his 'sincere feelings' (2000, 54). In frustration, Lurie replies that such questions are 'beyond the scope of the law' (55) and either an omniscient narrative voice or Lurie's interior monologue opines: 'Confessions, apologies: why this thirst for abasement? A hush falls. They circle around him like hunters who have cornered a strange beast and do not know how to finish it off' (56). The board's interrogation of Lurie's debasement of the codes of correct human behaviour is described in terms of the predatory instincts he is being accused of submitting to.

Lurie admits in his confession that the 'impulse' responsible for his actions with his student was 'far from ungovernable. I have denied similar impulses many times in the past, I am ashamed to say' (52). It is because we govern impulse and impound instinct that we then come to construct a false image of the kind of behaviour instincts and impulses promote. The aggressive human behaviour that Coetzee describes in the book, the interrogation of the academic council in the first section and the rape of Lucy in the second, is consistently differentiated from the behaviour of the animals. Whereas Kafka's story presents us with creatures burdened with very human dilemmas and crises mediated through a language of reason, Coetzee's novel conveys how human behaviour seems to be burdened by its stereotyping of instinct and impulse, characteristics that it frequently describes as expressive of the animal in us.

If 'the animal' becomes an 'artificial monstrosity' or an aggressive and destructive element, we also risk losing sight of the human. Coetzee may very well be using the animal to describe, what Leonard Lawlor refers to as 'the other in me' (170); he may even be supporting Aristotle's belief that animals possess a 'natural potentiality' akin to human 'knowledge, wisdom and sagacity', (210); but an animal that 'feels' it is trapped, like Kafka's creature in the burrow or like Coetzee's dog on the operating table, will always react as John Berger describes for the mouse in his 'A Mouse Story': as soon as it finds itself in a cage 'something in him never stops trembling' (4). Most of the animals in Kafka and Coetzee seem to be trembling. How do such moments allow for the human 'giving up of control' and the 'social subjectivity' that is essential for our relations with animals? When Lurie deliberates on his daily killing and disposing of dogs, he describes them as suffering most of all 'from their own fertility' (142):

> There are simply too many of them. When people bring a dog in they do not say straight out, 'I have brought you this dog to kill', but that is what is expected: that they will dispose of it, make it disappear, dispatch it to oblivion. What is being asked for is, in fact, *Lösung* (German always to hand with an appropriately blank abstraction): sublimation, as alcohol is sublimed from water, leaving no residue, no aftertaste. (2000, 142)

The dogs are being put down because they have responded to the impulse that Lurie has chided himself for 'governing' too frequently; their instinct for community and for life, what Kafka refers to as dogs' capacity to 'stick together', (Kafka, 1976, 529) has resulted in a dog population that is regarded as unmanageable by the humans that govern it.

This 'lack of fit' between the animals and the humans is also evident in the fact that the dog owners' language fails them in their final moments with their dogs. The animal is only recognized for what it is once language is discarded (As Derrida suggests, '[t]he real human sovereign is the signifier . . . this defect that the animal does not suffer from' [2009, 125]). The owners are unable to say 'I have brought you this dog to kill'; it would be equivalent to an admission, or confession, of guilt, guilt for both the dog's life they are giving up and for the instinctive and impulsive life that society deems must be 'governed' or 'dispatch[ed] into oblivion' in their own selves. Coetzee refers to the act of killing the dogs as an act of *Lösung*, or sublimation. The word connotes Freud, who adopts the term sublimation for a specific psychological practice: sublimation 'enables excessively strong excitations arising from particular sources of sexuality to find an outlet and use in other fields, so that a not inconsiderable increase in physical efficiency results from a disposition which in itself is perilous' (Freud, 1962, 271). The humans that kill these dogs, represented here by Lurie, live according to a work code that regards 'human rights' as necessitating the 'governing' of impulses and instincts. Unlike the dogs we kill, we struggle to live out the 'excessively strong excitations' that arise from 'particular sources of sexuality', and if we do so by understanding them solely in terms of aggression, society then demands that the guilty party demonstrates clearly how they have infringed on basic 'human rights': the statement that Lurie is asked to sign reads, 'I acknowledge without reservation serious abuses of the human rights of the complainant' (57).

Human rights,[1] then, are seriously abused when the human does not 'govern' or control his or her 'excessively strong excitations' or instinct. The daily killing of dogs for the crime of 'fertility' acts as a symbol for the fruits of 'ungoverned' attention to instinct. Coetzee's descriptions of Lurie's task offer an uncompromising account of how the life we deny animals in our 'governed' or controlled relations with them is a symptom of the instinctual life we deny ourselves. Coetzee is beginning to show us how we might give up control in our dealings with animals. He describes the actions of the dogs as consistently puzzling; they possess a sense of grace and a sensitivity for the moment in which they find themselves. Coetzee's detailing of an instinctual reaction to the moment that is unmediated by a governing rationality begins to enable us to reappraise our conception of the animal.

The end of the novel reinforces this reading of Coetzee's depiction of the relationship between the human and the animal:

> *It gets harder all the time*, Bev Shaw once said. Harder, yet easier too. One gets used to things getting harder; one ceases to be surprised that what used to be as hard as hard can be grows harder yet. He can save the young dog, if he wishes, for another week. But a time must come, it cannot be evaded, when he will have to bring him to Bev Shaw in her operating room (perhaps he will carry him in his arms, perhaps he will do that for him) and caress him and brush back the fur so that the needle can find the vein, and whisper to him and support him in the moment when, bewilderingly, his legs buckle; and then, when the soul is out, fold him up and pack him away in his bag, and the next day wheel the bag into the

flames and see that it is burnt, burnt up. He will do all that for him when his time comes. It will be little enough, less than little: nothing. . . .

Bearing him in his arms like a lamb, he re-enters the surgery. 'I thought you would save him for another week', says Bev Shaw. 'Are you giving him up?' (2000, 219–20).

The extract seems to begin with Lurie's own interior monologue. The italicized '*It gets harder all the time*' also appears to convey the immediacy of Lurie's painful duties. The extract then moves to what critics suggest is the perfective aspect. The perfective aspect expresses 'a temporal view of an event or state as a simple whole, apart from the consideration of the internal structure of the time in which it occurs'[2]; it says 'that in a given period of time, an event of a certain type occurs in its entirety' (Herweg, 363). Much biblical language can be described as perfective. Coetzee is perhaps trying to describe, like Kafka, an internal and an external time. He may be striving for an animalistic time of the 'eternal present' that he unravelled in Kafka. In describing the giving up of the dog, Coetzee may also be describing the 'giving up of control' that relations with animals necessitate. To describe the event as a 'simple whole' apart from the 'internal structure of the time in which it occurs' is perhaps as close to animal experience as a writer can draw. However, the reader will also discern here the uniquely human capacity Lurie is employing, a capacity to represent oneself to oneself in the contemplation and deliberation of an event, rehearsing an event as well as speaking afterwards at a time when the event's after-effects are still felt. The potentialities of animal and human time, as we may now understand them, merge here.

This style of narrative can also be regarded as allowing for the imaginative projection of the self into a future time, a human capacity sparked through the interaction with the involuntary, instinctual life of animals that expands the range of authority. This interaction gives us back, revitalized, our human potential, and thereby alerts us to what is most human – namely, the 'heartfelt', which is most viscerally experienced in those moments of compassion for the other in the face of death. It is a moment that also arises in *Diary*, when Anya mentally rehearses her care for a different kind of 'animal', the dying C: 'I will do that. I will hold his hand. I can't go with you, I will say to him, it is against the rules. I can't go with you but what I will do is hold your hand as far as the gate. At the gate you can let go and give me a smile to show you are a brave boy and get on the boat or whatever it is you have to do' (226). In refraining from giving us the 'mind' of an animal, as Kafka does, Coetzee details how human action – and the animal in the human – is affected by close encounters with animals. Just as Lurie recognizes, like Kafka, through his encounter with the animal, that 'the decisive moment of human development is everlasting', (578) so does Coetzee attempt to get this down for the reader. The emotion and care that become enlivened through the relation with the animal release what we have seen Kierkegaard refer to as the 'heartfelt' in humans and it is the 'heartfelt' that looks to the 'everlasting'. The most poignant expression of the 'heartfelt' is the expression of care that never realizes its own demise and is hence everlasting. It is a sense of prospective care that describes a time captured that does not look backwards in fear like the creature of 'The Burrow', or 'ahead-of-itself' in 'submission', but engages with the boundary event through a merging of the human and the animal around an admission of everlasting precariousness. At such moments in the narrative, characters like Lurie and Anya present us with this 'heartfelt' energy that allows them to commend lives they love to the future. It describes a capacity of an 'embodied soul', a state Elizabeth Costello describes animals as sharing in. Science, as we have seen, now describes the primary consciousness of animals in terms of an 'ability to create a scene in the "remembered present" in the absence of language' (476); it is a similar human capacity to remember in the lived present, despite distractions, the passing, death or weakness of the 'other' and the fellow-feeling or empathy it triggers that characters like Anya and Lurie appear to draw from the animal. The representation of such episodes imparts to fiction, and to the 'serious novelist', further gifts for expanding the range of authority, enabling it to admit something of the everlasting, 'decisive moment' of the animal.

Conclusion: Humane Weakness

The exploration of weakness can bring together secular and spiritual accounts of a shared, humane regard for life that works across traditions. It can speak for both the recognition of limits and a pragmatic sense of possibility. The body mediates these different accounts of weakness through appetite, vulnerability, survivability or precariousness, and the emotional and spiritual realizations that accompany these states have been explored by the works read above. Time and again writers and philosophers, from across traditions, return to weakness as a benchmark from which to begin again. Contemporary accounts of the body and of embodied life often neglect the emotional and spiritual dimensions of weakness; the body becomes either an object for a PET scan, a reminder of sin and salvation, or a 'weakest link'.

Of course, one can no longer presume to ground an ethic solely on a reading of literature and philosophy. Even though the weakness that is found in literature and narrative may offer a vision of the concrete that philosophy does not, it might be argued that weakness is always already formulated and legitimatized in society by institutional practices and discourses. A profound legalism and proceduralism very often sponsors and oversees the academic discourses that disseminate the theoretical and humanistic objections to oppression. Gayatri Spivak reminds us, in reference to Foucault and Deleuze, of the oversights of some of the most celebrated counter-hegemonic discourses. She argues that, in claiming to speak for the 'Other' by describing 'concrete experience' through a 'critique of the sovereign-subject', such discourses may only serve a more deep-set power dynamic: 'Indeed, the concrete experience that is the guarantor of the political appeal of prisoners, soldiers and schoolchildren is disclosed through the concrete experience of the intellectual, the one who diagnoses the episteme. Neither Deleuze nor Foucault seems aware that the intellectual within socialized capital, brandishing concrete experience, can help consolidate the international division of labor' (1988, 69). Spivak argues that Foucault did not go far enough in exploring the nature of power; because of the 'power of the word "power"' he often retreated to a 'heliocentric discourse' for power that only ever returns us to the 'sun of theory' (69). It must be recognized, then, that institutional tensions accompany any striving for a theoretical description of the 'Other' that might be amenable to 'Eastern' and 'Western' traditions, and that any accounting for 'concrete experience' through a reading of literature and philosophy risks claims of redundancy and idealization. However, I believe that narratives and stories that describe different aspects of weakness can always be traced to forms of oppression that create shared notions of precariousness and survivability, and that these, in turn, result in a shared appreciation of the 'authentic weakness of being'. Such narratives may not possess documentary realism or embedded, eyewitness immediacy, but they can offer believable archetypes for subjects struggling to conceptualize how perseverance and affirmation is still possible.

Humane weakness is weakness contemplated and embraced for the vision of hope it offers in times of crisis; it can also act as a ground for empathy's genesis since empathy as a basis for ethics cannot exist without an understanding of weakness. Weakness as 'wanting', 'need', or 'fallibility' (Ricoeur) might then be the last word to be exhausted by the politics of representation, the last to be reified. It can never be entirely Derrida's structuralist 'trace' or '*différance*', even though it might be argued that 'effacement constitutes it' (1973, 'Différance', 156) and that it is 'unnameable' (159), 'commands nothing, rules over nothing, and nowhere does it exercise any authority' (153). Indeed, 'structurally' it might be incredibly similar to trace and *différance*, differing only in that it does not privilege structure, but can there be a greater difference? Weakness is precariousness and surviving because it is a 'wanting', an asking and a realization, even if in the mud, that 'this creature is too intelligent to demand what is beyond my powers what then is not beyond my powers' (Beckett, *How It Is*, 87.105). It is an 'abiding' by the weak and the 'common' not because it is knowing 'your station', but because the 'common' is what such stations secretly crave; it is 'self-touching' and impotence as time-out from sexual performance, not as self-reproach, but as blossoming; it is 'weak mortality' where the 'new man' changes from 'rigidities to suppleness, from tightness to openness' (Nin, 1981, 52); it is a 'syntax of weakness' where the translator, in knowing something is lost, looks further into his or her own tongue; it is a plea to 'Enwreak us wrecks' (Joyce, 1992, 545.11–23) because there is no irremediable Fall for language so long as it has not been sold as 'cultural capital'; it is accepting of 'the animal' in us even if we put animals to sleep. Weakness cares less about textual 'play' since it never asks '[h]ow do we conceive of the outside of a text?' (Derrida, 1973, 158) Because of this care for need and 'wanting', its emergence in all its 'silent power' can never presume 'the necessarily violent transformation of this language' (157–8) or the 'so violent' 'passage through the truth of Being' (154) that the emergence of 'differance' inaugurates. Because it has recognized violence and reflected on its effects, it never wants its signs to presume violence. Its structure, sign or play is a taking stock, an engagement, an abiding and ultimately a giving.

In summing up, I would like to bring together some of the key ideas that have emerged from a thinking through of weakness across traditions around Spinoza's notion of virtue that sees 'the essence of the mind' as consisting in the fact 'that it affirms the actual existence of its body' (1996, 113). As we have seen, Spinoza's presentation of such states as the 'weakness of our bodies' is central to Michael Hardt and Antonio Negri's notion of the 'common'; they argue that Spinoza 'poses such states' as the weakness of bodies as 'the point of departure for a logic of transformation that moves us out of solitude and weakness by means of the construction of sociality and love' (53). In other words, the grappling with our 'nature' in the very act of self-preservation and in self-reflectively navigating a course through shame, indignation and the 'battle of life', allows us to see the stirrings of a strength and a life force that is most enduring. The acknowledgement of weakness through its framing and contemplation can then lead us to love and sociality and the strengths this human sharing affords. Spinoza privileges the body in his description of virtue. Virtue is 'the very essence, or nature, of man, insofar as he has the power of bringing about certain things, which can be understood through the laws of his nature alone' (117). For him, virtue is 'human power itself'; it is defined by man's 'essence alone, that is, solely by the striving by which man strives to persevere in his being' to the extent that 'the more each one strives, and is able, to preserve his being, the more he is endowed with virtue' (126). However, since 'the power of man' is always 'limited by the power of another thing and infinitely surpassed by the power of external causes', (118) it is to weakness we must turn in order to grasp the value of virtue as striving and perseverance. The contemplation of survivability, precariousness and the 'the authentic weakness of being' grant more profound insights into the nature and benefits of striving and persevering. The above writers, from Lao Tzu to Coetzee, remind us that any engagement with the nature of such striving must be linked to an engagement with, and abiding by, the 'weak', which guides us to a greater understanding of virtue as the means to self-preservation. Such virtue marks the point at which weakness and strength converge and the point at which strength can be seen to emerge once again. It begins like Joyce's 'words of silent power' and Keats's 'quiet power' and the only difficulty lies in accepting that we do not have to first experience a catastrophic fall before we can take it into our hearts.

Notes

Introduction

[1] Paul writes 'for when I am weak, then I am strong' (2 Cor 12.10), and Donald J. Munro argues in *The concept of man in early China* that for Lao Tzu 'life and death, good and bad, strength and weakness, beautiful and ugly are unified' (119).

[2] Derrida uses this phrase in describing the relationship between the equally troubling couple beast/sovereign (2009, 39).

[3] In Chapter 4 I examine in detail Gianni Vattimo's notion of weak philosophy.

[4] What Ian O'Neill describes as the 'Higgs boson treasure hunt' is directly linked to the 'LHC confirmation of the weak force': 'W (and Z) "gauge" bosons carry the weak force, one of the four fundamental forces known to exist in nature (the other forces are gravity, the electromagnetic and strong). The weak force is responsible for the decay of neutrons, producing proton and electron (or positron) decay products.' The elusive nature of the Higgs boson and its 'weak force' is causing some scientists to rethink the Standard Model. See http://news.discovery.com/space/jonathan-butterworth-lhc-higgs.html.

[5] This is from a talk entitled 'Who wants Chinese History? Take it out of the school curriculum?', which David Faure gave on 1 November 2011 at 'The Humanities and Public Discourse' conference at the Chinese University of Hong Kong.

Chapter 1

[1] Plato, *The Apology*. Plato I. The Loeb Classical Library. Trans. Harold North Fowler. Harvard: MA, 2001, p. 73: 18c. I use the Fowler translation in this instance as he uses the word 'weaker' whereas G. M. A. Grube uses 'worse'.

[2] Williams argues that Homer did not treat action in 'ineliminably ethical terms' (46). Homer's characters also lack a kind of psychological depth that Benjamin describes as creative of a kind of 'emptiness' in the work. Williams does note, however, that there *is* a psychological awareness in Homer and that events frequently describe what might be referred to as a psychological progression.

[3] Christopher Bobonich and Pierre Destrée write, in the introduction to their collection *Akrasia in Greek Philosophy*, that a rough description of *akrasia* would refer to a sense of 'lack of control' (xv). The Latin equivalent would be *incontinentia*. However, it is also generally used to describe two kinds of situations. The first applies to the situation of an individual who eats a cake that she generally believes to be bad for her where her knowledge of the fact that that particular cake was

bad for her at that time is not strong enough; it 'turns out to have been too weak at that time, or at least not strong enough to insure that she acts on it' (xv). The second situation – if we describe *akrasia* as a 'weakness of the will' – relates to the kind of situation where her 'appropriate, i.e. rational, desire to do what she thinks is better' is too weak and not 'effectively motivational' to 'lead the person to act rationally'. In other words, scholars appear to be split over the means by which an agent comes to be akratic. Bobonich and Destrée remind us that Plato never, in fact, 'uses the word *akrasia* which appears only in Xenophon, and later in Aristotle' (xix), and secondly, that 'in his so-called "middle" as well as "late" dialogues Plato explicitly and repeatedly reaffirms the famous motto – what Weiss takes issue with – "Nobody errs willingly" which is at the core of Socrates' (alleged) denial of *akrasia*' (xix). Aristotle, whom I examine later, is generally regarded as having described two types of *akrasia*: '"precipitate *akrasia*", where the agent doesn't deliberate at all, and "weak *akrasia*" where she does' (xvii).

[4] Desmond Lee translates the section as: 'There you are, curse you – a lovely sight! Have a real good look!' Danielle S. Allen in *The World of Prometheus* replaces the eyes with 'spirits': 'Look then, you evil spirits, and fill yourselves with the noble spectacle' (439e–40a) (245).

[5] Weiss does argue that 'Leontius is drawn by appetite to act in a way that reason regards as reprehensible, and spirit rushes to the side of reason to chastise appetite, here in the form of Leontius's eyes. It is surely not the case that Leontius's reason had determined, in a moment of weakness, that it was indeed best to look at the corpses', (fn. 177) but this does not explain how spirit in the form of one's 'eyes' can chastise. While the eyes must be regarded as staring, surely they cannot embody spirit or reason. It is far more likely that Leontius has turned the moment to his advantage. It appears to be true that reason did not determine in a moment of weakness that it was best to look at the corpses, for we are told that he was 'overpowered by appetite' and it was this that made him look. However, what I am arguing for is that the ferocity of his self-admonishing suggests that reason has now stepped in and taken control as he stares so that he can strive to teach himself a lesson that he won't forget.

[6] All references to Aristotle, unless otherwise stated, are from: *The Complete Works of Aristotle*. Vol II. The Revised Oxford Translation. Edited by Jonathan Barnes. Princeton Bollingen Series LXXI.2. Princeton: Princeton University Press, 1995.

[7] *Phronesis* or practical wisdom is the other important attribute for the continent man. It relates to 'the man who knows and concerns himself with his own interests' (1803) and is therefore a term that once again presumes a certain heightened and perceptive state of self-regard. Aristotle is clear that practical wisdom is not knowledge (1803). He goes so far as to state that the 'function of man' is achieved when he acts in accord with practical wisdom (1807), or as he puts it later in Book IX, 'we exist by virtue of activity (i.e. by living and acting), and then that handiwork *is* in a sense, the producer in activity; he loves his handiwork, therefore, because he loves existence' (1846).

[8] In the essay, 'Plotinus on *akrasia*: the neoplatonic synthesis', from the collection *Akrasia in Greek Philosophy* (Bobonich and Destrée), Lloyd Gerson focuses on Plotinus' reading of the Platonic distinction 'between the soul or true self

and the embodied composite human being' (xxvi). Gerson's point in his essay is that Plotinus assumes in a Platonic manner that 'wrongdoing or vice and *akrasia* are desires involving embodiment' and that 'such actions are possible owing to a weakness in one's self-identity' (xxvii). Gerson argues that for Plotinus, 'the weakness that is a turning away from the real good is based on a failure to separate the real good that one truly desires from the apparent goods proposed to the embodied person' (xxvii). This notion that embodiment, or put loosely, the flesh, is the root of all ills, is a notion that would be important for later Christian writers.

[9] Aristotle creates room for a degree of forgiveness in his descriptions of incontinence: 'Further, we forgive people more easily for following natural desires, since we forgive them more easily for following such appetites as are common to all men, and in so far as they are common; now anger and bad temper are more natural than the appetites for excess, i.e. for unnecessary objects' (1816).

Chapter 2

[1] In this chapter, the titles the *Tao te ching*, the *Lao tzu*, the *Daodejing* and the *Laozi* all refer to the same text. Lao Tzu and Laozi are names for the author of the work. Different translators and commentators use different names. I have tried to keep to the name a particular commentator uses when commenting on his reading. On all other occasions, I use the title, the *Lao tzu*.

[2] All extracts from the *Lao tzu* are from D. C. Lau's bilingual edition: *Tao Te Ching*. Hong Kong: The Chinese University Press, 2001.

[3] In *Confucianism and Christianity*, Xinzhong Yao argues that 'Confucianism is more concerned with the moral than with the natural order' (140).

[4] All extracts from Confucius are taken from D. C. Lau's translation (London: Penguin, 1979).

[5] Jean Calvin: Works and Correspondence. Electronic edition. *Institutes of the Christian Religion*: Books III.XX–IV.XX. 'The Nature and value of Prayer 1–3'. Intelex Corporation, p. 851.

[6] James J. Y. Liu questions the universality of logocentrism as claimed by Longxi Zhang for both the Dao and Logos: 'Zhang's comparison of dao to logos fails to take into account an important difference: in the West, logos is identified with God, but Lao Zi took great pains to say that dao is not the true name of the ultimate' [Liu 25].

Chapter 3

[1] Badiou's work has re-imagined our understanding of event. In his most recent work *Logic of Worlds*, the sequel to *Being and Event*, he describes an event as a 'real change such that the intensity of existence fleetingly ascribed to the site is maximal, and such that among the consequences of this site there is the maximal

becoming of the intensity of existence of what was the proper inexistent of the site. . . . The event is more than a (weak) singularity, which is itself more than a fact, which is in turn more than a modification [each of the words change, existence, site, maximal, inexistent, singularity, fact and modification have a specific meaning within Badiou's system]' (585).

[2] See Michel Henry's *Incarnation: une philosophie de la chair* (2000), and for an English introduction to the work of Henry, see my earlier book *Michel Henry: Incarnation, Barbarism and Belief.*

[3] For Jean-Luc Nancy in *Corpus* this mystery reveals, in an age where 'we have no sacrifices', (79) '*the body as revealed mystery*, the absolute sign of self and the essence of sense' (87).

[4] All references to the Bible are from the *New Revised Standard Version with Apocrypha*. London: Oxford University Press, 1989.

[5] Ann A. Pang-White, 'Augustine's doctrine of weakness of the will after 411' (1 January 1997). *Dissertations (1962–2010)* Access via Proquest Digital Dissertations. Paper AAI9811400. http://epublications.marquette.edu/dissertations/AAI9811400

Chapter 4

[1] In *Of Grammatology* Derrida admits that Heidegger's reading of Nietzsche may place Nietzsche '*within* metaphysics': 'To save Nietzsche from a reading of the Heideggerian type, it seems that we must above all not attempt to restore or make explicit a less naïve "ontology", composed of profound ontological intuitions acceding to some originary truth, an entire fundamentality hidden under the appearance of an empiricist or metaphysical text' (19).

[2] Deleuze explains beautifully how the man of *ressentiment* experiences others and he demonstrates clearly Nietzsche's sensitivity for psychological states that had not yet been named or scientifically analysed to the extent that would become common in the early twentieth century: 'The man of *ressentiment* experiences every being and object as an offence in exact proportion to its effect on him. Beauty and goodness are, for him, necessarily as outrageous as any pain or misfortune that he experiences. "One cannot get rid of anything, one cannot get over anything, one cannot repel anything – everything hurts. Men and things obtrude too closely; experiences strike one too deeply; memory becomes a festering wound" (*Ecco Homo*, I 6, p. 320)' (Deleuze, 116).

Chapter 5

[1] Rousseau is also, for Derrida, a writer who sets up the notion of 'pure breath' (*pneuma*) as what is representative of an 'intact life' and of 'pure vocalization'. However, it is a 'breath' that is 'no longer on the way to humanity' but on the 'way to superhumanity' (249). The relation of breath to self-transcendence is

important for Buddhism and its unique sense of passivity and non-action. Wordsworth also describes the 'might of souls' and 'what they do within themselves' that has nothing to do with 'outward things' such as 'words [and], signs' in terms of breath. In order to make contact with this domain, Wordsworth's speaker must 'make/Breathings for incommunicable powers' (*The Prelude*, Book 3, p. 100: 176–90 [1805]).

[2] I give an extensive reading of this aspect of Derrida in the first chapter of my book *The Incarnation of Language: Joyce, Proust and a Philosophy of the Flesh.*

Chapter 6

[1] In *The Communist Manifesto*, Marx explains why the relationship between work and 'nature' must be disconnected from any description that understands work from a 'supernatural' or mythic perspective: 'The bourgeois have very good reasons for imputing supernatural creative power to labour, since the fact that labour depends on nature has a direct correlate: a man whose only property is his labour must, in all societies and civilizations, be the slave of other people who have become proprietors of the material working conditions' (42).

[2] Helen Pidd. 'G2' 'Prostate Gland? What's that all about, then?' *The Guardian*, 22 March 2005, p. 8.

Chapter 7

[1] I take this phrase from line 389 of *The Fall of Hyperion* and I read the words of Keats's poet-dreamer here as semi-autobiographical since they echo so many of the themes in his letters.

[2] Bennett continues: 'As Dorothy Wordsworth and Elizabeth Fenwick suggest, for many years Wordsworth managed to maintain, against all odds – against the evidence of reviews, of sales-figures, even apparently against the opinion of his friends – that his poetry would survive, that his writing would "live"' (45).

[3] All references to the letters of Keats are from *The Letters of John Keats*. Edited by Hyder Edward Rollins. Cambridge: Cambridge University Press, 1958.

[4] Keats takes this phrase from Wordsworth's 'Tintern Abbey' where the speaker grasps that 'blessed mood' of poetic recollection where the 'burthen of the mystery' is 'lighted' and 'we are laid asleep/In body, and become a living soul' (37–46). Keats's 'weak mortality' would not allow him to completely renounce the body. He does, however, advise in a letter that we should not 'go hurrying about and collecting honey, bee-like buzzing here and there impatiently from a knowledge of what is to be aimed at' but should 'open our leaves like a flower and be passive and receptive'(Letter to J. H. Reynolds, 19 February 19 1818).

[5] As I discuss in Chapter 2, the Chinese character for weakness 弱 (*rùo*)is a pictograph of a fragile plant.

Chapter 8

[1] Harry Stone's 1965 article 'Dickens and Interior Monologue' argues that Dickens's narratives were already employing other typically modernist developments in narrative. For Stone, 'Dickens's very real achievements in the area of interior monologue are partially obscured' (64), even though Dickens recognized that interior monologue was a 'useful additional device . . . for understanding man, revealing character, and recording the nature of the universe' (64).

[2] Michael Slater has described in the later narrative style of Dickens, the Dickens of *Bleak House,* as one that uses 'many of the rhetorical forms such as free indirect speech and apostrophe, whether to his readers or to one of his own characters' to great effect (332). He argues that the first-person voice of *David Copperfield* 'curtailed' this later rhetorical mastery from showing itself (*Charles Dickens.* London: Yale University Press, 2009).

[3] In *Dombey and Son*, Dickens employs the figures of 'golden water' and of a 'river' to describe both an understanding of the afterlife and also an involuntary force of life that seems to flow about all the characters. When Florence reflects on her relationship to her father after the death of her brother Paul, she hears the voice of her brother describing her as a medium through which this current of life flows: 'Then a prospect opened, and a river flowed, and a plaintive voice she knew, cried, "It is running on, Floy! It has never stopped! You are moving with it!"' (591). Florence also retains the memory of the 'golden water she remembered on the wall' (427) from the time of Paul's death as a reminder of this involuntary force in all that will later enable her to save her father from himself: 'The golden water she remembered on the wall, appeared to Florence, in the light of such reflections, only as a current flowing on to rest, and to a region where the dear ones, gone before, were waiting hand in hand' (427).

[4] The involuntary sense being described here is broader than the Aristotelian description of the involuntary act. Aristotle argues: 'Since that which is done under compulsion or by reason of ignorance is involuntary, the voluntary would seem to be that of which the moving principle is in the agent himself, he being aware of the particular circumstances of the action' (*The Complete Works of Aristotle,* 1754). The sense of the involuntary being described here is not solely related to a compulsory act or to an act done in 'ignorance'. Since the psychological and existential state of the agent in Aristotle's theory of involuntary acts is to a certain extent taken for granted, it is inadequate for detailing the nature of the involuntary being described here in this battle of life.

[5] Little Nell's death scene is, of course, very different from that of Quilp's. When Nell dies we read: 'She was dead. No sleep so beautiful and calm, so free from trace of pain, so fair to look upon. She seemed a creature fresh from the hand of God, and waiting for the breath of life; not one who had lived and suffered death' (539). Dickens is treating her death with such reverence that her body is described as if it has not yet experienced the 'breath of life' that is denied Quilp's 'carcase'. Her body without life is also very different from Quilp's 'blazing ruin': 'And still her former self lay there, unaltered in this change . . . So shall we know the angels in their majesty, after death' (540). It would seem then that the good

character's body retains the likeness of the living 'self' while the bad character's body becomes a sordid 'carcase' or 'ruin'.

[6] Dickens's understanding of life may have grown starker in his later work. In *The Mystery of Edwin Drood* the omniscient narrator, in commenting on how the citizens of Cloisterham fear ghosts, gives a rather peculiar description of why such fear exists. Dickens writes that '[t]he cause of this [fear] is not to be found in any local superstition that attaches to the Precincts ... but it is to be sought in the innate shrinking of dust with the breath of life in it from dust out of which the breath of life has passed' (134). The situation in this final work in relation to the corpse or the 'carcase' from which the 'breath of life' has passed appears to have moved beyond the more sentimental tone surrounding Little Nell's death where people stay with her cold body for as long as possible. That the common ingredient of the animated body and the corpse has now been reduced to mere 'dust' is telling.

[7] In a recent article entitled 'The Paradox of Fiction and the Ethics of Empathy: Reconceiving Dickens's Realism', Mary-Catherine Harrison reads Dickens's work in the light of what she describes as the 'ethics of narrative empathy' (257). She argues that Dickens's work is 'a particularly salient case of how narrative empathy can inform our study of literary history' (258). Harrison employs a 'synecdochal model of interpretation' (261) to argue that '[a]lthough readers can, like Harold Skimpole, insulate their aesthetic appreciation from their ethical commitments, Dickens insists that fiction penetrate the "jeweller's cotton" that would shut out the suffering of the modern world' (269).

Chapter 9

[1] All references are from *Finnegans Wake* (1992). Introduction by Seamus Deane. London: Penguin.

[2] Gilles Deleuze. *Proust and Signs* (2008). London: Continuum, p. 16.

[3] Gilles Deleuze. *Difference & Repetition* (2004). London: Continuum, p. 175.

[4] Ibid., p. 397.19.

[5] Roland McHugh, *Annotations to Finnegans Wake* (1980). London: Routledge & Kegan Paul, p. 399.

[6] Ibid., p. 348.7.

[7] Ibid., p. 348

Chapter 10

[1] An earlier version of this chapter appears in James Carney, Leonard Madden, Michael O'Sullivan and Karl White (eds). *Beckett Re-Membered: After the Centenary* (forthcoming). Newcastle: Cambridge Scholars Publishing.

[2] samuel-beckett.net

[3] Reid, 11.

[4] In a letter to Günter Albrecht, dated 30 March 1937, Beckett mentions receiving Karl Ballmer's book *Aber Herr Heidegger* (Beckett misspelt Heidegger as 'Heidigger') from the actor Eggers-Kestner.

Chapter 11

[1] Agamben continues: 'What is man, if he is always the place – and at the same time, the result – of ceaseless divisions and caesurae? It is more urgent to work on these divisions, to ask in what way – within man – has man been separated from non-man, and animal from the human, than it is to take positions of the great issues, on so-called human rights and values' (16).

[2] http://www.sil.org/linguistics/GlossaryOfLinguisticTerms.htm

Works Cited

Agamben, Giorgio (1998), *Homo Sacer: Sovereign Power and Bare Life*. Translated by Daniel Heller-Roazen. Stanford, CA: Stanford University Press.

— (1999), *Potentialities: Collected Essays in Philosophy*. Edited and translated by Daniel Heller-Roazen. Stanford, CA: Stanford University Press.

— (2004), *The Open: Man and Animal*. Stanford, CA: Stanford University Press.

Ames, Roger T. (2011), *Confucian Role Ethics: A Vocabulary*. Hong Kong: The Chinese University Press.

Aquinas, St Thomas (1969), *Summa Theologica*. Translated John Fearon, O.P. Vol. 25. Blackfriars. New York: McGraw-Hill.

Aristotle (1995), *The Complete Works of Aristotle*. Edited by Jonathan Barnes. Vol. 2. Princeton/Bollingen Series LXXI.2. Princeton, NJ: Princeton University Press.

— (2000), *Nicomachean Ethics*. Introduction by Roger Crisp. Cambridge: Cambridge University Press.

— (2004), *History of Animals*. Whitefish, MT: Kessinger Publishing.

Arnold, Matthew (1971), *Selected Poems & Prose*. London: Heinemann.

Athanasius, St (1996), *On the Incarnation*. Crestwood, NY: St. Vladimir's Seminary Press.

Auerbach, Erich (1974), *Mimesis: The Representation of Reality in Western Literature*. Translated by William R. Trask. Princeton, NJ: Princeton University Press.

Augustine, St (1948), *Basic Writings of Saint Augustine*. Vol. 2. New York: Random House.

— (1998), *The City of God against the Pagans*. Edited and translated by Robert W. Dyson. Cambridge Texts in the History of Political Thought. Cambridge: Cambridge University Press.

Badiou, A. (2003), *Saint Paul: The Foundations of Universalism*. Stanford, CA: Stanford University Press.

— (2009), *Logic of Worlds: Being and Event, 2*. London: Continuum.

Banfield, Ann (2003), 'Beckett's Tattered Syntax'. *Representations*, 84.1, 6–29.

Barthes, Roland (1977), 'The Death of the Author'. *Image-Music-Text*. Translated by Stephen Heath. London: Hill and Wang, pp. 142–8.

Beckett, Samuel (1990), *The Complete Dramatic Works*. London: Faber & Faber.

— (1994), *Trilogy: Molloy, Malone Dies, The Unnamable*. London: Calder Publications.

— (1999a), *Proust and Three Dialogues with George Duthuit*. London: John Calder.

— (1999b), *Collected Poems 1930–78*. London: Calder Publications.

— (2001), *Samuel Beckett Comment C'est How It Is and/et L'image: A critical-genetic edition*. Edited and Translated by Edouard Magessa O'Reilly. London: Routledge.

Bennett, Andrew (1999), *Romantic Poets and the Culture of Posterity*. Cambridge: Cambridge University Press.

Berger, John (2009), *Why Look at Animals?* London: Penguin.

Bergson, Henri (1944), *Creative Evolution*. Translated by Arthur Mitchell. New York: The Modern Library.

Blake, William (1978), *The Complete Poems*. Edited by Alicia Ostriker. London: Penguin.

— (2002), *Collected Poems*. London: Routledge.

Bobonich, Christopher and Pierre Destrée (eds) (2007), *Akrasia in Greek Philosophy: From Socrates to Plotinus*. New York: Brill.

Brown, Peter (2008), *The Body and Society: Men, Women and Sexual Renunciation in Early Christianity*. 2nd edn. New York: Columbia University Press.

Budgen, Frank (1960), *James Joyce and the Making of Ulysses*. Bloomington, IN: Indiana University Press.

Butler, Judith (2009), *Frames of War: When is Life Grievable?* London: Verso.

Caputo, John D. (2006), *The Weakness of God: A Theology of the Event*. Bloomington, IN: Indiana Univesity Press.

Casanova, Pascale (2006), *Samuel Beckett: Anatomy of a Literary Revolution*. London: Verso.

Cassirer, Ernst (1979), *The Philosophy of the Enlightenment*. Princeton, NJ: Princeton University Press.

Chan, Wing-tsit (1963), *A Source Book in Chinese Philosophy*. Princeton, NJ: Princeton University Press.

Coetzee, John M. (1981), 'Time, Tense and Aspect in Kafka's "The Burrow"'. *MLN*, 96.3, German Issue, 556–79.

— (1992), *Doubling the Point: Essays and Interviews*. Edited by David Attwell. Cambridge, MA: Harvard University Press.

— (2000), *Disgrace*. London: Vintage.

— (2003), *Elizabeth Costello*. London: Vintage.

— (2007), *Diary of a Bad Year*. London: Harvill Secker.

Coetzee, John M. and Amu Gutmann (1999), *Lives of Animals*. Princeton, NJ: Princeton University Press.

Cohn, Dorrit (1968), 'Kafka's Eternal Present: Narrative Tense in "Ein Landarzt" and Other First-Person Stories', *PMLA*, 83, 144–50.

Confucius (1979), *The Analects*. Translated and introduced by D. C. Lau. London: Penguin.

Connor, Steven (1989), '"*Traduttore*, traditore": Samuel Beckett's Translation of *Mercier et Camier*'. *Journal of Beckett Studies*, 11–12, 17–46.

Cross, Richard (2002), *The Metaphysics of the Incarnation: Thomas Aquinas to Duns Scotus*. Oxford: Oxford University Press.

Cyril of Alexandria, St (1995), *On the Unity of Christ*. Crestwood, NY: St. Vladimir's Seminary Press.

Danta, Chris (2007), '"Like a dog...like a lamb": Becoming Sacrificial Animal in Kafka and Coetzee'. *New Literary History*, 38.4, 721–37.

Davidson, Donald (2006), 'How is Weakness of the Will Possible?' In *The Essential Davidson*. Oxford: Oxford University Press, pp. 72–89.

De Beauvoir, Simone (1976), *The Second Sex*. London: Penguin.

De Man, Paul (1989), *Critical Writings 1953–78*. Minneapolis, MN: University of Minnesota Press.

De Vries, Hent (1999), *Philosophy and the Turn to Religion*. London: The Johns Hopkins University Press.

Deleuze, Gilles (1976), *Proust et les signes*. Paris: Presses Universitaires de France.

— (2005), *Pure Immanence: Essays on a Life*. Introd. John Rajchman. Translated by Anne Boyman. New York: Zone Books.

— (2006), *Nietzsche and Philosophy*. Translated by Hugh Tomlinson. New York: Columbia University Press.

Deleuze, Gilles and Felix Guattari (2004), *Anti-Oepidus: Capitalism and Schizophrenia*. London: Continuum.

Derrida, Jacques (1973), *Speech and Phenomena: And Other Essays on Husserl's Theory of Signs*. Translated and introduced by David B. Allison. Preface by Newton Garver. Evanston, IL: Northwestern University Press.

— (1974), 'White Mythology: Metaphor in the Text of Philosophy'. *New Literary History*, 6, 11–74.

— (1982), *Margins of Philosophy*. Translated by Alan Bass. Chicago, IL: The University of Chicago Press.

— (1989), *Edmund Husserl's Origin of Geometry: An Introduction*. John P. Leavey Jr. (translation, preface and afterword). London: University of Nebraska Press.

— (1998), *Of Grammatology*. Translated by Gayatri C. Spivak. Baltimore, MD: Johns Hopkins.

— (2002a), *Writing and Difference*. Translated by Alan Bass. London: Routledge.

— (2002b), *Acts of Religion*. Edited by Gil Anidjar. London: Routledge.

— (2003), *The Problem of Genesis in Husserl's Philosophy*. Translated by Marian Hobson. Chicago, IL: The University of Chicago Press.

— (2008a), *The Gift of Death and Literature in Secret*. 2nd edn. Translated by David Wills. Chicago, IL: University of Chicago Press.

— (2008b), *The Animal that Therefore I am*. New York: Fordham University Press.

— (2009), *The Beast & The Sovereign. The Seminars of Jacques Derrida*. Vol. 1. Translated by Geoffrey Bennington. Chicago, IL: The University of Chicago Press.

Dickens, Charles (1846), *The Battle of Life*. London: Bradbury & Evans.

— (1985a), *Selected Letters of Charles Dickens*. Edited and arranged by David Paroissien. London: MacMillan.

— (1985b), *Dombey and Son*. Edited and introduced by Raymond Williams. London: Penguin Classics.

— (1997), *Our Mutual Friend*. Edited and introduced by Adrian Poole. London: Penguin Classics.

— (2000), *The Old Curiosity Shop*. Edited and introduced by Norman Page. London: Penguin Classics.

— (2002), *The Mystery of Edwin Drood*. Edited and introduced by. David Paroissien. London: Penguin Classics.

— (2003a), *Oliver Twist*. Edited and introduced by Philip Horne. London: Penguin Classics.

— (2003b), *Little Dorrit*. Edited and introduced by Stephen Wall. London: Penguin Classics.

— (2003c), *Hard Times*. Edited and introduced by Kate Flint. London: Penguin.

Earle, Bo (2002), 'Involuntary Narration, Narrating Involition: Proust on Death, Repetition and Self-Becoming'. *MLN*, 117.5, 943–70.

Edelman, David B. and Anil K. Seth (2009), 'Animal Consciousness: A Synthetic Approach'. *Trends in Neuroscience*, 32.9, 476–84.

Fehsenfeld, Martha D. and Lois M. Overbeck (eds) (2009), *The Letters of Samuel Beckett 1929–40*. Cambridge: Cambridge University Press.

Feuerbach, Ludwig (2008), *The Essence of Christianity*. Dover Philosophical Classics. New York: Dover.

Foucault, Michel (1977), 'What Is an Author?' In *Language, Counter-Memory, Practice*. Edited by Donald F. Bouchard. Ithaca, NY: Cornell University Press, pp. 113–38.

— (2001), 'L'hermeneutique du Sujet, Cours du 17 Mars 1982', *Cours au College de France 1981–82*. Cours du 17 mars. Paris: Seuil, pp. 395–434.

Fraser, Antonia (1985), *The Weaker Vessel: Woman's Lot in Seventeenth-Century England*. London: Methuen.

Freud, Sigmund (1991), *The Essentials of Psycho-Analysis: The Definitive Collection of Sigmund's Freud's Essays*. Edited and introduced by Anna Freud. Translated by James Strachey. London: Penguin.

Fung, Yu-Lan (1976), *A Short History of Chinese Philosophy*. Edited by Derk Boode. New York: The Free Press.

Gadamer, Hans G. (1995), *Truth and Method*. 2nd rev. edn. Translated by Joel Weinsheimer and Donald G. Marshall. New York: Continuum.

Gasché, Rodolphe (2002), 'Kafka's Law: In the Field of Forces Between Judaism and Hellenism'. *MLN*, 117, 971–1002.

Gilbert, Sandra M. (2011), *Rereading Women: Thirty Years of Exploring Our Literary Traditions*. New York: W. W. Norton.

Gosling, Justin (1990), *Weakness of the Will*. London: Routledge.

Greer, Germaine (1999), *The Female Eunuch*. London: Flamingo.

Grodzinsky, Yosef (2000), 'The Neurology of Syntax: Language use without Broca's Area'. *Behavioural Brain Science*, 23, 1–21.

Habermas, Jurgen (1987), *The Theory of Communicative Action - Vol. 2 - Lifeworld and System: A Critique of Functionalist Reason*. Translated by Thomas McCarthy. Boston, MA: Beacon Press.

Hardt, Michael and Antonio Negri (2009), *Commonwealth*. Cambridge, MA: The Belknap Press of Harvard University Press.

Harrison, Gary (1994), *Wordsworth's Vagrant Muse: Poetry, Poverty and Power*. Detroit, MI: Wayne State University Press.

Harrison, Mary-Catherine (2008), 'The Paradox of Fiction and the Ethics of Empathy: Reconceiving Dickens's Realism'. *Narrative*, 16.3, 256–78.

Hart, Clive (1962), *Structure and Motif in Finnegans Wake*. London: Faber and Faber.

Harvey, Lawrence (1970), *Samuel Beckett: Poet and Critic*. Princeton, NJ: Princeton University Press.

Heidegger, Martin (1991), *Nietzsche*. Vols. 1 and 2. Translated by David Farrell Krell. New York: HarperCollins.

— (1997), *Being and Time*. Translated by John Macquarre and Edward Robinson. London: Blackwell.

Heller, Erich (1974), *Kafka*. Fontana Modern Masters. Glasgow: Fontana.

Henry, Michel (1973), *The Essence of Manifestation*. Translated by Girard Etzkorn. The Hague: Martinus Nijhoff.

— (2000), Incarnation; une philosophie de la chair. Paris: Seuil.

— (2003), *I Am the Truth*. Translated by Susan Emmanuel. Stanford, CA: Stanford University Press.

Herweg, Michael (1991), 'A Critical Examination of Two Classical Approaches to Aspect'. *Journal of Semantics* 8.4, 363–402.

Hill, Raymond Thompson (1912), 'Enueg'. *PMLA*, 27.2, 265–95.

Husserl, Edmund (1970), *Logical Investigations*. 2 Vols. Translated by John N. Findlay. London: Routledge & Kegan Paul.

Hyde, Lewis (2007), *The Gift: Creativity and the Artist in the Modern World*. New York: Vintage.

Irigaray, Luce (1985a), *This Sex Which Is Not One*. Translated by Catherine Porter with Carolyn Bourke. Ithaca, NY: Cornell University Press.

— (1985b), *Speculum of the Other Woman*. Ithaca, NY: Cornell University Press.

— (2004), *An Ethics of Sexual Difference*. London: Continuum.

Janicaud, Dominique, Jean-François Courtine, Jean-Louis Chrétien, Jean-Luc Marion, Michel Henry and Paul Ricoeur (2000), *Phenomenology and the 'Theological Turn': The French Debate*. Translated by Bernard G. Prusak and Jeffrey L. Kosky. New York: Fordham University Press.

Joyce, James (1967), *Letters of James Joyce*. Edited by Richard Ellmann. New York: Viking Press.

— (1986), *Ulysses*. The Corrected Text. Edited by Hans-Walter Gabler with Wolfhard Steppe and Clause Melchior. New York: Random House.

— (1992a), *Finnegans Wake*. Introduction by Seamus Deane. London: Penguin.

— (1992b), *Ulysses*. Introduction by Declan Kiberd. London: Penguin.

Jung, Carl Gustav (2009), *Aspects of the Feminine*. London: Routledge.

Kafka, Franz (1975), *The Diaries of Franz Kafka*. Edited by Max Brod. London: Penguin.

— (1976), 'Investigations of a Dog'. *Franz Kafka*. London: Secker and Warburg, pp. 529–51.

— (1988), 'The Burrow'. *Franz Kafka: The Collected Short Stories of Franz Kafka*. Edited by Nahum N. Glatzer. Translated by Willa and Edwin Muir. London: Penguin, pp. 325–59.

Kaufmann, Walter (1974), *Nietzsche: Philosopher, Psychologist, Antichrist*. 4th edn. Princeton, NJ: Princeton University Press.

Keats, John (1951), *The Complete Poetry and Selected Prose of Keats*. Edited by Harold E. Briggs. The Modern Library. New York: Random House.

— (1958), *The Letters of John Keats*. 2 Vols. Edited by Hyder Edward Rollins. Cambridge, MA: Harvard University Press.

Kermode, Frank (1972), *Romantic Image*. London: Routledge and Kegan Paul.

Kierkegaard, Søren (1961), *Christian Discourses & The Lilies of the Field & the Birds of the Air & The Discourses at the Communion on Fridays*. Translated by Walter Lowrie. New York: Oxford University Press.

— (1983), *Sickness Unto Death: A Christian Psychological Exposition for Upbuilding and Awakening*. Editedand translated by Howard V. Hong and Edna H. Hong. Princeton, NJ: Princeton University Press.

— (1985), *Two Discourses at the Communion on Fridays. Without Authority*. Edited and introduced by Howard V. Hong and Edna H. Hong. Princeton, NJ: Princeton University Press, pp. 161–88.

— (1992), *Either/Or: A Fragment of Life*. London: Penguin, 1992.

— (2010), *Spiritual Writings*. Edited and translated by George Pattison. London: HarperCollins.

Knowlson, James (1996), *Damned to Fame*. New York, NY: Simon & Schuster.

— (1997), *Damned To Fame: The Life of Samuel Beckett*. London: Bloomsbury.

Knowlson, James and Elizabeth Knowlson (eds) (2006), *Beckett Remembering Remembering Beckett: A Centenary Celebration*. New York: Arcade Publishing.

Knowlson, James and John Haynes (2003), Images of Beckett. Cambridge: Cambridge UP.

Kristeva, Julia (1994), *Le temps sensible: Proust et l'expérience littéraire*. Paris: Gallimard.

Lakoff, George and Mark Johnson (1980), *Metaphors We Live By*. Chicago, IL: University of Chicago Press.

—(2003), *Metaphors We Live By*. Chicago, IL: University of Chicago Press.

Lau, D. C. (1958), 'The Treatment of Opposites in *Lao Tzu*'. *BSOAS*, 21, 244–60.

— (1963), *Lao Tzu: Tao Te Ching*. London: Penguin.

— (1979), *Confucius: The Analects*. London: Penguin.

— (2001), *Tao Te Ching*. A Bilingual Edition. Hong Kong: The Chinese University Press.

Lawlor, Leonard (2008), 'Following the Rats: Becoming – Animal in Deleuze and Guattari'. *Substance*, 117(37.3), 168–87.

Le Guin, Ursula K. (2009), *Lao tzu: tao te ching: An English Version*. Boston, MA: Shambhala.

Lévinas, Emmanuel (1961), *Totalité et Infini: essai sur l'extériorité*. Paris: Martinus Nijhoff.

— (1990), *Difficult Freedom: Essays on Judaism*. Translated by Sean Hand. London: Athlone Press.

Lewis, Clive S. (1952), *Mere Christianity*. New York: Macmillan Publishing.

Lillyman, W. J. (1971), 'The Interior Monologue in James Joyce and Otto Ludwig'. *Comparative Literature*, 23.1, 45–54.

Lopez, Donald S., Jr. (2004), *Buddhist Scriptures*. London: Penguin.

MacKenzie, Norman and Jeanne MacKenzie (1979), *Dickens: A Life*. Oxford: Oxford University Press.

Mann, Thomas (1998), *Death in Venice and Other Stories*. Translation and Introduction. David Luke. London: Vintage.

Mansfield, Katherine (1966), *The Garden Party and Other Stories*. London: Penguin.

Marion, Jean-Luc (1998), *Reduction and Givenness: Investigations of Husserl, Heidegger, and Phenomenology*. Studies in Phenomenology and Existential Philosophy. Evanston, IL: Northwestern University Press.

Marx, Karl (1992), *Early Writings*. London: Penguin.

McGann, Jerome J. (1985), *The Romantic Ideology: A critical investigation*. Chicago, IL: University of Chicago Press.

McHugh, Roland (1980), Annotations to Finnegans Wake. London: The Johns Hopkins University Press; Revised edition, 1991.

McLaren, Angus (2007), *Impotence: A Cultural History*. Chicago, IL: University of Chicago Press.

Merleau-Ponty, M. (2003), *Phenomenology of Perception*. Translated by Colin Smith. London: Routledge.

Moi, Toril (1985), *Sexual/Textual Politics: Feminist Literary Theory*. London: Routledge.

Munro, Donald J. (1969), *The Concept of Man in Early China*. Stanford, CA: Stanford University Press.

Nagel, Thomas (1974), 'What Is It Like to Be a Bat?' *The Philosophical Review*, 83.4, 435–50.

Nancy, Jean-Luc (2008), *Corpus*. Perspectives in Continental Philosophy. New York: Fordham University Press.

Nietzsche, Friedrich (1968), *The Will to Power*. Edited by Walter Kaufmann. Translated by Walter Kaufman and Reginald J. Hollingdale. London: Vintage.

— (1984), *Human, All Too Human*. London: Penguin.

— (1990), *Twilight of the Idols/The Anti-Christ*. London: Penguin.

— (1993), *The Birth of Tragedy: Out of the Spirit of Music*. London: Penguin.

— (2003), *Thus Spoke Zarathustra*, London: Penguin, 1969.

— (2004), *Ecco Homo: How One Becomes What One Is*. London: Penguin.

— (2007), *On the Genealogy of Morality*. Cambridge: Cambridge University Press.

Nin, Anaïs (1981), *In Favour of the Sensitive Man.* London: W. H Allen.

Norris, Margot (1974), 'The Consequence of Deconstruction: A Technical Perspective of Joyce's *Finnegans Wake.' ELH,* 41.1, 130–48, 131.

Nussbaum, Martha (2001), *The Fragility of Goodness: Luck and Ethics in Greek Tragedy and Philosophy.* Cambridge: Cambridge University Press.

O'Sullivan, Michael (2006), *Michel Henry: Incarnation, Barbarism and Belief.* Oxford: Peter Lang.

— (2008), *The Incarnation of Language: Joyce, Proust and a Philosophy of the Flesh.* London: Continuum.

Olson, Charles (1970), *The Special View of History,* Edited and introduced by Ann Charters. Berkeley, CA: Oyez.

Ou, Li (2009), *Keats and Negative Capability.* London: Continuum.

Pang-White, Ann A. 'Augustine's doctrine of weakness of the will after 411' (January 1, 1997). Dissertations (1962–2010) Access via Proquest Digital Dissertations. Paper AAI9811400. http://epublications.marquette.edu/dissertations/AAI9811400.

Phillips, Adam and Barbara Taylor (2009), *On Kindness.* London: Penguin.

Philo (1953), *Questions on Genesis.* Loeb Classical Library. Cambridge, MA: Harvard University Press.

Plato (1997), *Complete Works.* Edited by John M. Cooper. Indianapolis, IN: Hackett.

— (2001), Plato I: *Euthyphro – Apology – Crito – Phaedo – Phaedrus.* The Loeb Classical Library. Translated by Harold North Fowler. Cambridge, MA: Harvard University Press.

— (2007), *The Republic.* Translated by Desmond Lee. London: Penguin.

Proust, M. (1932), *Remembrance of Things Past.* Translated by Charles K. Scott Moncrieff. 2 Vols. New York: Random House.

Rancière, Jacques (2004), *The Flesh of Words: The Politics of Writing.* Stanford, CA: Stanford University Press.

Reid, James H. (2003), *Proust, Beckett and Narration.* Cambridge: Cambridge University Press.

Ricoeur, Paul (1986), *Fallible Man.* New York: Fordham University Press.

Safranski, Rüdiger (2003), *Nietzsche: A Philosophical Biography.* London: Granta.

Scarry, Elaine (2007), 'Among Schoolchildren: The Use of Body Damage to Express Physical Pain' in *Pain and its Transformations: The Interface of Biology and Culture.* Edited by Sarah Coakley and Kay Kaufman Shelemay. London: Harvard University Press, pp. 279–316.

Schendler, Sylvan (1989), 'Heroic Work, Heroic Being: Avoid the Valedictory'. In Richard Ellmann and Susan Dick. *Essays for Richard Ellmann: OmniumGatherum,* pp. 1–3.

Scholem, Gershom (1997), *On the Possibility of Jewish Mysticism in Our Time and Other Essays.* Edited and introduced by Abraham Shapira. Translated by Jonathan Chipman. Philadelphia, PA: Jewish Publication Society.

Sennett, Richard (2009), *The Craftsman.* London: Penguin. London: W. W. Norton.

Shakespeare, William (1926), *The Complete Dramatic and Poetic Works of William Shakespeare.* Philadelphia, PA: The John C. Winston Company.

— (1997), *The Norton Shakespeare.* Edited by Stephen Greenblatt, Walter Cohen, Jean E. Howard and Katharine Eisaman Maus. New York: W.W. Norton & Co.

— (2009), *William Shakespeare: On Power.* Penguin Books – Great Ideas. London: Penguin.

Slater, Michael (2009), *Charles Dickens.* London: Yale University Press.

Snyder, Verne P. (1981), 'Kafka's "Burrow": A Speculative Analysis'. *Twentieth Century Literature,* 27.2, 113–26.

Spanos, William V. (1980), 'Charles Olson and Negative Capability: A Phenomenological Interpretation'. *Contemporary Literature*, 21.1, 38–80.

Spinoza, Benedict de (1996), *Ethics*. London: Penguin.

Spivak, Gayatri C. (1988), 'Can the Subaltern Speak?' *Marxism and the Interpretation of Culture*. Edited by C. Nelson and L. Grossberg. Basingstoke: MacMillan, pp. 271–313.

Stone, Harry (1995), 'Dickens and Interior Monologue'. *Philological Quarterly*, 38, 52–65.

Swinburne, Richard (2008), *Was Jesus God?* Oxford: Oxford University Press.

Taylor-Batty, Juliette (2007), 'Imperfect Mastery: The Failure of Grammar in Beckett's *L'Innommable*' *Journal of Modern Literature*, 30.2, 163–79.

Tertullian (1956), 'On Modesty'. *The Anti-Nicene Fathers: Translations of the Writings of the Fathers down to A. D. 325*. Eds. Rev. Alexander Roberts and James Donaldson. Grand Rapids, MI.: Eerdmans, pp. 74–101.

Turner, Victor (1969), *The Ritual Process: Structure and Anti-structure*. Chicago, IL: Aldine Pub. Co.

Uhlmann, Anthony (2006), *Samuel Beckett and the Philosophical Image*. Cambridge: Cambridge University Press.

Vattimo, Gianni (2006), 'Metaphysics and Violence', *Weakening Philosophy: Essays in Honour of Gianni Vattimo*. Edited by Santiago Zabala, pp. 400–22.

Wall, Thomas C. (1999), *Radical Passivity: Levinas, Blanchot and Agamben*. New York: State University of New York Press.

Wartenburger, Isabell (et al.) (2004), 'Neural Correlates of Syntactic Transformations'. *Human Brain Mapping*, 22, 72–81.

Weiss, Roslyn (2008), *The Socratic Paradox and its Enemies*. Chicago, IL: University of Chicago Press.

Williams, Bernard (2006), *The Sense of the Past: Essays in the History of Philosophy*. Princeton, NJ: Princeton University Press.

— (2008), *Shame and Necessity*. 2nd edition. Berkeley, CA: University of California Press.

Wollstonecraft, Mary (1967), A Vindication of the Rights of Woman. Ed. Charles W. Hagelman, Jr. New York: Norton.

Woolf, Virginia (1996), A Room of One's Own and Three Guineas. London: Vintage.

Wordsworth, William (1979), *The Prelude: 1799, 1805, 1850*. Edited by Jonathan Wordsworth, Meyer H. Abrams and Stephen Gill. London: W. W. Norton.

— (1981), *William Wordsworth: The Poems*. Edited by John Hayden. 2 Vols. New Haven: Yale University Press.

Wu, Duncan (2004), *Romanticism: An Anthology*. London: Blackwell.

Würbel, Hanno (2009), 'Ethology Applied to Animal Ethics'. *Applied Animal Behaviour Science*, 118, 118–27.

Yao, Xinzhong (1997), *Confucianism and Christianity: A Comparative Study of Jen and Agape*. Brighton: Sussex Academic Press.

Zhang, Longxi (1992), *The Tao and the Logos: Literary Hermeneutics East and West*. Durham, NC: Duke University Press.

— (1999), 'Qian Zhongshu on Philosophical and Mystical Paradoxes in the Laozi'. In *Religious and Philosophical Aspects of the Laozi*. Edited by Mark Csikszentmihalyi and Philip J. Ivanhoe. Albany, NY: State University of New York Press, pp. 97–126.

— (2005), *Allegoresis: Reading Canonical Literature East and West*. Ithaca, NY: Cornell University Press.

Index